D1156047

Judge Learned Hand

Courtesy of Mrs. Norris Darrell

Judge Learned Hand

JUDGE LEARNED HAND

and the Role of the Federal Judiciary

KATHRYN GRIFFITH

University of Oklahoma Press : Norman

347.7
G85j

Library of Congress Cataloging in Publication Data

Griffith, Kathryn P.   1923–
    Judge Learned Hand and the role of the Federal judiciary.
    Bibliography: p.
    1.   Hand, Learned, 1872–1961.   2.   Judicial power—
United States.   I.   Title.
KF373.H29G7   347'.747'0234   72–9254
ISBN 0–8061–1071–6

Copyright 1973 by the University of Oklahoma Press, Publishing Division of the University. Composed and printed at Norman, Oklahoma, U.S.A., by the University of Oklahoma Press. First edition.

To Alfred

JUL 22 '76

HUNT LIBRARY
CARNEGIE-MELLON UNIVERSITY

Preface

The year 1972 marked the one hundredth anniversary of Learned Hand's birth and the eleventh anniversary of his death. Many of his eighty-nine years were spent in public life and thoughtful reflection about the universe in which he lived and the system in which he worked.

Trained in philosophy as he was, he was acutely conscious that the views a man holds about questions of the most basic sort—about liberty and the existence of God—provide the ultimate guides for his life. What he believes and the way he behaves are interdependent.

Learned Hand has been referred to as a representative of the age of relativism, for his philosophy represents, on a relatively sophisticated and intellectual level, the more or less vulgarized and largely unexamined assumptions upon which much of the modern American system rests. Thus an understanding of the relationship between his philosophical assumptions and his practice in political life may illuminate some problems of contemporary American life. It was his devotion to a concept of relative values that prompted him to question opinions of the Supreme Court which appeared to place one value absolutely above the others, whether the value was that of individual freedom or equality or the protection of young people from obscene literature. He believed that each of these values must take a place in the whole constellation of values which prevails; and while in some cases one may dominate, it was inconceivable to him that it would or should always do so. His understanding that moral values are but human choices made him most reluctant to have them written into law. He considered them largely matters of taste and felt that they should not be made coercive. His advocacy of judicial restraint stemmed from a widely held positivist view that the Constitution and other forms of law are to be regarded primarily as historical compromises among competing interests; that they embody almost nothing in the way of durable principles and can contribute little to modifying the moral climate of the community; and that those who interpret them have only the task of discerning the meaning of the compromise. For him it was a fundamental judicial responsibility to provide objective standards which provide realistic guides to judges of lower courts, law-enforcement officers, and the public itself. He emphasized the importance of an objective standard in his obscenity cases, in his criminal protection cases, and in his individual-liberty cases.

Learned Hand had great hope that the American democratic experiment would prove to be a viable solution to the age-old problem of the governance of men. He understood the difficulties that seem to be inherent in such a system and faced them honestly. He also perceived that there are problems in such a system that can be overcome if they are properly understood. He explored these weaknesses courageously and challenged others to do likewise.

One of his great concerns was that the function of the courts would be altered by increasing politicization so that their institutional integrity would be threatened and thus rendered incapable of performing their unique role in the American system. Hand died before the activism of the Warren Court came into full flower, and his expressions of concern were probing and speculative. It seems probable that the Warren Court set a standard of judicial activism unparalleled in American history and served to sharpen the differences regarding the proper judicial function rather than ameliorate it. We may assume that the politicization of the Court has increased rather than decreased with the coming into being of the Burger Court and that, even if the Court should assume a less active role, a recurrence of the activism of the 1950's and 1960's in the foreseeable future is not outside the realm of the possible. Thus reflections regarding the implications of activism and restraint are as relevant —perhaps more so—as ever before. Judge Learned Hand's consistent and logical reasoning, based upon a patently contemporary philosophical view and not upon his approval or disapproval of the substantive results of each opinion, may contribute substantially to a fundamental understanding of the direction in which the Court is moving. His judicious determinations in antitrust and tax cases, in admiralty law, patent and copyright cases, in substantive and procedural criminal law, and especially in those First Amendment cases involving individual freedom as it relates to the needs of society provide a perspective from which to view the work of the emerging Court.

Learned Hand's standards for judicial office take on new importance in light of contemporary concern for the quality of those who preside over the highest court in the land. He believed that learning in the law and craftsmanship of the trade were only the beginning of the necessary qualities. Even more important to him was familiarity with the humanities—history, philosophy, literature—and the new tentativeness of the sciences so that judges understand their heritage and face their task with humility and the understanding that it is only by slow stages that man can gradually raise himself and ultimately society. Not only is the knowledge that comes from such a fine liberal education important but the temper of mind—the understanding that many points of view reflect some truth and a capacity for tolerance—so necessary in a democratic society emerges with it.

Kathryn Griffith

Wichita, Kansas
January 15, 1973

Contents

PART I : *The World of Learned Hand*

CHAPTER I : *The Man*

Billings Learned Hand was "born to the bar" when Lydia Coit Hand presented him to her husband, Samuel, on the twenty-seventh day of January, 1872. He came into a distinguished legal family; his father grandfather, uncles, and other forebears were eminent lawyers and judges in northern New York State. An early ancestor, John Hand, migrated to America from Kent, England, some time before 1645 with his earthly goods consisting of a Bible, a Psalm book, a sword, and a pistol. Augustus Hand, Learned Hand's grandfather, who was born in 1803, attended the first law school established in the United States and began his practice in Elizabethtown, New York, where Samuel was born in 1833. Augustus was surrogate of Essex County and then turned to Democratic politics and served in the United States House of Representatives and the New York State Senate at Albany, as an associate justice of the New York Supreme Court, and as a delegate to the Democratic National Convention in 1868. Samuel moved to Albany, where he became a prominent member of the bar and was appointed to the New York Court of Appeals, though his term was a brief one, for a Republican victory swept the Democrats out of office. Samuel died when Learned was fourteen years old.

The only son of Samuel and Lydia Hand attended a private school in Albany, where he studied well, played mediocre football, and served as the hunting and trapping editor of the school paper. He later admitted that he fancied himself as Deerslayer Hand, though most of his knowledge had been gleaned from books and magazines rather than from practical experience in the woods. Nevertheless, as soon as school was out each spring, he went to Elizabethtown, where his greatest boyhood friend, Gus, or Augustus Noble Hand, lived and Gus's father,

3

Richard Lockhard Hand, practiced law. Gus was a little more than two years older than Learned, who looked up to him then and thereafter throughout the long lives they shared as boon companions and judicial colleagues. During these summers the boys never tired of tramping the woods and endlessly planning their brief camping trips into the Adirondacks or just talking interminably. They sought out and listened to Civil War veterans and learned their songs, which much later Learned Hand recorded for the Library of Congress. From birth he was known as Billings, but sometime before he was thirty he decided that it was much too forbidding and pompous, useful only for being buried or sent to jail, and so exchanged it for Learned.

In 1889, Learned followed his cousin to Harvard, where, because he sported a large drooping mustache and a pointed black beard, a style popular on college campuses, he was known as the "Ancient Mongolian." He majored in philosophy and spent five exciting and provocative years under a faculty that included William James, Josiah Royce, and the brilliant young George Santayana. Hand was influenced for the rest of his life by these new currents that were stirring along the Charles River.

His intelligence and skills in language won for him the Phi Beta Kappa key, the editorship of the *Harvard Advocate*, and the honor of being the class orator when he graduated *summa cum laude* in 1893. The next year he earned his master of arts degree before turning to the study of law. He considered continuing in philosophy, and his speculative mind would have suited him for it; but his cousin had gone into law, and the legal tradition of the family prevailed. The Harvard Law School faculty was also an illustrious one; he studied under Christopher Columbus Landgell, James Barr Ames, James Bradley Thayer, and John Chipman Gray. Throughout his life as a judge, Hand's comprehension of his role was greatly influenced by Thayer's teaching regarding the nature of law and the proper function of the legislative and judicial branches of government. Hand was editor of the *Harvard Law Review*, which was founded while he was a student, and was graduated with honors in 1896. One year later he was admitted to practice law in the state of New York.

For a time Learned Hand practiced in Albany without notable success. Philip Hamburger quotes him as saying that "many times I felt like putting a gun to my head. Nothing but foreclosures, mortgages, settlement of estates. Everything was petty and formal. Nobody wanted to get *behind* a problem."[1] In 1902 he married Frances Finche, a graduate of Bryn Mawr, with whom he happily shared the rest of his life, and moved to New York City. His work there brought him financial success and the attention of many prominent members of the bar, but he did not regard his early years as a lawyer as happy ones professionally. The routine of a law office seemed dull and unstimulating after his challenging years at Harvard. Soon, however, he found an occupation which provided him a lifetime of joy and satisfaction. In April, 1909, President William Howard Taft, who had been in office scarcely more than a month, appointed him to the Federal District Court for Southern New York. Hand was only thirty-seven at the time, and one of the youngest men ever to receive a federal judgeship.

Shortly after his appointment he committed what he must have later come to believe was a great indiscretion for a federal judge. He not only became an active Bull Mooser, supporting Theodore Roosevelt's candidacy against the incumbent Taft, who had appointed him to office, but became the Progressive Party's candidate for chief judge of the state of New York, challenging the regular Republican candidate. Later he explained his action by saying that he "knew that we had to break away from the Hanna thing—the control of the nation by big business." This was Hand's sole political venture, and while he did not change his mind about the "Hanna thing," one can only guess how much he must have regretted his action in light of his subsequent position regarding the necessity of judges to remain uncommitted in political matters. Moreover, it may well have been the overriding reason why he was deprived of a place on the Supreme Court. Traditional Republicans, and especially William Howard Taft, would long remember what he did then.

For fifteen years Hand sat in the lowest federal court, and during that time he gained skill in presiding over a courtroom and learned the nature and problems of jury trials. For the first time he found himself confronted with cases from very specialized areas, and he set about becoming something of a specialist himself in the problems and prece-

[1] Philip Hamburger, "The Great Judge," *Life*, Vol. XXI (November 4, 1946), 125.

dents involved. His cousin, Augustus, was appointed to the same district court in 1914, and the boyhood companions were together again.

While he was still on the lower court, Learned's decisions commanded authority. Judge Charles E. Wyzanski, Jr., says of him that even then

> Judge Hand often touched the superlative. The *Corn Products* case may serve an an example. A generation in advance of the Supreme Court, it grasped the relevance of the Sherman Act to the second industrial revolution. Judge Hand's injunction against the postmaster's exclusion of *The Masses* from the mails, though reversed on appeal, is seen, in retrospect, as the precursor of the federal court's present protection of freedom of the press. . . . he could speak to laymen with such simple persuasiveness in civil-liberties cases that his charges were regarded as text-book models.[2]

In 1924, President Coolidge raised Learned Hand to the Federal Court of Appeals for the Second Circuit, where he remained until his retirement from active duty on July 1, 1951. To his delight, his cousin was appointed to that court in 1927. The two Hands were an exceptional judicial team. Both were fair, reasonable, and without fear in performance of their duty. Learned was brilliant and had a speculative mind, but it was thought in the Hand family that Augustus had better judgment, and Justice Robert H. Jackson once half playfully advised the legal fraternity to "Quote B; but follow Gus."

Except for his obvious affection for his charming wife and three lovely daughters, Learned Hand's greatest satisfactions and pleasures came from his associations with his colleagues on the bench. In addition to Gus, there was Judge Thomas Walter Swan, former dean of the Yale Law School, who sat with them for many years and in honor of whom Hand wrote an eloquent tribute on the twentieth anniversary of his appointment to the court. Others who shared that bench with him were Harrie Brigham Chase, Robert P. Patterson, Charles Edward Clark, and Jerome N. Frank.

Learned Hand's home, the brownstone residence he bought when he took his bride to New York City, was an exceptionally happy and

---

[2] Charles E. Wyzanski, Jr., "Learned Hand," *Atlantic Monthly*, Vol. CCVIII, No. 6 (December, 1961), 54–55.

satisfying one. The first floor was dominated by the library, which contained several thousand books on many subjects, including chemistry, physics, and geography. For many years the Hands spent their summers dashing through Europe, but later they more often went to their home on a wooded country lane in New Hampshire when the court was dismissed. There, at "Low Court," as it was called, he tramped in the woods and read. He was always an inveterate hiker and continued to walk the four miles from his home to his office each morning until he was past seventy-five.

Blessed with the capacity for self-discipline and dedication to his work, he also possessed the ability to relax and enjoy the simplest pleasures of family life. To his children and then his grandchildren he told stores of Br'er Rabbit while he went hippity-hopping across the room and regaled them with tales about an imaginary character named Marge, who was well intentioned but constantly in trouble with the law. Another favorite was his pantomime of the Crooked Mouth family, in which he took the part of each trying to blow out a candle. At the end he would wet his fingers and snuff out the flame. When he played cowboys and Indians with his grandchildren, he used a wastebasket for a headdress and, according to his son-in-law, was not one but a whole tribe of Indians cavorting around the house. As part of the annual family Christmas celebration he always sang songs from Gilbert and Sullivan.

Hand was devoted to Harvard University throughout his life and repeatedly returned to speak there. Twice he served as overseer, and he was president of the Alumni Association in the tercentenary year of the university's founding. His other primary interest away from the court was the American Law Institute, which officially recognizes him as a founder. He also belonged to the American Bar Association and the Bar Association of the City of New York, the Century Club, and the Harvard Club. Wherever he went or whatever he did, his professional life and pleasure were inseparable; he often joined his colleagues on a committee in singing or entertained them with his fine storytelling and gifted mimicry. Once, after delighting Justice Oliver Wendell Holmes with ribald sea chanteys, he said that he hoped that Holmes had not taken him for a "mere vaudevillian." In his office at noon he sang hymns in accompaniment to the church chimes next door. When in a puckish mood, he delighted his audiences with stories delivered in Irish, Yiddish, and Italian accents. His impersonation of William Jennings Bryan addressing a political meeting in Jersey City was a favorite of Justice Felix Frankfurter.

Above all, Hand loved good conversation, which he enjoyed with a wide and diverse circle of friends, including men of the arts and sciences, statesmen, and philosophers, as well as the greatest judges, legal scholars, and lawyers of his era. He was very moody and liked to have good companions around to stimulate and cheer him. It has been suggested that T. S. Eliot's description of Paul Valéry fits Hand very well. Eliot said that Valéry had "intelligence to the highest degree, and a type of intelligence which excludes the possibility of faith, implies profound melancholy."

As a youth Hand chose to forgo the certainties of divine absolutes, and his solitary and thoughtful moments were beset by doubts as he struggled with himself in pursuit of truth. Yet from the religion of his ancestors he inherited the highest ethical standards and great devotion to them. While his philosophy denied the eternal verities, his speeches show that the personality, the humanity, and the teachings of Jesus made a deep and lasting impression upon him. During the last years of his life he and Mrs. Hand read the Gospels aloud, though he remained troubled by the miracles reported in them.

His scrupulous honesty caused him once to declare a pair of old shoes that he had had half-soled in Europe when he passed customs. He could not abide waste, especially in government, and often debated with himself before sending a letter to a fellow judge whether to stamp it or affix his frank. In spite of his personal standards, he was not a moral crusader and often gently chided those who would impose their own values on others. He was an early advocate of the position that morals are matters of taste and custom and should be left at that except when the issue involves some overriding public concern. Presiding over the New York court meant that he heard many citizenship cases, and he was invariably bothered by the statutory requirement that a person prove his good moral character before he could be naturalized. On one occasion a government attorney argued before him that the admission by a thirty-nine-year-old bachelor that he had had sexual relations with unmarried women disqualified him for citizenship on grounds of moral character. The lawyer appealed to the judge, saying that he

surely would not want his daughter to marry such a man. Hand's immediate retort was, "I wouldn't want her to marry a man of thirty-nine who
hadn't had the impulse!"

Even though Judge Learned Hand was quoted by name in Supreme
Court opinions and in academic publications more often than any other
lower-court judge, and though he was "universally acknowledged as the
greatest living judge in the English-speaking world,"[3] he did not, in
Justice Frankfurter's words, "become Mr. Justice Hand." Holmes
would have welcomed him to the Supreme Court while he was still a
district judge, and it was widely agreed that he would have met the
"spacious requirements for a seat on the Supreme Court as very few
men in his time."[4]

It has been suggested that Hand's failure to win this high office
was due to bad luck, political distrust, and geographical accident. The
circumstances which deprived him of this honor were doubtless many
and varied, but one of them seems apparent. When he was considered
and rejected for the vacancy created by the resignation of Justice
Mahlon Pitney, former President Taft—who had appointed Hand to
the federal bench and against whom Hand had supported Theodore
Roosevelt—was then Chief Justice Taft. He wrote to President Warren
Harding, saying:

> There is a United States District Judge of proper age, Learned
> Hand. He is an able Judge and a hard worker. I appointed him on
> Wickersham's recommendation, but he turned out to be a wild Roose-
> velt man and a progressive, and though on the bench, he went into the
> campaign. If promoted to our Bench, he would most certainly herd
> with Brandeis and be a dissenter. I think it would be risking too much
> to appoint him.[5]

Much later, before President Franklin D. Roosevelt appointed
Wiley B. Rutledge to the Supreme Court, he acknowledged the error
of his 1937 attack upon the "nine old men," by saying, "B has just the
right intellectual age; can't you do anything about his chronological

[3] Charles E. Wyzanski, Jr., in his introduction to Learned Hand, *The Bill of Rights*, v.
[4] Felix Frankfurter, "Learned Hand," *Harvard Law Review*, Vol. LXXV, No. 1
(November, 1961), 3.
[5] Quoted from the Taft Papers in David J. Danielski, *A Supreme Court Justice is
Appointed*, 42.

age?"[6] Ironically, Rutledge, a much younger man, lived only six years, while Hand lived another eighteen.

Though he did not serve on the highest court in the land, Hand was interested in and influenced the entire national judicial system. His horizons, stemming from a broad liberal education, were without the confining boundaries of provincialism, narrow professionalism, and traditional mores. It was with this unrestricted vision that he sought to understand his role as a judge as it related not only to his immediate task but also to his place in the order of things—to the relevance of his work to the society in which he lived. Beyond that he sought to appraise that society itself in terms of its contribution to the development of man as he understood him.

When Learned Hand sat on the bench, lawyers watched his face intently, and many had occasion to do so with great trepidation. Once when he was sitting in moot court at Yale, a prize student rose to address him and then fell to the floor in a dead faint without uttering a single word. Hand was attentive in the courtroom only as long as the argument was germane and became restless when it grew loose or wordy. He was especially irritated by lawyers who sought to flatter the court and often interrupted them to administer a sharp rebuke. The unfortunate lawyer who sought to rest his case on what Hand regarded as "broad principles of eternal justice" was frequently greeted with a vehement "Rubbish!" Philip Hamburger wrote that Hand's reaction to an attorney enthralled by the sound of his own voice was often a scribbled note of protest to one of his colleagues on the bench. In one of these notes he recalled: "John Marshall once said that among the qualities of a great judge was the ability to look a lawyer straight in the eye and not hear one word he was saying."[7]

Not only was Hand a great judge, he looked like one. He was a formidable man with stocky figure and huge shoulders. His features were craggy, his eyes gleamed beneath heavy brows, and his face, noble and powerful, demanded attention. Yet, in spite of its great strength, his was a mobile face, alternating from repose to irritation to delight and deep melancholy, mirroring his quickly changing moods. The majesty

[6] Wyzanski, "Learned Hand," *Atlantic Monthly*, Vol. CCVIII, No. 6 (December, 1961), 58.

[7] Hamburger, "The Great Judge," *Life*, Vol. XXI (November 4, 1946), 125.

with which he presided over the courtroom belied the inner doubt and persistent uncertainty that plagued him. He disbelieved in absolute principles but was constantly in search of them. He was never certain of anything but was always driven to do the best that he could.

Hand always called each of his law clerks "Judge" and promoted him to "Mr. Justice" when he moved on to the Supreme Court. It is largely from the long line of clerks, all honor students from Harvard, that the Hand legend has grown. Before beginning to draft an opinion, he thought aloud with his clerk in order to develop a general outline. The clerk looked up all the references mentioned in a brief, and Hand later checked them himself. The clerk might offer possible lines of reasoning, but was never called upon to draft a decision. In this formative period Hand tried to state his own prejudices and then discount them—to search for all possible solutions. Once these initial stages were over, he withdrew with orders not to be disturbed, and the creative labors of a great judge were drawn into full play. He struggled over his opinions, known throughout the legal world for their brilliance and clarity, writing three or four drafts in longhand on long yellow tablets until both the language and the logic satisfied him. The final product went unerringly to the kernel of the issue, concisely but eloquently, setting forth the relevant facts and appropriate judicial principles in language that could be understood by all who read them.

A common thread ran through his decisions—his deep concern for justice according to the rules as he understood them. This unifying and guiding theme makes it impossible to classify his opinions in the ordinary categories of liberal and conservative and denies the easy assumption that they reflect his personal predilections. He was liberal in the classic sense of being humane and loving freedom but respectful of the limits of the judicial function, and he was capable of great intellectual detachment, which permitted him to distinguish between his personal and official positions.

Learned Hand's reputation as a judge grew slowly over the years as the vast accumulation of his cases won the respect and admiration of experts, lawyers, and judges who read and followed his decisions. In spite of the breadth of his wisdom and understanding he belonged chiefly to the bar and bench until the country was electrified by his address, "The Spirit of Liberty," given in the critical war year of 1944 to almost one and a half million Americans in New York's Central Park. In the speech, marking "I Am an American Day," he expressed his own personal faith that

> the spirit of liberty is the spirit which is not too sure that it is right; the spirit of liberty is the spirit which seeks to understand the minds of other men and women; the spirit of liberty is the spirit which weighs their interests alongside its own without bias; the spirit of liberty remembers that not even a sparrow falls to earth unheeded; the spirit of liberty is the spirit of Him who, near two thousand years ago, taught mankind that lesson it has never learned, but has never quite forgotten; that there may be a kingdom where the least shall be heard and considered side by side with the greatest.[8]

For a fleeting moment after he finished there was absolute silence, and then the audience, which included 150,000 newly naturalized citizens, burst forth with great applause. The speech was not quoted in the papers the next day, but its fame quickly spread, and soon it was reprinted in newspapers and magazines accompanied by stories about the judge who had given it. Among Learned Hand's papers were hundreds of letters from friends and peers, but one that he prized most highly came from an old friend, M. Speciale, who over the years had repaired his shoes and taught him Verdi and how to make spaghetti. It was scrawled in Italian:

> Illustrious Sir:
>
> I read very attentively your excellent speech given at Central Park.
>
> You do not know how excellent you are, but people should tell you of your qualities, and I would like to tell you how well suited you are to govern this great republic. You are a great judge, philosopher and philanthropist. You lack nothing in knowledge and intelligence, and you understand the needs of the people.
>
> I hope that you who are of such great caliber and have such an excellent character will live many many years on this earth, and forever in the hearts of the people.
>
> I remain your humble shoemaker,
>
> M. SPECIALE[9]

[8] Learned Hand, "The Spirit of Liberty," as reprinted in *The Spirit of Liberty* (Comp. and ed. by Irving Dilliard), (1st ed.), 190.

[9] Bill Davidson, "Judge Learned Hand: Titan of the Law," *Coronet*, Vol. XXVI (September, 1949), 114.

The Man

With such an auspicious introduction to the people of the nation, Learned Hand's fame grew quickly, and in 1947 his seventy-fifth birthday was marked by broad popular acclaim as well as by his colleagues in the law. An issue of the *Harvard Law Review* was dedicated to him, and the editors compiled a list of his decisions to date. The list was eighty pages long and contained thirty-four categories of cases. His formal retirement from the bench in 1951 was greeted with widely expressed public regret, though he continued to assist his heavily burdened court by handling a limited number of cases. Within a year Irving Dilliard edited a collection of Hand's nonlegal papers and addresses and published *The Spirit of Liberty*, which served to focus public attention on the philosophical aspect of Hand's thought, as well as to widen the audience which was gradually becoming aware of this man, his thought, and his contribution to the public life of the nation. In 1958 he delivered the Holmes Lectures at Harvard to the largest audience ever assembled for such an event. The lectures were published as the only book he wrote, *The Bill of Rights*. A year later his court held a special session to commemorate his fifty years of service on the federal bench. Chief Justice Warren spoke on this occasion, and there followed another spate of newspaper and magazine articles acknowledging him to be one of the greatest judges of this century.

Learned Hand was very ill for the last months of his life, his body broken and feeble. He frequently and wistfully hoped that it was only his body and not his mind that had succumbed to eighty-nine vigorous and vital years, for his zest for life and robust joy were matched only by the profound melancholy which overtook him as he struggled with the unanswerable problems of man's search for the good life. Though he missed the highest honor to which a judge can aspire, few men have been so highly acclaimed during their lifetimes as was Judge Learned Hand. Perhaps because he never reached the highest court, there was a subtle awareness on the part of those who knew of him that his authority came not from pre-eminent position, wealth, conniving, or public "image" but from a personal grandeur and the individual greatness of a man wholly devoted to the work before him—a man with a capacity for insight and understanding that itself commands authority. People found reflected in his life and work the highest ideals and aspirations

13

HUNT LIBRARY
CARNEGIE-MELLON UNIVERSITY

of a free, democratic, and humane society. Ten years before his death the *New Republic* said:

> He possesses knowledge, without which an individual cannot truly be free. He possesses wisdom, without which an individual cannot properly use the knowledge he may have. And he possesses compassion, without which an individual cannot properly relate his wisdom and knowledge to the world about him. But most of all, he possesses the ability to question his own first principles, to search out the truth wherever it may seem to lead.[10]

[10] Eugene Gressman, "With Vision and Grace," *New Republic*, Vol. CXXVI (June 2, 1952), 19.

CHAPTER II : *His World*

The world of Learned Hand was the universe, his home. His interests were wide-ranging and almost unlimited. In a more restricted sense his "world" was the legal and judicial one into which he was born, in which he grew and was nurtured, and to which he contributed substantially. In spite of his distaste for limits and boundaries, he acknowledged that there are physical and intellectual limits within which all men necessarily live and find their places. His professional world was especially important to him because he believed that the excellence of a judge came not simply from knowledge of the law but also from wisdom and understanding drawn from a sympathetic comprehension of the whole history of man—from an intimate acquaintance with the works of Plato, Aristophanes, Thucydides, Rabelais, Lord Acton, Frederic William Maitland, George Santayana, Alfred North Whitehead. It seemed to him that everything he did or learned might in some way enhance his capacity to judge. His breadth of interest makes his work of special relevance to students of political theory and philosophy, as well as of law.

Judge Hand served his country on a federal bench for over half a century and wrote more than two thousand opinions. His is a remarkable record of service; but longevity is not a claim to distinction or greatness, though it did enhance his reputation through the sheer volume of his contribution to American jurisprudence and the frequent reiteration of his understanding of the law. His comprehension of the problems inherent in the issues with which he dealt and his creativity allowed him to give old doctrines new meaning as he imaginatively translated them from cases of one kind into useful service in opinions in other areas. He preferred to adapt familiar legal principles to meet new problems rather than discard the principles.

His pre-eminence among judges came from his profound capacity to judge and from the happy circumstances which permitted him to sit on one of the most important courts in the land, one designated unofficially as "the Top U.S. Commercial Court." The time during which he served also contributed significantly to his importance in American jurisprudence, for his tenure spanned what William Swindler has described as the "Old Legality," which arose in response to changes in the last half of the nineteenth century and the cataclysms which followed 1932. Hand himself wrote in 1936 in the issue of *Harvard Law Review* marking the fiftieth year of its publication and coinciding with his own legal career up to that time, that it had been "the seeding-time for a crop of new ideas, based upon a revolutionary outlook."

Henry Steele Commager marks the "watershed of the nineties" as the dividing line between early and modern America, and it does seem to separate early American constitutional experience from that of the twentieth century. It was at this point in time—just one hundred years after the Constitution first went into effect—that problems created by the changing society permeated almost every aspect of American life and signaled the emergence of a vastly more sophisticated federalism.

Shortly after the Civil War events began to occur which unalterably changed the domestic and international environment of the United States. Among these were the disappearance of the frontier, the rise of vast interstate industrial complexes, the shift from rural to urban population, unprecedented breakthroughs in science and technology, and in the present century an incredible range of economic prosperity and depression, admission of vast new groups of political power, participation in two global wars and their periods of reconstruction, and the challenge of a militant totalitarianism—all of which was too much for traditional law. The laws called forth by these radically altered circumstances often came before Judge Hand's court for judicial interpretation before they were acted upon by the Supreme Court, and so it was frequently his interpretation that prevailed or at any rate had to be contended with by the higher court.

About 1880 state and local boards of health began to appear along with legislation expressing concern for the health and welfare of the people, especially women and children. Laws sought to regulate conditions of those working on dangerous machines in the newly mechanized factories, establish maximum hours for certain jobs, and provide fair wages and to deal with the problem of establishing employer liability for workers injured on the job. These contests took place between champions of the workers and employer but also sometimes pitted legislators against those judges who applied strict construction to legislation which changed common-law arrangements and thereby effectively nullified the new legislation. Judge Hand was guided by the doctrine of presumed validity, and he had an ultimate concern for legislative intent. As a result his opinions gave this new legislation and other new regulatory statutes the full scope intended by the legislature.

The individual became steadily less important in the developing mass market, and an awareness of the need for some public responsibility to protect the consumer from damaged, defective, or impure goods emerged. The interests to be protected were scattered and difficult to organize, and individual losses to the public were considerable. The first laws designed to protect the consumer were passed in 1906. Consumer protection, though a twentieth-century phenomenon dependent upon modern techniques of administrative regulation, was made possible by the sense of public responsibility which began to develop late in the nineteenth century.

Another even more subtle change occurred in the perception of what is essential to man's freedom. It began to be understood that those who were at the lowest end of the socioeconomic spectrum—the insane, the delinquent, the handicapped, the ignorant, or the drunkard—were somehow victims of their own limitations and at least partly incapable of altering their own circumstances because of disability or incapacity. Reports of welfare institutions began to recognize that this inability of people to rise above their circumstances was costly to society in terms of human waste and loss of needed human resources. New concepts of freedom fed upon America's nineteenth-century moralistic bias, as well as the pragmatic tendency to "do something" when a problem was identified. This moralistic tinge, which has always been a part of the American social conscience, accompanied Theodore Roosevelt's antitrust campaign, the Grange's war upon railroad price fixing, and the whole Progressive movement. Later, as fact-finding techniques were developed and a scientific orientation began to emerge in political thought, the moralistic approaches began to give way to social engineering.

These tendencies were only incipient throughout the latter half of the nineteenth century. Nevertheless, through the conduct of public affairs, through the laws that were passed, through the lines of administration that were established and the legal battles that were waged, new political principles seemed to be emerging. A record of choice, of experience, however unconscious, established the framework within which public policy was to develop throughout the first half of the twentieth century.

The Progressive movement resulted in creation of new institutions and procedures which put power into the hands of the large mass of people. The direct primary, initiative, referendum, and recall laid the basis for an increasingly democratic society, and the introduction of the short ballot was indicative of an effort to improve administrative efficiency. The Progressive movement waned, and the scientific-management approach made its impact upon political life through its emphasis on efficiency and technical competence.

While in American social, economic, and political life there remained a place for private action and enterprise, it was increasingly groups rather than individuals who exercised initiative. Democracy based on individualism began to give way to a group-oriented society. As pressure groups became more effective in pressing their demands, the traditional judicial doctrine of "presumptive validity"—that short of clear evidence to the contrary legislation should be given the benefit of doubt about its constitutionality—began to have new implications. This principle now appeared to concede the propriety of permitting private pressure groups to exercise a substantial role in initiating and defining public policy through legislative enactment. Hand believed that this interpretation was the logical outgrowth of a free democratic society and that as long as group activity was contained within the constitutional framework it must be regarded as legitimate.

The judicial doctrine of presumed validity had developed in deference to the concept of separation of powers, and the Supreme Court had early recognized in principle that it ought not to substitute its own weighing of values for the compromises struck by the legislature. However, as social legislation continued to increase, the doctrine of presumed constitutionality began to collide with the prevailing laissez-faire attitude in economic matters. The widening scope of social legislation was mitigated insofar as the judiciary continued to represent the laissez-faire position. Justice Holmes's notable dissents from this position written early in the twentieth century were generally based on the equally traditional doctrine of presumed validity. Judge Hand accepted the latter doctrine and continued to apply it with an evenhandedness that ultimately was to draw praise and blame alternately from proponents of laissez-faire and regulatory legislation.

The American federal system includes a unique, complicated, dual system of courts with the state and federal systems, coexisting, sometimes uneasily, as they share jurisdiction and responsibility for justice. The growth and development of the national judiciary has been innovative and exploratory, resting on minimal constitutional provisions, elaborated upon by Congress, and made effective by the courts. In comparison with state judicial systems which are in many ways independent of national supervision, the federal system has developed—both in fact and in the minds of most Americans—an exceptionally high degree of integrity, fairness, and capacity to administer justice, in terms of the system itself and the quality of the individual judges appointed to the federal bench. Federal judges will not give advisory opinions, nor will they decide abstract hypothetical or moot questions. An issue becomes a case only when a person who has standing asserts a claim in the proper form and presents it to a judge as a reasonably specific issue between two litigants who stand in adverse relationship to each other.

The Constitution provides that there shall be one supreme court and inferior courts as Congress shall establish. The system of national courts attests to the determination of the founding fathers that the central government have the capacity to adjudicate and enforce its own laws. Granting Congress large power to determine the structure and jurisdiction of the system assured flexibility that was denied to state courts, which are generally rigidly specified in state constitutions. Consistent with the republican principle and the separation of powers, the Constitution assured that there would be a mixing of the judicial function among the separate branches with a kind of ultimate authority residing in Congress through its power to determine jurisdiction and to a lesser degree with the president, through his power to nominate judges.

The First Judiciary Act established the federal system in 1789 and remained almost unchanged for about one hundred years. It established as courts of first instance the federal district courts with a rather limited jurisdiction and circuit courts with both original and appellate jurisdiction. Section 25 of the act held that under the supremacy clause of the Constitution the state courts were bound to enforce the Constitution, laws, and treaties of the United States and were to that extent subordinate agencies of the federal government.

The judicial system has always been hierarchical in structure, with courts of the first instance, intermediate appellate courts, and final Supreme Court review. Arrangements for personnel have varied over the years. Originally the circuit courts were composed of one district judge and two justices of the Supreme Court. Later the justices were reduced to one, and as the work of the Supreme Court increased, one district court judge often sat alone on the circuit court, thus denying the appellate concept, since the same judge might hear the case both in the first instance and on appeal. In spite of complaints about the inadequacy of this arrangement, it remained in effect until Congress provided a modest change in 1869 by creating a new panel of circuit judges to join with the district judges in holding court. The vast increase in judicial business following the Civil War meant that by the late 1880's about 90 per cent of each circuit court's docket was being disposed of by a single judge, usually a district judge, and the number of cases docketed annually by the Supreme Court increased from 1,315 to 1,800 between 1884 and 1890.

The first substantial change in the structure of the national court system came in 1891, when Congress established new circuit courts of appeal. Although the old district and circuit courts were retained, and while certain cases were permitted to go directly to the Supreme Court from the courts of the first instance, most cases that were appealed were finally disposed of by the new appellate courts subject to certification to the Supreme Court or issuance of a writ of certiorari by the high court. In 1912 the old circuit courts were abolished and the present structure was established, the district courts having original jurisdiction and the circuit courts of appeal having jurisdiction in most cases with the final appeal in some cases being to the Supreme Court.

Important administrative improvements made in the federal judicial structure in the twentieth century have provided a unifying force and vastly improved the efficiency of the federal system. The chief justice now has authority to reassign, usually on a temporary basis, district judges from one district to another when the work loads of the various districts indicate the need for such a redistribution. The judicial conference, composed of the senior circuit judge from each circuit, meets annually with the chief justice to discuss the functioning and problems of the national judicial system. Learned Hand was the senior judge of the second circuit after 1939 and as such participated in these judicial conferences.

In 1939, Congress passed the Administrative Office Act, which established the Administrative Office of the Federal Courts and made it responsible to the conference. The Administrative Office has responsibility for preparing the budgets for the lower federal courts, a job previously done by the Justice Department. It also gathers statistics regarding the work handled by the federal courts and facilitates the redistribution of judges to care for the shifting workloads in the district courts. The act also created a judicial council in each circuit, composed of all federal judges, and made it responsible for the efficiency of the business of the circuit. Under this law each circuit is required to hold an annual conference with representatives of the bar to consider the work of the courts and administrative improvement.

As the federal system has developed, there has been a vast increase in the original jurisdiction of the lower courts and a corresponding restriction of the right of appeal to the Supreme Court. By 1875, Congress had given the national courts the full range of constitutional jurisdiction. Any suit could be brought in federal court if the action asserted a right under the Constitution, laws or treaties of the United States, and any action initiated in the state courts could be removed to the federal courts if a question of constitutionality was raised. Since that time various efforts have been made to withdraw some of this broad jurisdiction, but the only limitation has been an increase in the minimum value of the issue in controversy between citizens of different states that may be brought in a federal court—from five hundred dollars in 1789 to the present ten thousand dollars. Matters of controversy involving less than ten thousand dollars are now brought in state courts in the first instance.

Today the jurisdiction of the Supreme Court reflects the understanding that it is not simply an ordinary appellate court. It is a tribunal with unique responsibilities for holding the federal balance in some reasonable adjustment, and if it is to be free to perform this function, it must be relieved of many of the ordinary cases that might be appealed. This special function was not fully acknowledged until 1891, when the law creating the circuit courts of appeal was enacted. Even then the appellate jurisdiction was not effectively curtailed, for there had developed over the years the assumption of the "right" to appeal each case involving a federal question to the highest court in the land. The law did establish the principle that there should be powerful intermediate appellate courts between the courts of first instance and the highest court and also that the Supreme Court itself should have broad discretion to deny or grant writs of certiorari through which many cases were brought to that court. It expressed the new idea that it was not the primary function of the Supreme Court to see that justice was done in every case but to decide the more important issues arising within the legal framework that related to the federal balance, relations between branches of government, and the fundamental rights of the individual with respect to the government.

The federal system is related to the independent state court systems primarily through the kinds of cases and manner of appeal from state to federal courts and the action of Congress giving state courts jurisdiction in some diversity of citizenship cases. Since 1916, Congress has drastically limited the review of state court decisions that deny claims of federal right. Review of state decisions may now be had as of *right* only when a state court declares an act of Congress or federal treaty unconstitutional or when the state court sustains a state statute against the allegation that it is in conflict with federal Constitution, law, or treaty. Conversely, the disappointed litigant has a *right* to Supreme Court review if a federal district court declares an act of Congress unconstitutional in a case in which the United States is a party, if a district court enjoins the enforcement of a state statute, or if a court of appeals declares a state statute unconstitutional or contrary to federal law or treaty. Even where there is a legal right to review, the Supreme Court retains substantial discretionary power, since it is the justices who determine whether the litigant does in fact have the right. Large numbers of cases in which appeal is made from state courts are denied by the Supreme Court on the basis that there is no substantial federal question at issue. Other appellate cases come to the Supreme Court when four justices deem them to be of sufficient importance and grant a writ of certiorari.

There is at least one federal district court in each state. A district has one or more judges, depending upon the volume of business. A case generally is heard by a single judge, but certain kinds of cases may be heard by a panel of three district judges. Jurisdiction covers both civil and criminal matters that arise under federal law, treaties, or Constitution and shares with state courts responsibility for disputes involving over ten thousand dollars between citizens of two states. Most federal cases begin in, and are settled by, the district courts.

There are ten circuit courts of appeal and one for the District of Columbia, each court having three or more judges. A case usually is heard by three judges. Except for a very limited number of cases that may be appealed directly from the district to the Supreme Court and those appealed from the circuit courts to the Supreme Court, all appeals rising out of the district courts are heard and disposed of by the circuit courts. In addition, circuit courts hear appeals from the regulatory commissions, such as the National Labor Relations Board and the Interstate Commerce Commission.

The Supreme Court has exclusive and original jurisdiction over controversies between states and all legal actions relating to diplomatic representatives of foreign states. It has original but not exclusive jurisdiction over controversies between states and the United States, actions brought by officials of foreign states, and actions by a state against citizens of another state or aliens. Original jurisdiction of the Supreme Court is established in the Constitution, and Congress may not alter it, but it may authorize other courts to exercise concurrent jurisdiction in these matters. This original jurisdiction is of much less importance than the appellate jurisdiction given by Congress.

Though the courts are arranged in a pyramidal structure, the

Supreme Court exercises much less supervision and control over subordinate courts than is the case in most hierarchical arrangements. The authority of the chief justice within the Supreme Court rests largely upon his ability and capacity for leadership. His vote in disposing of a case counts for no more and no less than that of the most junior justice. A majority of the Supreme Court can reverse decisions of lower courts and criticize their opinions, and there is a powerful incentive to follow the lead of the higher court in order to avoid having a decision overruled. On the other hand, the Supreme Court has no formal disciplinary power over subordinate judges who also hold tenure for terms of good behavior, have salaries which cannot be reduced, and receive their appointments from outside the judicial branch of government. While higher courts provide guidance and leadership for the lower courts, application of the mandates of the Supreme Court or the circuit courts is not a mechanical process and often requires the same kind of judgment and discretion at the lower levels as is exercised by the Supreme Court in interpreting ambiguous parts of the Constitution.

It has been estimated that 98 per cent of the cases that are of direct concern to business and industry stop at the circuit court. The annual docket of the Second Circuit, situated as it is in the heart of the country's greatest industrial and metropolitan complex, is not only the largest handled by a circuit court but includes many crucial issues being raised for the first time. Like all other appellate courts, it makes a significant impact through its leadership of the lower courts in matters that are not appealed (the district courts in the Second Circuit hear far more cases than those in any other circuit), since the district courts usually try to interpret the law as they think their appeals court would.

It is, of course, true that in terms of sheer power the Supreme Court has ultimate authority on all federal issues, but in 1951, John P. Frank noted that "the measure of ability is something else again. Were courts rated like baseball teams, no expert in judging could be found to rank the Supreme Court first, if only because of the number of rookies on its nine. . . . most expert judges of judges would choose the Court of Appeals for the Second Circuit . . . as the ablest court in the U.S."[1] The incredible variety and critical importance of the cases that

[1] John P. Frank, "The Top U.S. Commercial Court," *Fortune*, Vol. XLIII (January, 1951), 92.

come before the Second Circuit suggest the contribution its judges have made to American jurisprudence. It is clear that for many years Learned Hand led, if he did not dominate, that court.

In 1949, two years before Hand's retirement from active service, about forty-six hundred suits related to admiralty law were begun in district courts. Of these, twenty-seven hundred were initiated in trial courts in the Second Circuit and were generally disposed of in accordance with principles established by that court. Learned Hand became widely acclaimed as the court's foremost authority in cases involving marine collisions, by moving models about on his desk. He kept marine charts, a compass, a ruler, and magnifying glass nearby with which he located every spot mentioned in the opposing briefs and took special delight in catching a lawyer in a minor nautical error. In *Dauntless Towing Line* v. *Canal Lakes Towing Co.*, a typical case concerning a collision between two barges, he wrote:

> As usual the testimony as to the whistles is contradictory. . . . Perhaps the most reasonable estimate is that she first blew when somewhat east of buoy 3A, about 1,200 feet from the place of collision. The only testimony is that the mutual approach of the vessels was nine miles an hour; and if so, the signal must have been given nearly three minutes before collision (even if we disregard the slow bell of the Calatco). That was ample time for the *Dauntless* to go to starboard.[2]

On one occasion he was expounding his theory about such a collision to a colleague, who finally capitulated, saying, "Captain, I've followed your navigation from that desk for twenty years, and I suppose it's too late to abandon ship now."[3]

The Second Circuit has also specialized in patent and copyright cases. In 1950 a third of all such cases originating in the United States began in courts under its jurisdiction. While Hand was not a specialist in this area, his creative imagination and love of beauty gave him an affinity for authors and inventors. It allowed him to understand an intricate invention, literary effort, or musical score so that he was able to recognize the relevant points at issue, appraise them correctly, and

[2] *Dauntless Towing Line* v. *Canal Lakes*, 140 Fed. (2d) 215 (1944).
[3] Frank, "The Top U.S. Commercial Court," *Fortune*, Vol. XLIII (January, 1951), 96.

write an opinion stating the reason for his decision in language that was comprehensible to lawyers and businessmen, as well as the artist or the technically educated.

His sense of humor often found its way into his opinions. Once, when asked to determine whether a play had infringed upon the rights of another, he wrote: "There are but four characters common to both plays, the lovers and the fathers. The lovers . . . are loving and fertile; that is really all that can be said of them, and anyone else is quite within his rights if he puts loving and fertile lovers in a play of his own."[4] One of his law clerks recounted that when the court had before it the patent for a Kiddie Kar the noted Judge Hand mounted it and rode around the building to call upon his colleagues.

Tax cases handled by the Second Circuit are extremely important. Since the advent of the federal income tax and the increasing use of various corporate forms for conducting business, lawyers, administrators, and judges have been occupied with the degree of freedom a taxpayer should have to choose one legal form over another simply in the interest of tax avoidance. Free choice of form may permit a substantial reduction in the amount of taxes a person must pay, even though for all other economic purposes the forms may be essentially the same. It is generally agreed that the tax planner has some choice but that the Internal Revenue Service is not simply bound to accept the choice and may challenge an arrangement even though it follows the letter of the law.

The courts have found no single principle that has been consistently useful in deciding such cases. When they do not accept the taxpayer's choice of organization, they commonly hold that the form is inadequate because it does not have a substantive purpose other than tax avoidance. When they accept the form, it is on the principle that, as Hand held, "there is nothing sinister in so arranging one's affairs as to keep taxes as low as possible."[5]

In an article in the *Yale Law Journal* entitled "Learned Hand's Contribution to the Law of Tax Avoidance," Marvin A. Chirelstein commented:

---

[4] *Nichols v. Universal Pictures Corporation, et al.*, 45 Fed. (2d) 119, 122 (1930).
[5] *Commissioner v. Newman*, 159 F. (2d) 848, 850–51 (1947).

More perhaps than any other single judge or commentator, Learned Hand was instrumental in the development of [these] interpretative principles. . . . Beginning with an opinion involving the Corporate Excise Tax Act of 1909, and ending almost forty years later with an obscure and troublesome dissent in the much debated *Gilbert* case, the relationship between form and substance in tax law engaged Hand's attention at fairly regular intervals during the entire span of his judicial career. His effort throughout . . . was to draw the line between permissible and impermissible tax avoidance by determining when the taxpayer's choice of form was to be respected—when a literal construction of the statute was appropriate—and when not.[6]

Hand established his pre-eminence as a tax judge in *Helvering, Commissioner of Internal Revenue v. Gregory*, in which he wrote an opinion concerning business reorganization for the sole purpose of tax reduction that is still regarded as a foremost judicial statement on the subject. Hand refused to rely simply upon literal interpretation as a doctrine of statutory construction and based his reasoning on congressional intent. In review the Supreme Court commented that "the reasoning of the court below . . . leaves little to be said."[7]

The Gregory opinion seeks to limit permissible tax avoidance to those situations in which the taxpayer's objective is not in clear opposition to the intent of Congress. Hand's interpretation of the law required a business purpose in order to justify the particular form of reorganization. The result was that the Internal Revenue Code was given a liberal interpretation by relating it to congressional intent and thereby warned taxpayers that they could not hope to rely simply upon compliance with the letter of the law.

The difficulty of such an interpretation was quickly pointed out by critics. It left tax planners with little guidance about when a literal interpretation would be employed and when a liberal one would be used. As Hand decided subsequent cases, he seemed to be intent upon keeping this liberal construction within bounds. He did not view the doctrine of congressional intent as a grant of complete discretion, though he did not develop specific guidelines to limit its use.

In *Higgins v. Smith* the Supreme Court reversed a holding of the

[6] Marvin A. Chirelstein, "Learned Hand's Contribution to the Law of Tax Avoidance," *Yale Law Journal*, Vol. LXXVII (1968), 441.

[7] *Gregory v. Helvering*, 293 U.S. 469 (1935).

Second Circuit in which Hand had joined. In the opinion the Supreme Court limited the use of diverse legal forms for tax avoidance permitted by Gregory, while at the same time citing Gregory as the precedent. In *Higgins* v. *Smith* the Court seemed to be granting the commissioner of internal revenue full discretion to accept or deny transactions between a shareholder and his wholly owned corporation to permit the commissioner to minimize tax avoidance.

Hand seemed perplexed by this opinion but, as always, felt constrained to follow the lead of the high court insofar as he was able. He did not try to hide his difficulty with the opinion but "set about to apply the Smith decision in subsequent cases, stressing first one and then another of the several aspects of Justice Reed's loosely written opinion in an effort finally to comprehend its effect."[8] At first he proceeded as though Smith did in fact follow Gregory, but later acknowledged that "the decision may therefore make it possible for the Treasury at times to disregard transactions between its shareholders and [their] corporation even though it be a 'corporation' in the sense we mean, although it must be confessed that the differentia is left open."[9]

Pursuant to this concept of the Smith precedent, Hand attempted to extend the doctrine of congressional intent to tax cases where the independent status of the shareholders and corporation was otherwise unquestioned. These cases appear unclear and unsatisfactory and were severely criticized by tax planners for limiting options that had formerly been open.

In 1956, Hand wrote an opinion which seemed to highlight the difficulties encountered in a selective liberal interpretation of the Internal Revenue Code. In *Loewi* v. *Ryan* he used a strictly literal interpretation and did so without trying to provide an answer to the crucial question why formal compliance with the letter of the law is adequate in some cases and not in others. It appeared that Hand himself felt that the technique of adding judicial definitions to the code was not useful or adequate in all cases, especially after Smith, and, as Loewi showed, the issue of when the liberal interpretation should be used had not been resolved in any systematic way.

8 Chirelstein, "Learned Hand's Contribution," *Yale Law Journal*, Vol. LXXVII (1968) 450.
9 *Commissioner* v. *National Carbide Corp.*, 167 F. (2d) 304 (1951).

In Hand's final case dealing with tax avoidance, *Gilbert v. Commissioner*, he seemed to offer his resolution to the perplexing issues brought to court under the Internal Revenue Code in the light of the problems of corporate entity and precedents provided by the Supreme Court. His opinion reflected his understanding of the inadequacies of the Gregory technique without sufficient guides to aid in determining when liberal and literal interpretations were appropriate. This case involved an unprofitable corporation of two equal shareholders, one of whom had made loans to the corporation roughly equivalent to his investment. No payments had been made on either interest or principle when the corporation was dissolved and the assets, which were roughly equivalent to the original investment, were distributed. The taxpayer sought to deduct his loans to the corporation as bad debts.

In seeking to resolve the question whether the bad debts should be allowed as tax deductions, Hand observed that it would be possible to describe what had transpired accurately in more than one way. For instance, the payment could be regarded as payment of the debt rather than as distribution of assets. It could also be described as distribution of assets and cancellation of the debt by the creditor. Hand argued that, since either of these statements described what happened as well as the statement made by the taxpayer, there were several possible ways of characterizing the transaction and the commissioner was not bound to accept one rather than another. To avoid the apparently arbitrary selection of one over another, Hand restated and narrowed the Gregory requirement of business purpose as follows:

> I would therefore substitute this which seems to me to . . . state the doctrine adequately: 'When the petitioners decided to make their advances in the form of debts, rather than of capital advances, did they suppose that the difference would appreciably affect their beneficial interests in the venture, other than taxwise?' The burden will be on them to prove that they did so suppose.[10]

This minority opinion held that in a situation which appears to be ambiguous for purposes of taxation the commissioner may select the legal form which produces the higher tax rate unless the taxpayer can show how the form he chose was either expected to or did produce some

---

[10] *Gilbert v. Commissioner*, 248 F. (2d) 399, 412 (1957).

reasonable advantage other than through tax avoidance. The opinion reflected the problems he experienced in applying the Gregory formula, especially after Smith. It served to limit the range of choice open to the taxpayer and vested considerable discretionary power in the commissioner which was in line with Smith. The Supreme Court adopted Hand's reasoning in Gilbert in *Knetsch* v. *United States* in 1960.

This series of important cases handled by Learned Hand does not provide a completely satisfactory solution to the tax-avoidance cases. Nevertheless, as Chirelstein remarked:

> Hand's response to the Smith decision over a period of years is again a reminder that his "penchant for logical statement" made it difficult but also imperative for him to deal frankly with the subject of tax avoidance and the problems of consistency in statutory interpretation. . . . Hand was a system-builder, . . . and his contribution to the law of tax avoidance lay partly in his persistent effort to rationalize the administrative process. That effort, which certainly succeeded in some degree, is an important feature of our tax history; it seems not unlikely that it will be an element in our future as well.[11]

While technological changes do not necessarily require new legal patterns, those which occurred in the last half of the nineteenth century provided the basis for the creation of a whole new social structure and approach to political life, and the development of new legal relationships appeared to be imperative. Hand believed that the greater and more important part of the law involves legal relationships between the individual and the community which arise out of the production and distribution of property. His judicial tenure spanned a period of radical alteration in these relations brought about by the Industrial Revolution and the shift in American jurisprudence from a predominantly common-law to a primarily statutory-law basis.

Today every segment of modern industry depends upon co-operative effort which is in turn dependent upon regulation by law. For instance, after the Civil War the railroads provided almost the only means of transporting goods, and they were vital to the areas they served. Hand thought the decision of *Munn* v. *Illinois*, which ruled that

---

11 Chirelstein, "Learned Hand's Contribution," *Yale Law Journal*, Vol. LXXVII (1968) 474.

a person might assume public duties by devoting his property to public use even though he enjoyed no special franchise, had amazed the legal profession and opened almost unlimited possibilities. It was during this period also that it became the practice for business activity to be carried on by corporations and therefore without personal liability. The shareholder, who is now separate from the management and helpless to direct large corporations, must depend upon public regulation in a degree unthinkable to his forefathers.

In retrospect, the Sherman Act of 1890 seems to have marked an important turning point in public policy dealing with control of the market. It is, in fact, much more important today than it was when it was first passed. It has only been in this century that executive initiative and judicial inventiveness have given great impetus to public regulation of market conditions. There appeared to be no general public demand for such legislation at the time the bill was passed, the newspapers gave little attention to its progress in Congress, and there is some reason to believe that its generality can be attributed to a desire in Congress to avoid the difficult issues involved in a more precise law.

The act did provide a change of direction through congressional acknowledgment of the value of free competition and an obligation on the part of the government to maintain a degree of that freedom. Congress no doubt assumed that private suits would be the primary instrument for enforcement, but the bill provided the possibility of government initiative to bring suits to maintain a proper balance in the economy. It gave the nation's judges a policy-forming position and so placed lawyers and judges, rather than politicians, economists, or administrators, in charge of supervising the nation's antitrust policy.

In 1895 the Knight sugar-trust case provided a narrow interpretation of the Sherman Act and held that manufacture was a local matter, that combinations to control manufacture had only an indirect effect on interstate commerce, and that the Sherman Act did not cover such combinations. Implicit in the opinion was the understanding that had the act presumed to control manufacture it would have been unconstitutional. Congress did nothing to oppose this assumption. It was Progressive Theodore Roosevelt who encouraged the Department of Justice to bring suits which permitted the Court to reconsider the Knight opinion. In the Northern Securities case decided in 1904, the

Court repudiated the narrow interpretation of the Knight case and opened the door to vigorous antitrust policies. Roosevelt subsequently waged a battle against monopoly which brought public acceptance of trust busting in the United States.

Among the most important and far-reaching Hand decisions have been antitrust cases. Section I of the Sherman Act condemns every "combination . . . in restraint of trade," and Section II makes a person guilty who shall "monopolize or attempt to monopolize" trade. The courts had sought to define with some care what was intended by "combination in restraint of trade" but had not dealt fully with Section II. The result was that the government struck at the abuses of monopolies without getting at the cause. Judge Hand helped change this approach and gave direction for subsequent antitrust suits by providing an interpretation of the Sherman Act which courts since that time have used as a broad base for dealing with such cases.[12]

Early in the 1940's the government brought a case against the Associated Press charging that it was monopolistic in its distribution of the news. This case, *United States* v. *Associated Press*, considered one of the most important in the history of the American press, came to Learned Hand's court. After a year of study he wrote an opinion holding that a bylaw of the association which permitted members to veto admission of competing papers constituted an illegal monopolistic practice under the Sherman Act. He found that the restrictive bylaw was a sufficient burden to the public that the public aspect outweighed the benefit provided for the members.

Another case, *United States* v. *Aluminum Co. of America*, was appealed directly from the district court to the Supreme Court, where it was impossible to get a quorum of justices because so many of them had been involved in the case before it reached the Court. By a special act of Congress the case was referred to the Second Circuit, making it the court of last resort for this particular case. The original trial had taken two years, records totaling forty thousand pages, and an opinion which took the trial judge from September 30 to October 9 to read. *Life* photographed the dozens of volumes comprising the record, which showed that the Aluminum Company of America controlled 90 per cent of the aluminum for sale in the United States. Hand reversed the decision

12 "The Antitrust Campaign, *Fortune*, Vol. XXXVIII (July, 1948), 63.

of the lower court and held that this percentage did in fact constitute a monopoly, although 64 per cent might not and 33 per cent surely would not. Furthermore, he said, it was not possible to conceive of a monopoly which did not monopolize and which did not know what it was doing. His unwillingness to specify the lower limits of monopolistic control, since the case did not require him to do so, and his acknowledgment that he was not certain where it would fall suggests his pragmatic view that that would have to be determined by a reasonable appraisal of the facts in each case. In a concise twenty-eight-page opinion Hand told the whole story and held in a landmark decision that Congress had not distinguished between good and bad monopolies but had forbidden them all. His opinion destroyed for all time the idea that size is immune from control by law. He wrote:

> . . . it is no excuse for "monopolizing" a market that the monopoly has not been used to extract from the consumer more than a "fair" profit. The [Anti-Trust] Act has wider purposes. Indeed, even though we disregarded all but economic considerations, it would by no means follow that such concentration of producing power is to be desired, when it has not been used extortionately. Many people believe that possession of unchallenged economic power deadens initiative, discourages thrift and depresses energy; that immunity from competition is a narcotic, and rivalry is a stimulant, to industrial progress; that the spur of constant stress is necessary to counteract an inevitable disposition to let well enough alone. . . . True, it might have been thought adequate to condemn only those monopolies which could not show that they had exercised the highest possible ingenuity, had adopted every possible economy, had anticipated every conceivable improvement, stimulated every possible demand. . . . Be that as it may, that was not the way that Congress chose; it did not condone "good trusts" and condemn "bad" ones; it forbade all. Moreover, in so doing it was not necessarily actuated by economic motives alone. It is possible, because of its indirect social or moral effect, to prefer a system of small producers, each dependent for his success upon his own skill and character, to one in which the great mass of those engaged must accept the direction of a few.[13]

Thus he declared that, regardless of its intent, the Aluminum Company of America fell within the scope of the act because of its

---

[13] *United States* v. *Aluminum Co. of America*, 148 F. (2d) 416, 427 (1945).

great concentration of producing power. Again Hand demonstrated his creative capacity as a judge within the framework of his understanding of the judicial function. Had he been less confident of his understanding of his responsibility and the legislative intent, he might have stayed within the scope of existing precedent. He was making new law if measured against what the Supreme Court had already said. But he was certain that Congress would have chosen to legislate against the undesirable social and economic consequences of such powerful monopolies and was willing to so judge. Thus it is apparent that, while he believed clear and relevant precedent should be followed, he was not constrained to be subservient when congressional intent was clear and the problem seemed to require innovation and imagination. His opinion in this case may be regarded as a model of judicious interpretation.

Before long the Supreme Court had affirmed many of Hand's generalizations in the Aluminum case and pushed his reasoning to new grounds in a suit brought by the government against the three big tobacco companies which were theoretically competitive. The companies were accused of pursuing similar policies which tended to be prejudicial to competitors, and, following Hand, the high court determined that even though it is not used, the power to exclude competition is illegal—that it is not necessary to show formal collusion in order to show unlawful conspiracy. Together, the Aluminum and tobacco company cases represented a shifting away from the peripheral attack upon the abuses of monopoly and concentration upon the problem of what makes the abuses possible. A whole series of subsequent cases elaborated the original Aluminum case doctrine to make it applicable to related problems of monopoly and restraint of trade.

Judge Wyzanski credits Learned Hand with contributing more than any other lower court judge to the current interpretation of antitrust laws. It was his creative imagination that permitted the concept of the "rule of law" to be applied to private associations which the public sector was seeking to restrain. His opinion in the Aluminum case "suggests ways by which limitations may be placed upon clusters of combined strength, procedural fairness may be assured, power be divided, and adverse interests be marshalled."[14]

[14] Wyzanski, "Learned Hand," *Atlantic Monthly*, Vol. CCVIII, No. 6 (December, 1961), 55.

Judge Hand's contribution to jurisprudence was not limited to commercial or business law. His appointment to the district court in 1909 coincided with the beginning of a new era of federal criminal law. The U.S. Criminal Code was passed in that year and included many subjects that Congress had never before acted upon. It was the beginning of a vast expansion of federal law based on the authority of the commerce clause. At that time judicial emphasis on technical errors was being attacked from many sides, and Hand had an active role in the improvement of archaic procedural rules and interpretation of the substantive law of federal crime. He was neither a "hanging judge" nor a "defendant's judge," and provided

> not a one-sided approach to the criminal law, but a wise and impartial judgment which balances the public interest in prompt and efficient prosecution with the individual interest (which is not without its social importance) of each defendant in a fair trial. During the important period in federal criminal law which has marked his service on the bench, he has made a major contribution toward making that law an effective instrument of justice.[15]

Hand doubtless would have been less willing than the Warren Court to tie the hands of prosecutors and less willing to allow error or reversal on technical or legalistic grounds provided the trial had been reasonable and fair and the evidence clearly pointed to the defendant's guilt. He did believe that if judges were not realistic about the limits and restraints imposed upon the prosecution public opinion might well react and demand withdrawal of many of the protections which are generally taken for granted. He believed that this would in effect be preparing the way for despotism while giving the illusion of protecting freedom. The current emphasis upon law and order is partly a response to lawlessness in the streets but also, no doubt, reflects public uneasiness over what some regard as overprotection of those accused of crime.

Hand's concern for the form and substance of criminal law was apparent in his speeches and his contribution to the work of the American Law Institute, as well as on the Judicial Conference of Senior Circuit Judges. His knowledge of philosophy and human nature taught

[15] Orrin G. Judd, "Judge Learned Hand and the Criminal Law," *Harvard Law Review*, Vol. LX (February, 1947), 405, 422.

him that society is held together partly by persuasion and partly by coercion, and he acknowledged the necessity for both. He avoided oversentimentality for those convicted but insisted that the trial be fair. He made a major contribution to the developing criminal law through his efforts to improve procedures. In criminal matters this is extremely important since most cases relate to rulings on admitting or denying evidence and charges given to juries. Hand did not approve of letting minor or technical errors handicap the work of the courts and followed a philosophy of reason and fair play rather than formal legalism. In 1909 he stated his philosophy clearly:

> I do not in the least mean to reflect upon the wisdom of the counsel who filed these demurrers. To our great discredit, as I think, technicalities of the kind which it raises have been too often successful to permit a conscientious counsel to forego their trial, whenever his ingenuity devises them. . . . Any honest reasoning is quite legitimate, and the responsibility for mistakes must rest with the court. Nevertheless, I cannot resist saying that to adopt the construction which is suggested would, in my judgment, be to pervert the obvious meaning of the act quite unpardonably, and that, too, by a metaphysic which is fatuously verbal and naively nonsensical. . . . While the act is badly drawn, its intent—an intent not imputed, but drawn from the words—is perfectly obvious.[16]

At that time the form of the indictment was frequently challenged, and the first three criminal cases in which he wrote opinions involved such attacks. He denied each of them and made it clear that he would not defer to technical defenses. He maintained this position throughout his service as a district judge.

As a circuit judge, Hand continued to follow the rule of reason when called upon to review errors of the courts below. When the defendant was clearly guilty, Hand was not quick to discover error. He believed that the surest way to achieve a strong system of trial courts was to leave large responsibility to the judge. In *United States* v. *Cotter* he stated his position:

> Criminal prosecutions are not to test the trial judge's adeptness in answering questions of law, put to him in multitude, often in the heat

---

[16] *United States* v. *Franklin*, 174 Fed. 163, 164 (1909).

of sharp dispute. Trials are to winnow the chaff from the wheat; when the accused has had fair opportunity to answer the charge; when it has been lawfully proved, and fair men have found him guilty, our duties end.[17]

However, when there was evidence of partisanship on the part of the trial judge, Hand reversed the judgment, and when it appeared possible to him that the error in question might have altered the verdict, he was ready to acknowledge it. His sense of fair play required that evidence which might have been favorable to the defendant could not be withheld. In *United States* v. *Krulewitch* the defendant appealed to see a written statement made some time before the trial by one of the principal witnesses for the prosecution. The sealed statement had come to Hand as appeals judge, and upon examination he determined that it was in fact inconsistent with the witness's testimony at the trial. Hand ruled that the refusal to admit the written statement was a reversible error and that the defense should have been permitted to examine it. In the same spirit he ruled in *United States* v. *Andolschek* that the government could not claim that reports were privileged when they were the basis of the prosecution.

With regard to the documents that the judge had denied the defense permission to see in *United States* v. *Coplon*, he said:

> in truth, it is extremely unlikely that she suffered the slightest handicap from the judge's refusal. But, we cannot dispense with constitutional privileges because in a specific instance they may not in fact serve to protect any valid interest of their possessor. Back of this particular privilege lies a long chapter in the history of Anglo-American institutions. Few weapons in the arsenal of freedom are more useful than the power to compel a government to disclose the evidence on which it seeks to forfeit the liberty of its citizens.[18]

Hand's reluctance to find error in the evidence admitted or the charge to the jury is partly a result of his confidence in the jury's ability to reach fair conclusions in most situations. He was not unaware of the problems of juries, but he thought that minor errors in matters of evidence and charges to the juries generally would not alter the verdict.

[17] *United States* v. *Cotter*, 60 F. (2d) 698 (1932).
[18] *United States* v. *Coplon*, 185 F. (2d) 629 (1950).

He was, nevertheless, rigorous in maintaining the constitutional provisions regarding juries. He thought that trial in the locality where the crime was committed was very important and reversed for error in venue when it seemed appropriate.

His distaste for the formal legalism of the technical error as a means of escaping punishment did not deter him from giving vigorous protection to the procedural safeguards found among the constitutional rights. When they were abused, Hand was ready to defend the most squalid huckster. Jerome Frank, one of his colleagues on the Second Circuit Court of Appeals noted that Hand

> has been a doughty defender of the procedural provisions of the Constitution, whether contained in the Bill of Rights or elsewhere. . . . In particular, he has, in his decisions, enforced rigorously the Fourth Amendment's prohibition of unreasonable searches and seizures; our kind of society, he believes, cannot survive unless the courts prevent such incursions on the individual's privacy.[19]

In *United States* v. *Casino* he held that a search even under a warrant was illegal unless there was sufficient evidence to make the search reasonable. He said, "The Constitution protects the guilty along with the innocent. . . . It means to prevent violent entries till evidence is obtained independently of the entries themselves. . . . Were it not so, all seizures would be legal which turned out successful."[20] In *United States* v. *Kirschenblatt* he emphasized that the power to search under the Fourth Amendment must be limited to the "tools and the fruits of the crime" and that ransacking the defendant's home and going through papers not related to the crime violated rights the amendment was designed to protect.[21]

Hand's opinion in *United States* v. *Coplon* is a vigorous defense of the Fourth Amendment and meant the reversal of Judith Coplon's espionage conviction. Miss Coplon, an employee of the State Department, had been convicted of conspiring to defraud the United States by delivering material that she had made insistent efforts to obtain to Valentine Gubitchev, a citizen of a foreign country. Miss Coplon and

---

[19] Jerome Frank, "Some Reflections on Judge Learned Hand," *Chicago Law Review*, Vol. XXIV (1957), 690.

[20] *United States* v. *Casino*, 268 Fed. 976 (1923).

[21] *United States* v. *Kirschenblatt*, 16 F. (2d) 202 (1926).

Gubitchev were arrested without a warrant, and in her purse was found a sealed packet of incriminating documents which she would have had no occasion to carry if she had not intended to give them to Gubitchev. Hand agreed that the evidence would have convinced any fair-minded jury that she was engaged in a conspiracy as charged and that she fully intended to pass the material on to Gubitchev when the proper time came. But he noted that the statute under which she was being tried gives agents of the Federal Bureau of Investigation power to make arrests without warrant for felonies when there are reasonable grounds to believe that the person is guilty and when there is likelihood that the person may escape before a warrant for arrest can be obtained. While the judge before whom Miss Coplon was taken after her arrest found that she was likely to escape, Judge Hand found no reason to justify the assumption. He said:

> Moreover, there was not the slightest need of arresting her without a warrant, even if there had been danger that she might run away and hide. It is apparent that even in the morning the Bureau had decided to arrest her that day; and there was not the least need of doing so without a warrant. No sudden emergency forced the hand of the agents; they made everything ready except the one condition which would have made the arrest lawful: a warrant.
>
> The statute certainly required a warrant when there is time to obtain one; the dispensation is limited to occasions when it is not safe to wait. The only excuse that is suggested is that Gubitchev might have made off with the papers, and to it there are two answers. First, the condition is not that evidence shall be likely to escape, but that the person to be arrested shall be. Second, if a warrant had been obtained, the incriminating papers could as well have been seized. We have no alternative but to hold that the arrest was invalid, and concededly that made the packet incompetent against her.[22]

The rule that it is unreasonable not to obtain a warrant for arrest when there is time to do so has not always been honored by the Supreme Court, but it is an eminently logical one that if followed would provide an objective standard for the guidance of law officers. Taken together the Casino, Kirschenblatt, and Coplon cases would, if followed, provide a high degree of protection for Fourth Amendment rights. They

[22] *United States* v. *Coplon*, 185 F. (2d) 629 (1950).

provide consistent, objective, and predictable standards and reflect Judge Hand's belief that it is the responsibility of the courts to provide as specific standards as the subject matter permits.

While the number of cases dealing with substantive criminal law was fewer than those dealing with procedural problems, Hand had his share of the former. Orrin Judd suggested the scope of Hand's substantive criminal holdings as of 1947: they included sustaining the constitutionality of the Harrison Anti-Narcotic Law, upholding an indictment under the Espionage Act of 1917, hearing cases under the mail-fraud statute, and other crimes related to the increasing federal regulatory power. (His substantial contribution to the law of censorship is dealt with in a later chapter concerning the First Amendment.) In 1919 he heard a treason trial in which he directed a verdict in favor of the defendant on the grounds that there must be two witnesses to the overt act, a rule that was followed by the Supreme Court at the close of World War II.

As the number of federal crimes grew, the importance of federal law making it a crime to conspire to commit a crime also grew. Judd says that Learned Hand's decisions "contributed toward making conspiracy 'that darling of the modern prosecutor's nursery,' as he termed it."[23] While he did permit broad use of this technique for joining several defendants in one trial and using the testimony of one against the others, he was conscious of the problems of determining individual guilt in such trials and sought to establish rules for safeguarding individual defendants. For example, in *United States* v. *Crimmins* he ruled that a defendant had to understand the purposes of a conspiracy and join in those purposes before evidence could be admitted against him.

In the area of constitutional issues Hand doubtless made his unique contribution to American jurisprudence, and it is here that he attracted his most severe criticism. In matters of constitutional law he was primarily interested in the role of the court as the umpire between the nation and states, judicial review of substantive issues of legislation and administration, and the interpretation of the Bill of Rights. The focal point of this book is an examination of his position on these constitutional issues, its implications for the American system, and some criti-

[23] Judd, "Judge Learned Hand and the Criminal Law," *Harvard Law Review*, Vol. LX (February, 1947), 418–19.

cisms of his position. These matters will be dealt with more fully in subsequent chapters.

Learned Hand's personal predilection would have placed him alongside the judicial protectors of individual liberties, but his understanding of the American democratic system caused him to assume what by modern standards is a very conservative view of the court's role in this effort. The impact of his First Amendment opinions has ranged widely, and, except for his understanding of the proper function of judicial review which runs through them all and provides the principle of coherence, they might appear inconsistent. *Masses Publishing Co. v. Patten* was widely hailed as a libertarian judgment which in spite of public clamor held to the highest principles of free speech; his decision in *Dennis v. United States,* which upheld the conviction of Communist leaders, was greeted with mixed reactions; and his reversal of the conviction of Judith Coplon on procedural grounds attested to his loyalty to constitutional principles which he regarded as specific enough to serve as a basis for legal action.

His disagreement with the most active judicial defenders of liberty was not with the necessity of freedom to human life but with the proper function of a judge in a democratic society. He acted in accordance with his understanding of that function and did not assume the role of social or moral reformer. Even though he was criticized for what some in the legal and judicial circles thought was failure to exercise fully the authority to which he had access, he chose not to use judicial interpretation as a means of moving society closer to his own vision of the good life:

> For this role of prophet, innovator, and statesman Learned Hand has never billed himself. To him the judge who took the central role would have betrayed his trust. He was commissioned for a different part—a leader of the Greek chorus interpreting and appraising the drama. The artistry, the forbearance in judgment, and the faithfulness with which Learned Hand has performed that part are his principal contribution to the public law. . . . His use of allusion and suggestion, his scorn of didacticism disclose the detachment, skepticism, and tolerance which are for him cardinal virtues of the judge.[24]

[24] Stephen H. Philbin, "Judge Learned Hand and the Law of Patents and Copyrights," *Harvard Law Review,* Vol. LX (February, 1947), 396.

That his life and judgment were in close harmony with his philosophy is repeatedly attested to by his colleagues of the bar and bench. The human characteristics he held essential to the progress and happiness of man are the ones most often used to describe him and his work. Archibald Cox said:

> . . . at the heart of his work lies deep-seated tolerance. I say deep-seated to distinguish his tolerance from easy acquiescence in the view of others. It stems from knowledge, . . . from learning of the kind which he suggests may quiet the spirit of faction and expose the emptiness of catch-words, which too often have the explosive energy of faith behind them. Deep-seated, too, because Judge Hand's continuing search for truth yielded . . . the conclusion that the outlook of man on life depends in the end on arbitrary preferences. . . . because of it he does not put his own conclusions beyond question, and so is willing to try out the views of others. . . . Such a spirit finds in the freedom from words and canons of interpretation the opportunity to manifest in their particulars the ideals and purposes underlying legislation, even when they are quite different from our own. It does so, not in the despair which skepticism sometimes breeds but in the faith that, as by endlessly retesting its hypotheses reason may proceed towards truth, so by trial and error man proceeds.[25]

Judge Hand's authority was not limited to the jurisdiction of his court, for he contributed to the structure and spirit of American law through his participation in professional associations, the most significant one of which was the American Law Institute. He was vice-president, member of the council, and served as adviser on many codes and restatements, thereby making a substantial and influential impact upon the law in areas lying outside the scope of his federal judgeship.

The institute draws upon the talents of judges, lawyers, and law-school teachers to provide a continuing effort to clarify and simplify the law, to help adapt it better to meet new social needs, and conducts a program of legal education in co-operation with the American Bar Association. As part of this activity it prepares restatements of the law and drafts model codes for the assistance of legislatures. Hand con-

[25] Archibald Cox, "Judge Learned Hand and the Interpretation of Statutes," *Harvard Law Review*, Vol. LX (February, 1947), 392–93.

tributed to the Code of Criminal Procedure, the Model Code of Evidence, the Restatement of Torts, the Restatement of Conflicts of Law, and the Model Penal Code. It is difficult to measure accurately the degree of influence he exercised in these debates, but perhaps one instance will suggest some measure of his authority.

In 1955 the annual meeting of the institute had under consideration the proposed Model Penal Code, which was to provide guidance for state laws. As the discussion moved into the area of sex offenses, it seemed clear to most of those present that, since most states did not enforce their laws forbidding adultery, it should not continue to be considered a statutory crime. The institute finally limited criminal penalties for homosexual behavior to that "involving force, adult corruption of minors and public offense," thereby rejecting a clause branding a homosexual as one engaging in deviant behavior and, therefore, guilty of a crime.

The issue of sodomy proved to be more controversial, and both arguments for and against labeling it a crime against the state were set forth. In the course of the discussion Judge Hand expressed his position, saying, "I think it [sodomy] is a matter of morals, a matter very largely of taste, and it is not a matter that people should be put in prison about."[26] He then recalled that he had previously voted to retain the provision because he feared its elimination would produce a negative reaction to the code as a whole, but, since he had finally decided that the chance of its prejudicing the code was not too great, he cast his lot with those who would remove it from the list of crimes. The institute subsequently voted thirty-five to twenty-four to uphold the view he expressed and removed sodomy as well as adultery from the list of crimes against the state. It was this element of personal authority that Hand commanded, which was in many ways independent of official position, that led Justice Frankfurter to say of him:

> His jurisdiction was confined within Acts of Congress and the controlling precedents of his hierarchical superiors, but not his authority. His influence radiated to all the courts of the land and thereby improved the corpus and spirit of American law. Suffice it here to say that by his

26 "The Law," *Time*, Vol. LXV (May 30, 1955), 13.

opinions and his dominant role in shaping the various Restatements of the American Law Institute he magisterially affected doctrine in areas of the law lying wholly outside the scope of federal jurisprudence.[27]

[27] Frankfurter, "Learned Hand," *Harvard Law Review*, Vol. LXXV, No. 1 (November, 1961), 2.

PART II : *The Philosophy He Chose*

CHAPTER III : *The Nature of Man and His Values*

Man's actions and thoughts regarding the most important things invariably stem from fundamental assumptions about man and his place in the universe. Learned Hand attempted to understand, acknowledge, and articulate his own philosophical assumptions, and much of his nonjudicial writing was concerned with these deeper meanings, with developing and expounding his own philosophy, which profoundly affected his judicial opinions.

Hand's understanding of philosophy was a traditional one—that is, a quest for truth about man and the universe which provides a basis for rational thought and action. He believed that any interpretation of man was necessarily drawn from assumptions about the nature of man. He did not shrink from making such assumptions; and in the tradition of his teachers whom he admired so greatly, he had the courage "to bet his all on what was no more than the best guess he could make" about man and the universe in which he lives.[1] From this philosophical understanding he approached the problem of human values and political life and eventually the role of the judiciary in the American democratic system. Thus an examination of his assumptions about man and his values and the expression of his philosophy through actual legal decisions provides an opportunity to consider the implications of this philosophy for practical political life.

Hand believed that man is an evolving, intermediate creature whose upward path is uncertain and difficult. His origin is clear—he is

that old Adam who, from the first flicker of sentience and in the midst

[1] Learned Hand, "At Fourscore," *Harvard Alumni Bulletin*, Vol. LIV, No. 10 (February, 1952), as reprinted in Hand, *The Spirit of Liberty* (3d ed.), 259.

of the appalling tragedy of existence, has striven to endure, and in spite of all still goes on. Man's upward course from the first amoeba which felt a conscious thrill, is no more than the effort to affirm the meanings of his own strange self, to divine his significance, and to make it manifest in the little hour vouchsafed him.[2]

Man's rise from his remote forerunners has been a groping, searching movement along a murky path strewn with violence and immeasurable waste. What he gains in the future will be achieved in the same searching, groping, inefficient fashion.

Hand was always hopeful for the successful achievement of man's desires, yet he did not think progress in this direction was guaranteed by the nature of things. It depends, rather, upon man's constant and unremitting struggle to pull himself upward, to create, and to achieve the good life from among the resources available to him. Man can ill afford to rely upon some concept of necessary progress or benevolent nature. The provisional character of man's progress results from the creativity of the individual and the finality of his choice.

According to the dictionary, evolution may be "any process which exhibits a direction of change." This was Hand's understanding of human evolution, and it is in evidence throughout his writings. He did not believe that it was by accident, fortuitous variation in the reproductive process, mechanical causation, or cataclysmal evolution that man had come into being. Humanity developed as a result of both chance and man's own free efforts through pragmatic doubt, trial, and tentative conclusion. As he gropes along his path there are no absolute criteria by which he may judge the truth or wisdom of his choices or whether they are in fact leading him to greater happiness and satisfaction. Thus he is forced to create his own values, and to vindicate them he must rely upon trial and error—pragmatic incursions into reality. He must experiment time and again, but if he is persistent and honest in his effort, his reward will be closer concurrence between his choices and reality. The method by which Hand believed human development came about reflected his high regard for the methodology of science and his long association with the early American pragmatists.

---

[2] Learned Hand, "Mr. Justice Holmes," *Harvard Law Review*, Vol. XLIII (April, 1930), as reprinted in *The Spirit of Liberty* (3d ed.), 60.

Judge Hand's view of the nature of man was an expansive one which left open the possibility of great creativity and achievement, as well as the occasional or even persistent domination of his lower animal instincts. Though trial and error be the lot of man, each advancement does provide a new base from which to strive for some further step. Thus man is not limited in action or choice by his primeval animal needs. In the long reaches of man's growing humanity the satisfaction of basic wants has pointed in turn to new goals and desires—luxuries have become necessities, ends have become means; and there seems to be no limit to human desire and thus no discernible limit to the human drive and creativity necessary to satisfy it. Man's progress is intimately related to the development and expansion of his needs, from the satisfaction of his primitive bodily demands to the satiation of his craving for the luxuries of civilization. Potential achievement has been greatly enhanced by science, which also contains the possibility of the ultimate destruction of what is called civilization. Hand's optimism about the future of man was tempered by his belief in man's right to choose for himself and an almost sanguine acceptance that this choice might in the end prove to be destructive. Nonetheless, he believed that man had the capacity to achieve a better world and a better life by his own unassisted powers. His advice was to

> beware then of the heathen gods; have no confidence in principles that come to us in the trappings of the eternal. Meet them with gentle irony, friendly scepticism and an open soul. Nor be cast down, for it is always dawn. Day breaks forever, and above the eastern horizon the sun is now about to peep. Full light of day? No, perhaps not ever. But yet it grows lighter, and the paths that were so blind will, if one watches sharply enough, become hourly plainer. We shall learn to walk straighter. Yes, it is always dawn.[3]

Nature is grandly indifferent to man, it may at times appear friendly or hostile. The universe is incomplete, open, subject to whatever order man can impose. Even though his home is a "great and awful Universe, where man is so little and fate so relentless, . . . his hands reach

---

[3] Learned Hand, "Democracy: Its Presumptions and Realities," *Federal Bar Association Journal*, Vol. I, No. 2 (March, 1932), reprinted in *The Spirit of Liberty* (3d ed.), 101–102.

out towards all of nature on which to impose the forms which his busy brain contrives; and so he literally creates his world, fabricating now this, now that, for the mere joy of creation."[4] There is within man some unaccountable urge toward creativity, a compulsion to leave his own impression on the flux of his world—to impose form and order upon the universe in which he lives. Not only does the world become coherent through man's creative effort, it is through the satisfactions of this conscious desire to impose himself upon an indifferent universe that man achieves satisfaction as a human being.

Learned Hand viewed human life as a struggle to create the meaning of man and that of the universe. For those rare individuals who are able to cope with the awful freedom there is great satisfaction in this creation. It is this self-assertion which not only gives meaning to the universe and to human life but also provides the potential capacity to control and exploit nature to gratify growing desires and to find the good life. Man's future and purpose is undefined except as he determines it for himself. Hand believed human purpose is based on desire and guided by experience arising from those choices which provide the greatest satisfactions. If man can only discover what he truly wants, there is reason to hope that, through modern science, he may achieve it with a degree of success yet undreamed—that he may further confine the power of the physical world to limit his choices.

Even though an evolutionary view suggests that there is only a difference in degree between man and his animal forebears, Learned Hand found something almost sacred in man. He is significant and interesting because of his creativity, his almost limitless capacity for achievement, and his ability to look into the future and to choose and plan what he will be in that future. Hand's belief in the supreme importance of the individual was derived from his assumption that man, being undetermined and without a definable "nature" or "essence" in the traditional sense of Plato and Aristotle, creates his own essence; that is, he is what he chooses to be and is guided by the values and standards he selects—he imposes upon the world whatever meaning it has. Hand believed that man has an existence and certain given

---

[4] Hand, "Mr. Justice Holmes," *Harvard Law Review*, Vol. XLIII (April, 1930), as reprinted in *The Spirit of Liberty* (3d ed.), 63, 61.

potentialities—that there is a universal human condition—but that what each one does with it depends upon his own individual choice.

It is as man creates the universe and his own place in it that Hand thought human freedom essential within certain basic and irreducible limits. An important limiting factor is man's own human condition— the bounds of physical necessity, human rationality, and the tentativeness of all knowledge. In addition to this inner limit there are external bounds to man's freedom to create. He is limited by the "outside world," as Hand called it. While man has learned by his own great scientific discoveries that much of nature is subject to his control and mastery, there are certain physical realities in the world which are given and upon which he cannot impose his own choice or image. Futhermore, since he seeks association with his fellow men, the requirements of society place additional restrictions on his freedom. It is within this framework that man must seek to satisfy his physical, spiritual, and intellectual impulses.

While an open or undetermined system makes man's progress or success tentative and uncertain, it has the advantage of imposing no objective limits on the potential achievements of man. From Hand's point of view, one can accurately speak of progress only in terms of some specific chosen goal. Since there is no natural end for man by which human progress can be judged, progress must be relative to specific goals that he has freely chosen. Hand spoke frequently of the good life and assumed that all men desire it, but since the definition of the good life is confined to personal choice, it does not afford a general standard by which progress can be measured.

To be human is to choose, but man's partial identification with the brutes means that he, like them, has physical desires, passions, and instincts and that these bodily needs will be factors in his choice and may provide the initial stimuli for all action. Hand's definition of man includes this understanding. But while man's action may be motivated by these primary animal needs and desires, his humanity requires that he choose the appropriate manner to achieve their satisfaction. This facility of choosing and the possibility of rational thought entering into the choice is the quality that sets man off from his arboreal ancestors. "Life is a dicer's throw; and reason, a smoky torch. We move by what light we have; but some light we need to move at all."[5] Man's rationality is relative and incomplete—it suggests solutions to be tested so that through the pragmatic method of trial and error suitable means may be discovered to those ends first demanded by his passions. Man can only discover what is useful through trial and error, and so to know both success and failure is an essential part of human experience. This pragmatic view regards reason as essentially purposive and primarily an instrument in the evolutionary struggle. It is a means of solving man's immediate problems and, insofar as he has the power, of reshaping his environment to make it better serve his needs and desires. Even a strictly instrumental view of reason affirms its incredible importance in the search for solutions to some of man's fundamental problems.

Hand was conscious of the great variations in men's capacity to reason and may well have thought that the limits of this human power were still unknown. The progress of mankind did not seem to him to require that all men be truly creative or highly rational. It seemed enough that the opportunity remain open to those who have the capacity and desire to create. He regretted what he thought was a current tendency to discredit reason, for he was certain that the improvement of man's condition was dependent upon reason and that anything which tended to destroy that capacity threatened his humanity. He noted that ideas are as infectious and spread as rapidly as disease. Men become attached to them without comprehending what they imply or where they lead. "Such habits are not conducive to the life of reason; that kind of devotion is not the method by which man has raised himself from a savage. Rather by quite another way, by doubt, by trial, by tentative conclusion."[6] Man's use of his reason accounts for the direction of his own transformation and that of nature. Will or desire may provide the first impulse to action, but reason has guided that impulse in a way that has caused man to be what he is today.

Ultimate choices of purposes and values cannot be rationally determined according to Hand because he denied that there is a standard outside man by which they can be measured. Rational thought is the

---

[5] Learned Hand, "At the Harvard Tercentenary Observance," *Harvard Alumni Bulletin,* Vol. XXXIX (September, 1936), as reprinted in *The Spirit of Liberty* (3d ed.), 122.

[6] Learned Hand, "Sources of Tolerance," *Pennsylvania Law Review,* Vol. LXXIX (November, 1930), as reprinted in *The Spirit of Liberty* (3d ed.), 75.

instrument of some human goal. The criterion of reason is outside of reason since the success or failure of thought is determined by whether or not it contributes to achievement of a desired goal.

Man exhibits the human characteristic of conscious choice only as he pauses and reflects before choosing. Since choice determines the direction of his creation, if not its purpose or end, it is a highly significant if not impelling human characteristic. But it is the nature of man that he is not consistently guided by his reason. Man's mind is a part of his human body and is forever tied to and limited by it.

The importance of free choice to human life suggests the need for tolerance of other choices. Upon his retirement Judge Hand observed that the key to his philosophy was found in Oliver Cromwell's plea before the Battle of Dunbar: "I beseech ye in the bowels of Christ, think that ye may be mistaken. . . . for it seems to me that if we are to be saved it must be through skepticism."[7] Skepticism and doubt are essential to pragmatic trial and error, to knowledge through experience, and to a spirit of tolerance. But man is not naturally endowed with skepticism, and while it may be acquired, it always remains an alien. In spite of this, Hand believed man's happiness was dependent upon his ability to overcome what appears to be a natural instinct to suppress all ideas and opinions that differ from his own. So it is not sufficient that man merely acknowledge his lowly animal origins—he must repress much of this inheritance if he is to achieve what seemed to Learned Hand a satisfactory human life. He believed that experience itself encourages the qualities needed for further experimentation, for the attempt to discover for one's self often leads to humility, tolerance, and skepticism.

Learned Hand believed that man has become human through his freedom to create, to reason, to experiment, to find meaning to his life, and to impose order upon the world; and so human society is conditioned upon the continuing opportunity for free creation and rational choice. His belief in the profound necessity for tolerance and the open mind for human life follows naturally. He said:

> For I submit that it is only by trial and error, by insistent scrutiny and by readiness to re-examine presently accredited conclusions, that we have risen, so far as in fact we have risen, from our brutish ancestors; and I believe that in our loyalty to these habits lies our only chance, not merely

[7] Hand, "The Spirit of Liberty," as reprinted in *The Spirit of Liberty* (1st ed.), xxiv–v.

53

of progress, but even of survival. They are not, indeed, a part of our aboriginal endowment. . . . Obviously, enough of us did manage to get through; but it has been a statistical survival.[8]

Since man is simply what he makes of himself, there are many inconsistencies in individual men and profound inconsistencies and divergences in man as a class. He is what he proves to be in any given situation. He may be rational, noble, creative, and virtuous today and irrational, contemptible, fearful, and without honor tomorrow. These differences are surpassed only by the differences in values men choose.

Nietzsche's defiant and strident declaration that "God is dead!" provided the basis for much twentieth-century philosophy. Man, if thus released from the bonds of Christian or divine morality, might create his own values. Insofar as faith in God has in fact declined, divine meaning or purpose to life has also declined. The emerging philosophy has been that man is the creator of all values and all law. This belief is apparent in Learned Hand's writings. He was emphatic in his belief that as the creator of the universe man must create his own values. He asserted this again and again, and it properly followed from his understanding of man. He said, "Outside ourselves there is no value; what we desire is the sole measure of right and wrong, of Heaven and Hell."[9]

If human values are based solely on arbitrary choice, desire, liking, or preference without reference to external standards, they can be thought of as absolute for each individual and incapable of being subsumed under any higher order of values. Hand believed that in this sense they are ultimate—once the preference is expressed, a value created and declared, there is nothing more to say.

He was not dismayed by the existence of many conflicting values but accepted this as inevitable. He argued that as man became aware of the relative, changing, and even arbitrary nature of his own choices he would become tolerant of others. Surely a generation that had seen even the sciences of its fathers become outmoded would not speak in "apocalyptic verities" or scourge those who prize different values. He

[8] Learned Hand, "A Fanfare for Prometheus," as reprinted in *The Spirit of Liberty* (3d ed.), 294.
[9] Hand, "Mr. Justice Holmes," *Harvard Law Review*, Vol. XLIII (April, 1930), as reprinted in *The Spirit of Liberty* (3d ed.), 61.

knew such tolerance was not a fact, however, and in a less optimistic moment acknowledged that factions caused by disagreement about values might ultimately destroy the pluralistic democratic society which he believed essential to the good life for man.

If Judge Hand acknowledged no external standards, what did "the truth" mean to him? It appeared to be some illusory quality dancing always beyond man's grasp which was such a beguiling enchantress that he was impelled to try to bring her within his reach. This was the truth which he believed Charles Peirce, William James, and John Dewey pursued, forsaking all claim to absolutes or values outside themselves and trusting only pragmatic experience. It is in the search of this truth that man faces "the discords of the Tower of Babel" with equanimity, and tolerance becomes both possible and necessary as a guiding principle in human life.

Hand believed that man must have faith in the values he holds if he is to defend them against attack. This is so for individuals and for whole communities. The test of faith in a belief is whether or not one is willing to act on it. Insofar as man acts on the basis of his beliefs he has faith in them; and to the extent that the actions are successful the beliefs are true and have value because they have provided the basis for a successful experience or progress toward a desired goal.

Truth as a pragmatic concept is measured by the success of internally chosen values in the outside world. Man may create his own moral standards or values through an exercise of his own free will or arbitrary choice, but the test of their "truth" or validity lies in their experienced consequences relative to assumed goals. The creation is internal, but the test of truth is external. There are no substantive, objective, or eternal truths or permanent answers to the problems of man. What is true today may be proved false tomorrow.[10] Learned Hand described the

---

[10] William James defined "truth" and "right" in a way that appears compatible with Hand's use of these terms. James wrote: " *'The true,' to put it very briefly, is only the expedient in the way of our thinking, just as 'the right' is only the expedient in the way of our behaving. Expedient in almost any fashion; and expedient in the long run and on the whole of course; for what meets expediently all the experience in sight won't necessarily meet all farther experiences equally satisfactorily. Experience, as we know, has ways of boiling over, and making us correct our present formulas. . . . Meanwhile we have to live to-day by what truth we can get to-day, and be ready to-morrow to call it falsehood."* William James, *Pragmatism*, 145.

kind of man who is capable of approaching his goal of truth when he said of Judge Samuel Williston:

> He was an innovator throughout his subject, but by steps, and in response to an intellectual detachment which stifled overwhelming loyalties or the afflatus of revelation. Such men certainly never figure among the Luthers of the world, and no doubt the world owes much to its Luthers; abuses get deeply rooted and entwine so much that to tear them out will fetch along much that is good. The eruptive energy necessary can apparently be nurtured only upon burning concepts, arrived at intuitively, coming with the impact of absolute certainty. But whatever their services, revolutionaries obstruct the path to truth; the qualities which clear it are wholly inconsistent with theirs; scepticism, tolerance, discrimination, urbanity, some—but not too much— reserve towards change, insistence upon proportion, and, above all, humility before the vast unknown.[11]

Dedication to the truth requires intellectual detachment and denial of overwhelming loyalties. Man's highest effort is search for truth. Only thus can he discover what is worthy of loyalty and devotion because it leads to the good life. But the search appears to be incompatible with the capacity to defend the values man chooses as a result of this search for truth. He must have sufficient faith to act upon his choices and to support them when they are confronted by alien doctrines, but this appears to lead to intolerance and away from the truth.

Hand's philosophy of relative human values nourished by tolerance, skepticism, and intellectual detachment from the burning controversies of the day is challenged as inadequate by A. A. Berle, Jr., who asked:

> how does any man find possibility of achieving this state of grace or any fraction thereof? How is he defended in impartiality, protected against unbearable pressure, safeguarded in pursuing without interruption the course of his self-directed mind? . . . One can be coolly serene and tolerant of this [Communist] view of course—but only if defended from it and safely kept beyond its scope. Other, less spectacular forces deny Hand's premises and seek to drive any who hold them into final silence.

[11] Learned Hand, "Foreword to Williston's Life and Law," *Life and Law*, as reprinted in *The Spirit of Liberty* (3d ed.), 142.

Historically, in Anglo-Saxon and American life, the existing measure of peace and order within which some fragment of this Olympian
hope may be realized has been attained only by centuries of passionate,
and often bloody, struggle.[12]

Berle argued that freedom to search for the truth is sustained not
only by detachment, skepticism, and tolerance but also by devotion,
loyalty, and courage in seeking, protecting, and even crusading for the
way of life which protects that search.

Hand did not deny that a man passionately devoted to an idea or
belief may contribute to human well-being—"no doubt the world owes
much to its Luthers." But he warned that such devotion may also
"convert him into a fanatical zealot, ready to torture and destroy and
to suffer mutilation and death for an obscene faith, baseless in fact and
morally monstrous,"[13] and thus may contribute either to man's happiness or to his despair and destruction. This appears to be an inherent
tension between the demands of philosophy (search for the truth) and
the demands of a political society for absolute loyalty to the beliefs upon
which the society is based. It appears to be another aspect of Hand's
dilemma in arguing that all men can achieve the skepticism and
tolerance bred in the scientific search for truth and that these can,
therefore, become guiding principles in human society. He was aware of
the problems of a society based on relative values but considered the
alternative to be contrary to his understanding of the needs of humanity
which he appeared to accept as a kind of objective standard. He affirmed
the value of democratic choice but as a member of society remained
free to question the wisdom of choices actually arrived at by this means.

Once he visited a Hollywood movie studio and was deeply im-
pressed with the marvels of man's modern technical and mechanical
achievement. But he found the uses to which this marvel had been put

> were beyond endurance tawdry, trite, dreary and childish. . . . The whole
> seemed to have been designed on the theory that one thing was as good
> as another provided it could, and would, be consumed. That was the
> vital fallacy. There is no democracy among human values, however

[12] A. A. Berle, Jr., review of *The Spirit of Liberty: Papers and Addresses of Learned
Hand, Columbia Law Review*, Vol. LII, No. 6 (June, 1952), 813.

[13] Learned Hand, "Mr. Justice Brandeis," as reprinted in *The Spirit of Liberty* (3d
ed.), 173.

each may cry out for an equal vote. It is the business of the soul to impose her own order upon the clamorous rout; to establish a hierarchy appropriate to the demand of her own nature, and by the mere fiat of her absolute choice, if that be based upon self-knowledge. . . . it is the cause that counts; and that must not be acquisition or affluence or power; but that, knowing herself, the soul shall be free, free to be herself; that, should she achieve success and learn the pattern of her needs, she may safely trust her will.[14]

But by what standard did Hand judge the use of this technical marvel of the movie studio to be unworthy? What of choice based on ignorance rather than self-knowledge? What if the cause *is* acquisition, affluence, or power? What of the soul that demands freedom without self-knowledge? If, lacking any ultimate standard of values that is valid for all men, each is entitled to define his own values, make his own choices, and enjoy the freedom to act upon them, and if these values are ultimate and not capable of being subjected to any common denominator, what is the basis of society? Hand might insist on a standard of self-knowledge so that man may safely trust his own will, but this is a personal, not a universal or even majority choice. Insofar as Hand provided an answer, it appears to be found in the determination of community values through the democratic process. This is apparent not only in his essays but in his judicial decisions as well. His understanding of the procedure of democracy included the freedom of each to work within the prescribed framework to secure community acceptance of his personally chosen values. Democracy in this light appears as a mutually accepted expediency for maintaining peace and order while each person or group seeks to impose his will upon the whole. Given the assumption of relative, man-created values and purposes, there appears to be no other basis for acquiescence in community values which one does not accept.

Berle suggested that Hand's thought and action were not altogether consistent, for, while he spoke of skepticism and detachment, he was not always tolerant of enemies of freedom or skeptical about the worth of freedom and the institutions which make it possible. Hand did sometimes speak as if his own values were absolute. Early in 1945, just

[14] Learned Hand, "To the Harvard Alumni Association," *Harvard Alumni Bulletin*, Vol. XXXVIII (July 3, 1936), reprinted in *The Spirit of Liberty* (3rd ed.), 113–14.

before the end of World War II, he spoke of the necessity of continuing the battle until Americans had done their part to fashion a better world in which "right," "justice," and "brotherhood of man" made the human association something more than a den of thieves. One is entitled to ask by what standard Hand sought to impose his notion of right, justice, and brotherhood upon other men if they were simply his own values. And again, what is the source of certainty with which he proclaimed the importance of free discussion?

> Risk for risk, for myself I had rather take my chance that some traitors will escape detention than spread abroad a spirit of general suspicion and distrust, which accepts rumor and gossip in place of undismayed and unintimidated inquiry. . . . The mutual confidence on which all depends can be maintained only by an open mind and a brave reliance upon free discussion. I do not say that these will suffice; who knows but we may be on a slope which leads down to aboriginal savagery. But of this I am sure: if we are to escape, we must not yield a foot upon demanding a fair field and an honest race to all ideas.[15]

According to pragmatic thought, intellectual dedication to a relative concept of values does not deny one the right or necessity of advocacy. Consistent with his assumption that man creates values, Hand chose his own. He had great faith in their validity and spoke of them in unconditional language. Repression of freedom by force and authority or even social pressure vitiates the opportunity of what Justice Holmes called "the best test of truth . . . the power of the thought to get itself accepted in the competition of the market"[16] and were thus incompatible with Hand's thesis. All goals and the diverse means to them must have an opportunity to compete regardless of their infinite variety or incompatibility, since truth will be discovered only through trial and error.

It has often been pointed out that the value of a free market in ideas assumes that all opinions will have an opportunity to be represented on a basis of equality in that market. Hand expressed great concern with the increasing tendency of the power of mass media and propaganda to destroy meaningful debate. As a purely personal choice

---

[15] Learned Hand, "A Plea for the Open Mind and Free Discussion," reprinted in *The Spirit of Liberty* (3d ed.), 284.

[16] *Abrams* v. *United States*, 250 U.S. 630 (1919).

he would rely on free expression, but he was not confident of the outcome and acknowledged the right and necessity of society to protect itself. Even though he retained his personal faith in freedom, in his capacity as judge he rendered decisions which limited freedom of expression when a prior judgment had been made by a proper authority that such a restraint was necessary.

Tolerance of all choices is the basic principle of a society based upon relative human values, and intolerance can be countenanced only insofar as it does not destroy the principle. Some absolute values appear to inhere in this position, and opposing values may be allowed only insofar as they are not destructive of the primary requisites of man as a creative and thus human animal. The limits Hand placed on choice are similar to those John Stuart Mill placed upon freedom when he denied the freedom to destroy liberty or the social and political structure which protected it.

In spite of Hand's insistence on the relativity of all values, there were some conditions he regarded as essential to humanity: freedom to choose or create according to one's own will, a degree of rationality implicit in conscious choice, and tolerance, without which there can be no real human freedom in society. He argued not that these conditions will always prevail or dominate but simply that insofar as they do not man's humanity is threatened. He stopped short of saying that these values provide an absolute standard for human life and must prevail, but it is clear that he believed they should. He might insist that these were his own values and others might choose different ones, but he would maintain that, if his own choices were justified by experience, selection of any other values would necessarily be based either upon a different set of criteria for judging the experience or upon arbitrary will opposed to experience. The issue would then become the standard by which experience is judged. While he always implied that his values were selected on the basis of experience, there is some obscurity and vagueness about the standards by which he ultimately evaluated the consequences of his "experiments." Arnold Brecht highlighted the problem when he wrote of pragmatists generally:

> Of course, pragmatists were inimical to value judgments made
> *a priori*, as they were to all a-priori statements. There was, however, no

outspoken tendency on their side to bar value judgments when arrived at *a posteriori*. On the contrary, they seemed to look to value judgments made *post factum* with confidence. Their major concern . . . was the emphasis on the practical consequences of different ideas and actions. The standards finally to be applied in evaluating these consequences played little if any role. Pragmatists seemed ever to repeat, "Let us watch the consequences and *then* judge, or rejudge; let us do things and see what happens, and then revise our concepts and ideas." It generally remained obscure, or at least undecided, whether they meant to say that when it came to evaluating the consequences there could be ultimately no difference of opinion, a view that would betray absolutistic tendencies in the tacit assumption of some highest standard of judgment, such as happiness of the individual or of some group; or whether they recognized that final controversies in evaluation could not be resolved with scientific means . . . or whether they would refer supra-individual evaluation to democratic procedure (majority decision after full discussion), which would be a political, not a scientific, solution of the problem and not help us in scientific controversies with those who in good faith do not agree with the majority principle.[17]

This criticism seems to apply in part to Hand. While he did not assert that there could be no differences in opinion in the evaluation of consequences of scientific investigation, he sometimes appeared to assume that the evaluation was implicit in the consequences themselves. He insisted upon the correctness of his own philosophical assumptions, which he regarded as not open to question. Ultimate values, by definition, are not subject to scientific proof or disproof but are matters of choice and of the will. He did believe that the experience and the trial and error which are part of the scientific methodology supported the validity of his assumptions, even though they could not prove that validity beyond scientific doubt.

It appears that, while it is possible to defend a concept of relative values on a theoretical basis and to affirm it intellectually, it may be very difficult to translate universal skepticism into a basis for action in a viable political society. The statesman-philosopher Cicero, himself a Skeptic, taught the Stoic doctrine to the Roman people, for he under-

[17] Arnold Brecht, *Political Theory: The Foundations of Twentieth Century Political Thought*, 192.

stood that universal skepticism regarding the very basis of society could lead to its destruction. Learned Hand possessed supreme self-restraint and self-discipline and was firmly devoted to his belief in the need for tolerance in a free society. The difficulty he had in maintaining a posture of complete skepticism and open-mindedness about his own values suggests a measure of the problem such a view poses for a whole society.

CHAPTER IV : *Cornerstones of Political Life*

As man aspires to rise above his crude beginnings and somehow to leave his own impression upon the universe, he is forced to create his own values and goals, to choose his own moral standards, and to create the world of good and evil according to his own desires. If man is to fulfill his human destiny as Hand understood it, he must be free—free to create, to desire, to pursue the truth wherever it may lead. Man's self-realization and self-affirmation depend upon such freedom.

Learned Hand knew that many concepts of liberty have been prized by man. Each of them seems to be charged with passion, and the record of the defense of liberty is one of great suffering and heroism. Liberty seems to touch the inner life of man so closely that he who will fight and die for anything will fight and die for it. It has been the rallying cry for those who attach contrary meanings to it, so that opponents in battle have both fought in the name of liberty. It is sometimes merely a negative term or the battle cry of empty, futile, or misunderstood convictions. It may be a useful catchword for those who are "conscious of constraint; but once set free, their lives may prove more inane than when they were hemmed about. . . . To most of us . . . freedom is a curse; we slink back into our cages however narrow, and our disciplines however archaic. They are the defenses against the intolerable agony of facing ourselves. We prate of freedom; we are in deadly fear of life, as much of our own American scene betrays."[1]

The fearsomeness of liberty is implied in these brief sentences. Most immediate is apprehension of loss of the constraints that give the limits and meaning to life. Convention, Hand once suggested, is like

[1] Hand, "Mr. Justice Holmes," *Harvard Law Review*, Vol. LII (April, 1930), as reprinted in *The Spirit of Liberty* (3d ed.), 59.

the shell of a chick, a protection until he is strong enough to break through. But once man has destroyed the bonds of convention and restraint, his life is often suddenly without meaning. He is struck with the deeper implications of liberty: that man is undetermined and without values except as he creates and chooses them—the existential understanding that he has no external justification for his values and that he is condemned to be free and thus totally responsible for his choices. Liberty is truly appreciated only by those who understand the great opportunity it offers and have the courage and capacity to avail themselves of it for creative purposes: for the self-assertion that is life itself and for the imprint that they may leave upon the universe.

The limits placed upon man's freedom by the natural universe are irrelevant to the problem of liberty in society, which is concerned with human hindrances. It was clear to Learned Hand that there must be limits of freedom in society, but the question remained, What is the nature of the limitations? To assert that there must be compromise merely states the problem. He illustrated the difficulty with an example from Plato's *Republic*. The high civilization and glorious life of the Athenian aristocrats necessitated the exploitation of slaves. It is often asserted that this concept was wrong because oppression and justice are inherently antithetical and injustice can never be right. Hand agreed with the conclusion but did not believe there was any way to reach this conclusion objectively. He was certain there was no way that a balance of the goods and evils of Athenian society could be struck. While man may find such a balance for himself in the present, he finds difficulty even in this if he includes his own future. The idea that it can be done for a whole community of many millions of persons seemed completely unrealistic to Hand. He regarded the resulting problem of discord and confusion as serious enough to suggest the practicability of instilling in all the belief that each achieves his highest good by completely submerging himself in the community. There would seem to be no denial of liberty, for no one would feel himself constrained. Man is malleable and might be taught to find satisfaction in a life dedicated to a common fate. But whatever contentment or tranquillity he might achieve in such a society would suppress what Hand believed to be the most precious part of man's nature—his inherent willfulness and self-assertion. This he thought must be preserved. He would not purchase social peace at the expense of progress toward man's creativity and a society appropriate to him. Hand could not claim this as an objective standard for he knew that social reformers reject it, but it was the standard by which he judged human society. He understood that man could be constrained without being conscious of constraint, but he believed that the collective fate of the community depends upon the "irrespressible fertility of the individual, and the finality of what he chooses to call good."[2]

In a more pragmatic vein Judge Hand contended that the only meaning of liberty that can survive in society is that it represents the degree of latitude the powerful choose to grant the weak. He could discover no principle which would alter this fact. Thus the limits of legitimate coercion seem to depend upon human forbearance. But if this is all, there is no substance to liberty, and man is forced into intolerable submission to a mass, perhaps mediocre conscience whose standards he may look upon with contempt. Hand viewed the paradoxical character of liberty in terms of the conflicting assumptions of human society found in Alexander Hamilton and Thomas Jefferson. He understood Jefferson's fear of the subjection of the individual to the domination of whatever the current notion of propriety might be. He believed that Jefferson had found the essential conditions of the good life in freedom of expression for each individual, the ability to determine the terms of his own life, and the right to enjoy the fruits of his own labor. While government was necessary to man it was also a constant threat to his freedom.

Hamilton thought government consisted of combinations based on self-interest and that liberty did not rest on anarchy. Man required an ordered society, which included not only individual concerns but collective interests and which permitted human life to rise above that of the savage and made possible joint efforts and thus more comfort, security, and leisure for a better life. He believed that while Jacobins cried for liberty what they really wanted was to exercise their own tyranny over the mob. It appeared to Learned Hand that history had proved Hamilton right. He approved this verdict and the expanded

[2] Learned Hand, "Liberty," *Yale Alumni Magazine*, Vol. IV (June, 1941), as reprinted in *The Spirit of Liberty* (3d ed.), 149, 151–52.

opportunities that have followed, though he acknowledged that a price had been paid in terms of personal freedom.

To Hand it seemed that the conditions of freedom change as man continues to refine and define for himself his goals and standards, his hopes and aspirations. If the American goal was once the pioneer absence of interference, in modern times it might be the development of a complex society which is able to contribute substantially to man's wants and desires yet which will leave for each individual a large sphere in which he may create and choose for himself. Liberty is not lack of restraint simply, but lack of restraint in those areas that are essential to the dynamic character of man—to his creativity and self-determination.

If there is a side of liberty that appears to be selfish because it is self-centered, dominated by the idea of self-assertion, the right to choose, the right to establish one's own goals, values, and standards based simply on individual preference, there is another side of liberty—that which makes possible a liberal democratic society. The former appears as an absolute if the individual is to be unimpaired in his choice of values. Supposedly, then, if man lived in isolation and without need of human association, his ideal would be complete freedom to determine his own individual future. Occasionally Hand spoke as if this were what he meant, but he also knew that man had long lived "in time and amid his kind; he looks before and after, his days are bound each to each, and he has his being only as a member of a group. That continuity and that communal nature clip his wings and cage his flights."[3] Thus if man is to continue his search for greater humanity and also satisfy an insistent desire for human association, this absolute freedom to create and choose must be moderated to encompass not only individuality but also society.

The spirit of liberty necessary to a political society which permits human creativity requires that each member of that society, while demanding those freedoms that are essential to his own nature, respect the same rights in other individuals. This is the tentative, tolerant, social aspect of liberty which must in the last analysis be found in the hearts of men and women. It is "not the ruthless, the unbridled will; it is not freedom to do as one likes. That is the denial of liberty, and

---

[3] Hand, "At the Harvard Tercentenary Observance," *Harvard Alumni Bulletin*, Vol. XXXIX (September, 1936), as reprinted in *The Spirit of Liberty* (3d ed.), 118–19.

leads straight to its overthrow. A society in which men recognize no check upon their freedom soon becomes a society where freedom is the possession of only a savage few, as we have learned to our sorrow."[4]

Thus Hand, prompted to seek the condition which makes freedom possible, found that the spirit of liberty is identified with a tolerance which is fearful of all orthodoxies and assumed that Americans have staked their hopes on the unverified thesis that the "path towards the Good Life is to assure unimpeded utterance to every opinion, to be fearful of all orthodoxies and to face the discords of the Tower of Babel; all with the hope that in the end the dross will somehow be automatically strained out, and we shall be left with the golden nuggets of truth."[5] Judge Hand was sensitively aware of the dichotomy between individual freedom and freedom provided by society. Both are essential to man, yet there is a permanent tension between the two. Hand, the pragmatist, left it unresolved except as it is worked out in each instance through experience. This is the condition of man, and the best he can do is meet each situation with the faith that trial and error will provide at least adequate answers as specific situations demand them. He believed that the problem of social freedom was not amenable to a permanent solution and would depend upon the tolerance and reason brought to bear upon the resolution of each conflict. He knew that it was not possible for man to become completely detached from his own special personal interests and desires. However, the tension between freedom to pursue individual concerns and the needs of society may be ameliorated as man learns that he must partly overcome his initial selfishness and intolerance if he is to achieve a satisfactory human life. Hand did not contend that the solution at any time would be satisfactory for all but believed that when it became sufficiently unpalatable to people with enough power to alter it, there was hope that the balance could be re-established without the dissolution of society. Throughout it all, the measure of man's freedom would be his own creativity.

Man learns to live in society and becomes aware of the relative nature of his own choices through the knowledge that they have been asserted before but have now generally disappeared. A sense of history

[4] Hand, "The Spirit of Liberty," as reprinted in *The Spirit of Liberty* (1st ed.), 190.
[5] Hand, "At Fourscore," *Harvard Alumni Bulletin*, Vol. LIV, No. 10 (February, 1952), as reprinted in *The Spirit of Liberty* (3d ed.), 257.

and of the culture of other peoples will help avoid the greatest danger in modern American society, "the disposition to take the immediate for the eternal, to press the advantage of present numbers to the full, to ignore dissenters and regard them as heretics."[6] Judge Hand offered this avenue to tolerance and liberty almost hesitatingly, aware of the difficulties it presented for the great multitude of people yet hopeful that some impress could be made upon the large numbers of young people flocking to the colleges and universities. Only in some such way could people hope to contend with the high-powered salesmanship of "political patent medicine."

To Hand a workable balance between the needs of the individual for freedom and the requirements of society appeared to rest in distinguishing between areas of common interest and concern, which should be subject to common decisions, and those of individual concern, which must remain the sole province of the individual self. This discrimination and delineation between public and private is, he believed, a part of the continuing growth and development of the community and depends upon man's rationality and his ability to make intelligent judgments about his future welfare.

For Learned Hand the idea of liberty had many facets which must be brought into proper relationship with each other. There is the liberty of the individual and of the society in which he lives. There is the negative freedom from interference but also the freedom of an ordered society which provides the conditions and opportunities that are necessary for creativity. There is the unbending spirit—the unassailable right to create all values—but also the tolerance that is necessary to the maintenance of liberty for all. Liberty is essential for spontaneity and creativity but requires discipline and concern for others.

To champion one aspect of liberty at the expense of others would be to destroy or deny its richness and magnitude. Hand sought not to make the complex and complicated simple by means of selective inclusion or exclusion but to comprehend its many diverse elements and their importance to man. This effort appears to be characteristic of him in all that he did. Justice Frankfurter described Hand's refusal to oversimplify in this way:

[6] Hand, "Sources of Tolerance," *Pennsylvania Law Review*, Vol. LXXIX (November, 1930), as reprinted in *The Spirit of Liberty* (3d ed.), 80.

When considerations of such magnitude influence if they do not under-
lie the accommodations that determine important adjudications, it is
not surprising that on occasion we find in Learned Hand, as in Holmes,
a certain vagueness of formulation and a penumbral scope to decisions.
This is a manifestation of clarity of thought. It is the kind of clarity,
which, in Professor Whitehead's phrase, "leaves the darkness unob-
scured." Analysis of a difficult problem may still be incomplete or its
solution as yet unattained. The search for truth at a given time may
require even of a judge avowed agnosticism or inexplicitness of statement. I believe it was Artemus Ward who said "it is better not to know
so many things than to know so many things that ain't so." Learned
Hand knows what he does not know; and he knows the importance of
not obstructing deeper analysis tomorrow by the illusory certainty of
obsolete or premature generalization. When he rejects, he has taken in
what he rejects, which is different from rejecting without understanding.
In short, he does not meet difficulties by evading them. Intricate problems do not appear simple to him, nor does he make them appear simple
to others by verbal legerdemain. He does not have the treacherous
strength that draws on jaunty confidence in one's power to solve
problems. He has that rarer strength which comes from readiness to
grapple fearlessly with issues defying sleazy answers.[7]

The concept of liberty is of fundamental importance in Learned
Hand's philosophy. It is consistent with his views of man, his universe
and values, and is a necessary presupposition for the dynamic creativity
which is the organizing principle of his whole doctrine. It is the essential
condition for man's creativity through which he gives meaning to
himself and the universe; it is the foundation of all humanistically
determined values. It was obvious to Hand that any society which
is good for man must permit individual freedom; this necessary condition of the development of man's humanity was the primary criterion
by which he measured democracy and more particularly American
democracy.

The question Hand posed in evaluating democracy might be stated
thus: Does it encourage the spirit of tolerance which alone will permit
the freedom necessary to man and yet create sufficient loyalty and
attachment to common goals to constitute a viable system? As with

[7] Felix Frankfurter, "Judge Learned Hand," *Harvard Law Review*, Vol. LX (February,
1947), 326–27.

other fundamental problems of men, he did not offer a final answer but affirmed democracy on the basis of his knowledge of human experience as the most satisfactory way of life man has yet conceived.

His approach to the understanding of democracy appears to be on two different levels, one theoretical or ideal and the other pragmatic and practical. He spoke and wrote about both the highest aspirations of a democratic society and the pragmatic truth of its actual operation. It seemed to him that the ideal presuppositions of traditional American democracy have not been borne out in practice. He understood those presuppositions to include intelligent concern for the public good which all judge alike and share in the same way so that the welfare of the individual is identified with that of the community. The traditional model of a democratic society does not include breakdown into classes, each of which presses its private demands without regard for the general welfare.

But in place of intelligent attention and capacity he saw apathy so deep no scandal, no disclosures of corruption seemed to stir the voters. It was conceivable to him that things might become "uncomfortable enough to arouse them, but, given reasonable opportunity for personal favors, and a not too irksome control, they are content to abdicate their sovereignty and to be fleeced, if the shepherds will only shear them in their sleep."[8]

This view of man as citizen is vastly different from his description of man as a being who creates for the "mere joy of creation." Did he mean to imply that man's inherent selfishness directs his energies, resourcefulness, and creativity to personal ends so what is the concern of all is the concern of none? That is possible, but his answer to the question would doubtless have been that man is a recalcitrant, willful creature who fits into no single mold. He may be creative or apathetic, and his energies may be directed toward either private or public concerns.

The problem of apathy in political life is not unrelated to another which was of equal concern to Learned Hand—that of conformity. It

[8] Learned Hand, "Democracy: Its Presumptions and Realities," *Federal Bar Association Journal*, Vol. I, No. 2 (March, 1932), as reprinted in *The Spirit of Liberty* (3d ed.), 94.

might even be possible to argue that the former grows out of the latter. He recalled that Jefferson sought to supplement the formal limits on governmental power to encroach upon man's realm of private liberty by a social structure based upon small communities of farmers which he thought could not be swept by uniformity or mob hysteria. Jeffersonian isolation has failed, and it is no longer possible to conceive of a modern society in terms of rural communities. But beyond that, even isolated communities are no longer free from the threat of mass hysteria, for the modern "levelers"—the press, the radio, and television—penetrate into the most remote areas of the land. There is no turning away from mass society and mass production with its relative affluence. But what are the implications of mass production, which has served so well in material goods, when one moves to the world of ideas, of morals, of religion, and of amusement?

It is partly the very closeness to one's fellow men (the condition Jefferson sought to avoid), the creations of a society dominated by mass production, and a life made easier and more pleasurable by new scientific advances which created the possibility of mass propaganda and the tendency to fall into comfortable patterns identical with those of one's fellows, that threatens man's individuality and his ability to think and act independently—to be creative and inventive.

The problem is closely related to the matter of preserving liberty in modern democratic society. The danger of comfortable conformity is that it makes freedom appear less vital and essential. If man does not exercise his liberty, it may atrophy, so that when life in a mass society loses its appeal either from monotony or abuse of authority, man may find himself so confined that he no longer has freedom to choose. Liberty must be constantly exercised if it is to be preserved.

Hand's answer to the pertinent question of how far liberty is consistent with the methods of Madison Avenue's high-power salesmanship, which are greatly enhanced by mass communication, was not reassuring. He said:

> our increasingly efficient and pervasive apparatus of mass suggestion is planing off individual differences, and making us more and more facile for mass manipulation. . . . Man is a gregarious animal, extremely sensitive to authority; if it will only indoctrinate him thoroughly in

his childhood and youth, he can be made to espouse any kind of orthodoxy.[9]

He believed that Hitler had proved the efficiency of this device, at least for the short run. No society, even a relatively sophisticated one, is free from the threats of manipulation.

If mass suggestion can contribute to a good society and make government easier in the way mass production has made our physical life more comfortable, why should its use be eschewed? How can one justify the limitation of scientific knowledge to control the natural world when our fellow men represent the most important part of our environment? These questions are especially relevant inasmuch as Hand admitted that men may not be happier when they are devoted to the democratic faith of tolerance and free expression than they are when they are under the spell of absolute orthodoxy which is protected from all heresy. His response was clear and unequivocal:

> My thesis is that any organization of society which depresses free and spontaneous meddling is on the decline, however showy its immediate spoils. . . . Even in the very technology on which they so much pride themselves, the totalitarians in the end will fail; for they stand upon the shoulders of generations of free inquiry. . . . Where heterodoxy in what men prize most is a crime, fresh thinking about anything will disappear.[10]

It seemed to Hand that the best argument against totalitarian regimes is not their immorality—though he thought they were immoral—but that they are unstable because they discourage the creative impulse in man. Any society that stifles creativity, either through conditions which dull his desire to create or through totalitarian controls, will, Hand believed, ultimately destroy the conditions of human happiness and satisfaction. He believed that a democratic society provides the best means to the good life but does not necessarily guarantee it. The problem is to discover a way to prevent democracy—the means devised to preserve liberty—from subverting and destroying it. Hand's hope for some mediation of the dilemma was in the open mind—in

[9] Hand, "Liberty," *Yale Alumni Magazine*, Vol. IV (June, 1941), as reprinted in *The Spirit of Liberty* (3d ed.), 149–50.
[10] *Ibid.*, 153–54.

tolerance and detachment alien to man's native impulse. "Upon the failure of this necessary detachment right judgment is most often wrecked; its achievement most strains our animal nature; it is the last habit to be acquired and the first to be lost."[11]

It appeared to him that there is something with almost the quality of an absolute—right judgment—that comes from a certain habit of the rational mind, a habit he designated "detachment." If some judgments are right, by implication some must be wrong. How is this compatible with the understanding that values are relative? Hand appeared to be asserting that pragmatic experience has shown that judgments made by those with open minds most often contribute to man's happiness.

Judge Hand described the attributes of detachment idealized by the true scholar: He is aloof from burning issues; he resists the impulse to jump into the fray against oppression or injustice in order that he may preserve an open mind to each disconcerting fact or cold doubt; he seeks truth but does not become an advocate of his own view. One must be acutely conscious of human failures in these matters, and Hand himself believed that complete detachment is a fiction. This is only the ideal of detachment, which if attained by the whole of society would perhaps destroy the vitality of democracy and contribute to apathy or neglect of public affairs, which would be destructive of the system. The distinction appears to be between "necessary" and "entire" detachment—a matter of degree. The ideal of objective, rational, disinterested choice is impossible for society, yet Hand thought that no democracy could survive unless it achieved a degree of this ideal in practice. The urgency with which he felt this necessity helps to explain his insistence that the courts observe these ideals in adjudication and thus assure at least some measure of objective rationality in a democratic society.

The open mind is the human facility which is most difficult to acquire and so fragile that it is easily lost. A realistic concept of political society must take this into account. Learned Hand's theory assumed that something approximating the common good will result from the democratic process as such. He did not believe that the ends of society and man were identical or that there was one end toward which all men and society necessarily moved. He thought, rather, that the good

[11] Learned Hand, "On Receiving an Honorary Degree," *Harvard Alumni Bulletin*, Vol. XLI (July, 1934), as reprinted in *The Spirit of Liberty* (3d ed.), 136–37.

of man could be best served if all men were free to pursue their own ends as they understood them within the limiting framework of a democratic society. Like the truths which emerged from conflicting opinons, the best attainable solutions for the community would be the outcome of this individual self-assertion. In spite of evidence that the original ideal assumptions about democracy at the time of independence included a belief in a "common weal," democracy has always been in practice a means of achieving the resolution of differences in society by combinations resting on self-interest. This explanation of democracy regards the group as the basic unit of political activity. Hand appeared not to accept this as desirable insofar as it denies that the individual is the primary focus of society, though he did accept it as an actual operating fact and thus true for democratic systems. He said:

> Nor would there still be many, though doubtless some there are, who would deny that government must be the compromise of conflicting interests. . . . While there lingers in political platforms and other declamatory compositions the notion that each man, if only he could be disabused of false doctrine, would act and vote with an enlightened eye to the public weal, few really believe it. . . . we must be content with compromises in which the more powerful combination will prevail. . . . in government as in marriage, in the end the more insistent will prevails.[12]

It seemed clear to him that self-interest would dominate in the political arena and inevitable that government was on the way to becoming an agent which reacted to pressures of economic or social classes. But for society to persist, he thought that the concept of self-interest shared by its members must include an awareness that each gains certain advantages from the community and thus must contribute to its well-being. "A society in which each is willing to surrender only that for which he can see a personal equivalent, is not a society at all; it is a group already in process of dissolution. . . . No Utopia . . . will automatically emerge from a regime of unbridled individualism, be it ever so rugged."[13]

[12] Hand, "Sources of Tolerance," *Pennsylvania Law Review*, Vol. LXXIX (November, 1930), as reprinted in *The Spirit of Liberty* (3d ed.), 71.
[13] Hand, "Liberty," *Yale Alumni Magazine*, Vol. IV (June, 1941), as reprinted in *The Spirit of Liberty* (3d ed.), 150.

Learned Hand's preference for democracy was based on his belief that in the long history of man's efforts to raise himself from his animal forebears no other way of life had permitted such great achievement; that if the system ultimately fails man will be the better for having reached beyond his capacity; and, most important, that if man can but learn tolerance he may achieve freedom in a democratic society. In order to secure the democratic process, Hand was even willing to accept, at least to a point, the domination of the stronger. Perhaps this attitude followed naturally from his insistence that all values are equally legitimate and that the dominance of those held by the stronger is in no way negation of "better" or "higher" values but is simply a manner of peacefully determining which values shall prevail in a given society at a given time. He asked:

> ... why must we hold altogether illegitimate the advantage that cohesion, assiduity and persistence bring in government as elsewhere? By what right do we count those who have not the energy or intelligence to make themselves felt, equivalents of those who have? ... Given an opportunity to impose our will, a ground where we may test our mettle, we get the sense that there is some propriety in yielding to those who impose upon us. There has been an outlet, a place of reckoning, a means not of counting heads, but of matching wits and courage. If these are fairly measured, most of us acquiesce; we are conscious of a stronger power which it is idle to resist, until we in turn have organized in more formidable array and can impress ourselves in turn.[14]

Learned Hand's view of democracy is in accord with his basic assumptions about the nature of man and the universe. It is man's proper destiny to be creative. To do so he must have freedom to express himself in his own way. But man also seeks companionship, and so some order must be imposed upon his liberty. The key to the melding of his freedom as an individual and in society is tolerance. This suggests a democratic society in which all are free but must respect the limits of freedom as determined by the necessary requirements of society. A democratic government sits most easily on the shoulders of a free man, but it also makes great demands upon him and requires that he over-

[14] Hand, "Democracy: Its Presumptions and Realities," *Federal Bar Association Journal*, Vol. I, No. 2 (March, 1932), as reprinted in *The Spirit of Liberty* (3d ed.), 97–99.

come his extreme selfishness and intolerance. Judge Hand himself might have preferred to live in an idealized democracy where the common good was determined rationally by those who had achieved a degree of wisdom and personal detachment, but he would also be comfortable in a society in which the strong could be kept from having their way without restraint.

Judge Learned Hand's theory of democratic society and the law which governs it was the product of a gradual change in man's belief, and few who today share his view are aware, as he was, of the magnitude and implications of the change. This change has come about largely because of increased skepticism about the existence of a supreme being and thus the necessity for man to establish the meaning of himself and his world and the values that are to guide him. It was Judge Hand's knowledgeable acceptance of this modern concept that makes his appraisal especially significant for the American system. He understood fully the implications and difficulties it implied but accepted it and defended it ably. Judge Hand would have been in complete accord with his teacher John Chipman Gray, who asserted:

> The great gain in its fundamental conceptions which Jurisprudence made during the last century was the recognition of the truth that the law of a State or other organized body is not an ideal, but something which actually exists. It is not that which is in accordance with religion, or nature, or morality; it is not that which ought to be, but that which is.[15]

Hand thought that experience did not support belief in natural law. Furthermore, the assumption that there was such would have been completely antithetical to his belief that all values and standards are human creations and thus relative.

He gave little credence to the traditional idea of a common will which all understood and shared alike. At most he would have admitted that there may conceivably be some matters on which a majority of people agree—there may be agreeing wills, but the will itself is individual. If a common will is not essential for the existence of law, there may be in fact a majority opposed to it. When this opposed majority makes itself effective in the manner prescribed by society, it may succeed in changing the law.

[15] John Chipman Gray, *The Nature and Sources of the Law*, 94.

Americans have fallen into the habit of accepting the action of their officials as expressing the common will and have made this acceptance a basic part of their political structure. The common law is a prime example of combined custom and successive adaptation by the nation's judges. If the common will implies assent of a majority of living men and women, Hand thought it obvious that the common law is not an expression of it. Many look to the legislature for the enunciation of the common will, but in fact most legislation represents the will of an aggressive minority. Man occasionally creates something that resembles the common will through propaganda and modern salesmanship, but it has no real substance to support the law that flows from it. Even the skills of the pollsters contribute little to the understanding of a common will, since their techniques for counting noses are purely formal and there is little real agreement on the meaning of the results.

Apathy and pressure of personal concern estops most citizens from involving themselves in public affairs until things become so irritating that they are finally teased into action. In the meanwhile and for a great majority of the time, they go along with what is without consciously accepting or having any opinion or will about the matter. Hand believed that apathy as such was not necessarily destructive of democracy provided there continued to be a means for the usually quiescent to reassert themselves when their interests were flagrantly disregarded. For him it was simply necessary to keep open access to political change through an accepted and peaceful process. The complete and full involvement of each individual in the political process might well be destructive of it and lead to anarchy. He was certain that

> of the contrivances which mankind has devised to lift itself from savagery there are few to compare with the habit of assent, not to a factitious common will, but to the law as it is. . . . we can say with him [Hobbes] that the state of nature is "short, brutish and nasty," and that it chiefly differs from civilized society in that the will of each is by habit and training turned to accept some public, fixed and ascertainable standard of reference by which conduct can be judged and to which in the main it will conform.[16]

[16] Learned Hand, "Is There a Common Will? *Michigan Law Review,* Vol. XXVIII (November, 1929), as reprinted in *The Spirit of Liberty,* 55–56.

This interpretation of man's attitude toward the rules of society was an important one for Learned Hand. Here apathy acquired another connotation—a habit of assent. This implied that there has been either consciously or subconsciously a choice made by which people select assent as a pattern of behavior on the rational grounds that society was created to mitigate conflict and that acquiescence is to be chosen until an issue become sufficiently critical to warrant an effort to upset the existing law. He did not deny that the habit was supported and sustained by pure apathy but believed the habit of assent or self-restraint is an affirmative rather than a negative basis for noninvolvement. The habit of assent retains within itself the element of choice, and this is its fundamental distinction both from pure apathy and from the mass society that has been taught by effective modern propaganda to accept official dogma without question. Attention should be called to the fact that Hand's assent was not to a common will but to "law as it is."

Law was not the law of nature or of nature's God, nor was it the product of a common will for Judge Learned Hand. He conceived of law as

> the conduct which government, whether it is a king or a popular assembly, will compel individuals to conform to, or to which it will at least provide forcible means to secure conformity. . . . The law is the command of the government, and it must be ascertainable in some form if it is to be enforced at all.[17]

There are judges in all civilized countries (and perhaps in all political societies) whose duty it is to say precisely what the government has in fact commanded in every case. Once this judgment has been given, the force behind the law will be used.

Much of the law that governs a people is the result of the compromises of conflicts long forgotten, and the meaning of that final formal expression and its real relevance to the problems of today are often difficult if not impossible to determine. In such cases it cannot be argued that there is any actual assent, but merely the habit of assent, for it may not be a consciously accepted rule at all. Lacking sufficient challenge to change them, laws endure. They become custom or habit,

[17] Learned Hand, "How Far Is a Judge Free in Rendering a Decision?" as reprinted in *The Spirit of Liberty* (3d ed.), 104.

and man accepts the convention with the hope of avoiding sudden or violent change.

Not all law, however, is either ancient or the gradual accumulation of successive generations of judicial decision. There is also the enacted law of today—the most recent compromises of currently waged conflicts. By enacted law Judge Hand meant

> any authoritative command of an organ of government purposely made responsive to the pressure of the interests affected. I shall assume that before enacted law is passed these interests have opportunity in the press, in public meeting, by appearance before committees or the like and in any other lawful way, to exert their influence.[18]

Enacted law is in no sense the embodiment of permanent principles, but it may be relatively stable and rests always upon the assumption that it may be changed if there is a sufficient shift in political power. It is that to which all will accede at least until they can organize to overcome it in the way prescribed by the rules of the society itself. As such it cannot even be cast "to accord with the aspirations of the best of our time. . . . it must fit more easily upon prevailing conventions and even prejudices; it must not be a divine code handed down from Sinai."[19]

Judge Hand recognized the pragmatic source of law and the occasions which cause it to come into being. He was aware of its limits, but he was in no way contemptuous of it or of its contributions to man in society. Far from it. Whether the law prevails because of apathy or the habit of assent, whether it embodies the will of the stronger who continues to make his will effective, or whether, perchance, it somehow accords with the interest of all, it is essential to man's progress and to the growth of his humanity.

> Despite its inconsistencies, its crudities, its delays and its weakness, law still embodies so much of the results of that disposition as we can collectively impose. Without it we cannot live; only with it can we insure the future which by right is ours. The best of man's hopes are enmeshed in its success; when it fails they must fail.[20]

[18] Learned Hand, "The Contribution of Independent Judiciary to Civilization," as reprinted in *The Spirit of Liberty* (3d ed.), 155–56.

[19] Hand, "Is There a Common Will?" *Michigan Law Review*, Vol. XXVIII (November, 1929), as reprinted in *The Spirit of Liberty* (3d ed.), 56.

[20] Learned Land, "To Yale Law Graduates," as reprinted in *The Spirit of Liberty* (3d ed.), 88.

Judge Hand's understanding of law as the resolution of conflicts in society was consistent with his theory of democracy as a process by which differences are moderated and concluded at least temporarily and with his concept of liberty. It was compatible with his assumption that man is a self-assertive creative creature, capable of but not dominated by rational thought, and that all values and purposes arise from human choice. In it there was no place for a substantive notion of a higher law or of a tangible common will as the directing force of society.

The law must be adequate to claim assent, but it could not hope to impose the highest aspirations of a society. It must have a degree of permanence for stability, but it must be amenable to change when the temper of the people requires change. It must deal in generalizations but provide guidance for resolution of specific questions. As in the entire human realm, law contained no absolutes or final answers.

PART III : *The Federal Judiciary—Motor or Brake?*

CHAPTER V : *The Judge and the Power of Judgment*

Few students of the American judiciary would take issue with Alexander Hamilton's assertion that "the judiciary . . . may truly be said to have neither *force* nor *will*, but merely judgment."[1] The implications of this terse assertion can claim no such unanimity. Rather, definition of the proper function of the federal courts and especially the Supreme Court has not been far from the center of controversy since that historic day when John Marshall enunciated the principle of judicial review in *Marbury v. Madison*. In spite of the widespread belief that the issue has finally been settled and the controversy put aside, the evidence is to the contrary. It seems inevitable that shifts in the court as well as in the mood and temper of the people make this an "eternally recurring" subject.

Many scholars and jurists have contributed to the debate through the years, but Judge Hand's position is especially entitled to consideration. His reasoning was not dependent upon his approval or disapproval of the results in specific cases. Rather, he denied that it is a proper ground upon which to rest the issue and thus raised the discussion to a debate regarding the constitutional function of the federal courts. He insisted that the role of the judges and the courts must be defined in terms of the agreement hammered out at the Constitutional Convention and with concern for the maintenance of the system as conceived by that compromise. Hand did not deny the need for or the utility of change in the system but adhered strictly to the position that the constitutional compromise provides the proper means through which that change should occur and that, to be legitimate, it must follow the rules

[1] Alexander Hamilton, John Jay, and James Madison, "Federalist, No. 78," *The Federalist: A Commentary on the Constitution of the United States*, 504.

contained therein. Throughout society today there is a preoccupation with change and thus the necessity to be concerned with the legitimate limits of change and the procedures through which it may reasonably be permitted. It is appropriate that we examine Learned Hand's understanding of the power of judgment as it relates to the problem of change.

If there was one characteristic which dominated Learned Hand's philosophy and life, it was that of moderation—of temperance and tolerance combined with a profound understanding that many points of view may contain some truth and a determination not to foreclose any that might contribute toward a better solution to the problems of man. This attitude prevailed throughout his judicial career, which was marked by deference to others without loss of strong convictions and dedication to his own standards. He thought that a judge must decide in accordance with decisions arrived at through the political process without attempting to impose his own values. When it seemed appropriate to him, he deferred to the higher court, to the legislature, to administrative tribunals, and to the spirit of the time. This temper of moderation was not the product of indecisiveness or lack of comprehension but was a fundamental acknowledgment of the complexity of the problems of man which defy easy or complete answers. From this awareness followed his acquiescence, when necessary for the continuity of society, to values or standards he thought were inferior to his own.

Learned Hand believed that it was the primary function of the courts to settle disputes between litigants but that there were two opposing views concerning the judicial method appropriate to the resolution of these conflicts. According to one position, a judge should observe the letter of the law with care and never depart from the literal meaning of the written words. This school he referred to as the "dictionary school," but he did not believe that any judge had ever actually carried out this spirit literally or that he would long be tolerated if he did.

Exponents of the "dictionary school" regard the judge as a passive interpreter and see his absolute loyalty to authoritative law as the price he must pay for freedom from political pressure and his continued security of tenure. The aim of such a judge must be to understand the law as he finds it. It is in no way his responsibility to seek results that keep pace with changing public aspirations because, since they are still unformulated, they are necessarily vague and fragmentary. Hand did not regard this position as completely disinterested because it tended toward the protection of property and for many years meant the slowing of social regulation. He thought that if the laws encouraged economic and social reform these same conservatives might endorse judicial initiative. It appears to be true that attitudes regarding strict and literal constitutional interpretation are most often based on approval or disapproval of the substantive results of the two approaches.

The absurdity of the "dictionary school" he illustrated by a case in which a clearly guilty man escaped because the indictment against him had omitted the word "the," alleging that what he did was "against the peace of state," rather than as the law prescribed, "against the peace of *the* state." Even though the statute had specified the terms of conviction, it was obvious that it did not intend a guilty man should go free because the word "the" had been omitted in the indictment. It was not enough, Hand thought, for a judge to follow the dictionary, for that might lead to a result that was the opposite of what was intended and contradict or leave unfulfilled the obvious purpose of the law.[2]

According to the opposing view, the judge should follow the dictates of his own conscience and not be bound by "technical rules" which have no relationship to what is naturally right or wrong. It denies that judges in the past have ever really followed the law but asserts that they have and should have assumed almost complete latitude in arriving at their decisions. It is a judge's responsibility to make the verdict conform to what honest men regard as right, and he may best seek this answer in his own heart. But if the dictionary school provides too little leeway, this one provides too much.

A judge must tread the narrow path between slavish adherence to the letter of the law and license in substituting his own choice for that already expressed by the government. It seemed inevitable to Hand that, as a judge interprets the words of the law and seeks to determine what the government intended but did not say, he will find what he believes it ought to have said. This process, he acknowledged, is very close to substituting what he thinks to be right. "Let him beware, however, or he will usurp the office of government, even though in a small

---

[2] Hand, "How Far Is a Judge Free in Rendering a Decision?" as reprinted in *The Spirit of Liberty* (3d ed.), 106.

way he must do so in order to execute its real commands at all."[3] It is a difficult distinction for a judge to make and an even more difficult one to translate into meaningful terms for laymen.

It was Hand's belief that in the power structure of the American political society the judge stands low, and he is not entitled to act contrary to the last formal expression of public opinion. Hand suited his action to his words, Judge Wyzanski said:

> Judge Hand's view of the judge was austere, even Austinian. He regarded it as his chief obligation to be a disinterested interpreter of other men's wills. He was to remain detached, not merely from immediate partisanship, but also from any ultimate passion for reform. Such abstinence he regarded as the only condition from which appointed judges could properly be tolerated in a democracy. For judges to offer themselves as Platonic guardians would wrongly lead the laity to expect of judges more than they could perform, and would impair such limited authority as they might properly enjoy.[4]

Louis L. Jaffe thought that perhaps Hand "reified" the notion of power—that he associated it primarily with the masses whom he feared because he was an aristocrat and scorned because he was an artist, and also because of his

> remarkable prescience of the innate, ineradicable savagery of man. . . . Constantly echoing Hobbes, he is afraid that frustration of organized power will bring civil war . . . [and that] it is dangerous and irresponsible for the judiciary, which is without power, to interpose its veto on the operations of power.[5]

It is true that Hand believed judges have "neither *force* nor *will*, but merely judgment," but it seems improbable, especially in view of his *Masses* decision, that his reluctance to "use himself as a measure" of legislation arose from fear, as Jaffe seems to suggest. It seems rather to have come from his philosophical pragmatism and intellectual conviction that the constitutional allocation of function makes it the duty and responsibility of the courts to apply the law fairly and to determine

---

[3] *Ibid.*, 108.

[4] Wyzanski, in his introduction to Hand, *The Bill of Rights*, vi.

[5] Louis L. Jaffe, review of *The Spirit of Liberty: Papers and Addresses of Learned Hand*, *Harvard Law Review*, Vol. LXVI, No. 5 (March, 1953), 942.

the constitutionality and not the wisdom of legislation. In *Dennis* v. *United States* he said:

> Once the question is answered whether the Smith Act is valid, and whether there was evidence before the jury from which they might hold it violated, we find no privilege and no right denied them which had substance. . . . it is not for us to say whether such a prosecution makes against the [Communist] movement, or, on the contrary, only creates more disciples; ours is only to apply the law as we find it.[6]

This is not so much a matter of power as the comprehension that the wisdom and constitutionality of a statute are not congruent.

Archibald Cox believed that Hand's reluctance to review the wisdom of choices arrived at through legitimate democratic procedure resulted from his understanding that society itself is dependent upon acceptance of the law "as it is," that it will not tolerate even a wise judge who accepts no legal standards except his own personal sense of justice.[7] The continued authority of the courts and their judges depends upon the assumption that they speak not for themselves alone but for the whole of society, or at least the portion which has made good its claim to be heard. A judge's pronouncement must have greater weight than any individual personal reputation or character can command. He must enhance his authority by drawing upon the past and maintaining a continuity between it and the emerging trends of his time.

It is true that, where the legislature has not acted, the courts, while remaining loyal to precedent, must shape the law to meet current needs and aspirations within the confines of that which is generally accepted by the society. In dealing with problems covered by statutes, the courts do not have the same responsibility, for the interests have already been evaluated and adjusted by the legislature, and there remains less need for the courts to strike the balance. Even in cases where the intent or relationship of the law to the case is not entirely clear there is some general purpose which provides a guiding framework for the work of the judges.

Hand believed that judges should not impose their own solutions upon the basic conflicts of society that remain unresolved by the

---

[6] *United States* v. *Dennis*, 183 F. (2d) 201, 234 (1950).

[7] Cox, "Judge Learned Hand and the Interpretation of Statutes," *Harvard Law Review*, Vol. LX (February, 1947), 373.

legislative process. There may be times and societies in which the community is in basic harmony when it is appropriate for judges to elaborate the unformulated consensus:

> But what if it [society] be riven by contentions going to the very heart, and if the bench by birth and training be interested parties? How can such then be spokesmen of a harmony not realized, and perhaps not realizable? Let them beware of playing Procrustes. The decisive conflicts are not for their solution; they must be content to accept commands which may violate their dearest prepossessions.[8]

When there has been no agreement achieved upon a matter of fundamental importance or if the old compromise has become inadequate, the courts must await a new resolution. The continued authority of the judges depends upon resisting changes that are not yet acceptable, resolving inconsistencies, eliminating confusions, and spelling out unrecognized implications, thus making modest advances. But where the purpose of the community is evident, though perhaps not clearly defined, the judge does have a responsibility to assist in spelling out that meaning and applying it to specific problems in society so that the original intent is carried out. Here there is latitude for judges to engage in courageous experiments. Hand knew that the nation's judges were not without imagination to divine solutions to the nation's problems in accordance with their own interests and philosophy. He feared that their failure might lie in the inability to understand the confines of the judicial function and to exercise their creativity within those boundaries. Hand's description of Robert P. Patterson's attitude toward his judicial responsibilities mirrored his own. He said that Patterson's opinions

> disclosed his underlying attitude to his duties, his understanding of the position of a judge, as interpreter. . . . he recognized that he was the mouthpiece of a purpose, which he was bound to treat as authoritative, and to which he must therefore conform; that he had no mission to set right what he might not approve; and that it was not the function of courts to resolve the major conflicts of interest in a democratic society. He had a well-settled and an unconcealed scorn for that temper . . .

---

[8] Learned Hand, review of *Collected Legal Papers*, by Oliver Wendell Holmes, *Political Science Quarterly*, Vol. XXXVI, No. 3 (September, 1921), 530.

which transfigures a judge into a crusader for righteousness as righteousness as righteousness may appear to his incandescent conscience.[9]

Learned Hand's strong conviction that judges should refrain from imposing their own views on the law was supported by his belief that they are generally drawn from a privileged class and are not representative of the society as a whole. Though he asserted that judges were from the "propertied" class, he did not necessarily mean the very wealthy but rather a class that was privileged because it possessed the substance to enjoy the fruits of an excellent education and an opportunity for public service and recognition. The need for restraint has been heightened with the increase of popular domestic participation in political life. Until very recently

> the American bench and bar could utter justice without misgiving or constraint. Differences of course there were, but the self-conscious elements of society were homogeneous and the divergences not fundamentally distracting. At least, such genuine distraction as there was was latent, class grievances were inaudible. . . . Lawyers got by a kind of natural right the authority to interpret justice, since they were in a broad sense genuine representatives of all that could achieve representation.
>
> All this has changed; the profession is still drawn, and so far as we can see, will always be drawn, from the propertied class, but other classes have awakened to conscious control of their fate, their demands are vocal which before were dumb, and they will no longer be disregarded.[10]

It seemed to Hand that when the country was governed by a kind of natural aristocracy or even by a single propertied class it might have been permissible to allow judges to share to some extent in the resolution of basic conflicts in society. Assuming, as he did, that those who belong to the same class will share a basic understanding of the good life, the result would likely be very much the same whether or not a functional separation of powers is rigidly followed.

Even though many of them assumed a natural governing elite, the men who created the American system thought it essential to separate

---

[9] Learned Hand, "Robert P. Patterson," as reprinted in *The Spirit of Liberty* (3d ed.), 265.

[10] Learned Hand, "The Speech of Justice," *Harvard Law Review*, Vol. XXIX (April, 1916), as reprinted in *The Spirit of Liberty* (3d ed.), 16–17.

the powers of government to prevent abuse. Judge Hand thought that experience had proved their wisdom. Since all classes are now entitled to participate fully in the process of government, the law must be spelled out by representatives whom the people elect and can replace. Judges are not subject to direct popular control. He believed that they must be expected to express the points of view of the class to which they belong rather than that of the whole community. Thus careful adherence to the original functional separation of power between making the law and adjudication of rights under the law is more important today than when the nation was founded, for

> if justice be a passable accommodation between the vital and self-conscious interests of society, it has taken on a meaning not known before. But the profession has not yet learned to adapt itself to the change; that most difficult of adjustments has not been made, an understanding of and sympathy with the purposes and ideals of those parts of the common society whose interests are discordant with its own.[11]

Hand believed that in modern times justice is conceived of as the peaceful solution to conflict that has been accepted by the self-conscious interests in society. To him the difference between a society where there was a single class which could impose its will and one in which many groups seek to participate was obvious. He believed that if the judge is to continue to enjoy a place of authority in the community he must somehow discern the underlying will of all without giving undue weight to his own. He must be a part of the community—integrated, enmeshed, involved, feeling, desiring, and choosing, at least for purposes of judging, as the community chooses.

Notwithstanding the changed conditions of American democracy which have deprived the propertied class of the right to rule, Hand believed it might still be appropriate for a large share of the country's judges to be drawn from that class (assuming they exercise self-restraint), for the law "is the precipitate of a long past of active controversy and cannot be successfully administered by those to whom equilibrium has no proper values of its own."[12] The courts with their

[11] *Ibid.*, 17.

[12] Learned Hand, "Mr. Justice Holmes at Eighty-Five," *New York World*, March 8, 1926, as reprinted in *The Spirit of Liberty* (3d ed.), 24.

sensitivity to tradition and understanding of the importance of continuity in society provide a proper institutional balance for the legislatures which seek to reflect or achieve a compromise between currently competing interests. However, judges should not place themselves in the balance and lend additional weight to the conservative interest of which Hand thought they were a part. To do so would be to violate the trust placed in them and jeopardize their competence to perform the unique function of adjudication.

At least one study supported Hand's contention that Supreme Court justices are drawn not only from a privileged class but also from a relatively wealthy group. John R. Schmidhauser made a detailed study of the family backgrounds of the ninety-one men who have served on the high court and concluded that only a handful of them were of humble origin. He wrote, "The remaining eighty-two (90 per cent) were not only from families in comfortable economic circumstances, but were chosen overwhelmingly from the socially-prestigeful and politically-influential gentry class in the late eighteenth and early nineteenth century or the professionalized upper middle-class thereafter."[13] According to his study a high percentage of the justices came from families with an aristocratic tradition of political obligation and social responsibility and not simply political activism. Schmidhauser also found that the educational opportunities of Supreme Court justices have generally been beyond the capacity of families outside the upper economic classes.

It is true that this study involved only justices of the Supreme Court and does not apply to all federal judges. However, the factors which seemed to be important in the selection of members of the Supreme Court also apply, if to a lesser extent, to lower federal judgeships. Educational opportunity and political participation are obvious examples, and while both of these advantages are more accessible to young men of modest means today than ever before, both are enhanced by economic advantage. Schmidhauser concluded that if the Supreme Court "is the keeper of the American conscience, it is essentially the conscience of the American upper middle-class sharpened by the imperative of individual social responsibility and political activism, and

[13] John R. Schmidhauser, "The Justices of the Supreme Court: A Collective Portrait," *Midwest Journal of Political Science*, Vol. III (February, 1959), 9.

conditioned by the conservative impact of legal training and professional legal attitudes and association."[14]

Hand's assumption that judges are likely to impose their class predilections if they are involved in determination of the fundamental issues of society seems to be more speculative, and Hand himself insisted that some men are free from such bias. He was not as much concerned with the grosser economic or material interests of judges as with their more basic understanding of what constitutes the good life. Hand believed that most judges did not use their power for personal gain but that it was often difficult for them to maintain an open mind to ideas which challenge their basic faith and most profound assumptions. He felt that these fundamental predispositions would almost invariably be part of a decision in which a judge sought to interpret vague and ill-defined pronouncements of the public will. He did not argue that judges can or should divest themselves of their basic beliefs but only that they should exercise self-restraint so that they do not make their own beliefs the criteria of the basic values of society. According to Hand's understanding of the American system, the court was not the proper forum for a confrontation of fundamental "interests" in either the material or the ideological sense.

Schmidhauser suggested that there have generally been two contemporary approaches to the study of the courts: the interest-group theory and the elitist theory. Hand's view touched both. He thought that the American bench was in a very real sense an elite and also that if judges were free to impose their own ideals or interests through judicial legislation the result might be a corruption of the democratic process. This concern appears to account in part for his insistence upon great judicial restraint.

Learned Hand was both a trial and an appellate judge but was always subject to the ultimate authority of the Supreme Court and was extremely conscious of his place within the judicial hierarchy. His deference to others with whom he shared the responsibility of judging emphasizes another facet of his self-restraint, as well as his appreciation of the roles of tradition, consistency, and unanimity in maintaining the authority of the law.

Since he viewed the Supreme Court as the source of all final and

[14] *Ibid.*, 49.

authoritative judgments within the sphere of the federal judiciary, he felt bound to accept its judgment when it was clearly relevant, even though he personally believed it to be in error. In *Phelps Dodge Corp.* v. *National Labor Relations Board* he said, "Having taken part in that decision and my notions being then overruled, I regard it as authoritative."[15] Judge Wyzanski said of Hand:

> Few judges of his capacity have been so conscientious in abiding by a precise precedent. . . . And no one can so briefly and accurately summarize the evolutionary process, showing the nexus of each prior decision to the case at bar. Witness his unequalled drawing of the genealogical tree of the Associated Press and Aluminum Company decisions.[16]

Hand's attitude was clearly apparent in *Spector Motor Service* v. *Walsh* when he dissented from an opinion which broke with the clearly established precedent of the Supreme Court on the basis of "trends [which] . . . have gone further in several specific cases fundamentally close to this and in divisions in the Court itself, which are certainly not without significance in forecasting the future course of the law. And our function cannot be limited to a mere blind adherence to precedent."[17] Judge Hand said, in opposition to this position:

> It is always embarrassing for a lower court to say whether the time has come to disregard decisions of a higher court, not yet explicitly overruled, because they parallel others in which the higher court has expressed a contrary view. I agree that one should not wait for formal retraction in the face of changes plainly foreshadowed. . . . But nothing has yet appeared which satisfies me that the case at bar is of that kind. . . . Nor is it desirable for a lower court to embrace the exhilarating opportunity of anticipating a doctrine which may be in the womb of time, but whose birth is distant; on the contrary I conceive that the measure of its duty is to divine, as best it can, what would be the event of an appeal in the case before it.[18]

This assumption is apparent in many of Hand's opinions. When-

[15] *Phelps Dodge Corp.* v. *National Labor Relations Board*, 113 F. (2d) 202, 207 (1940).

[16] Charles E. Wyzanski, Jr., "Judge Learned Hand's Contribution to Public Law," *Harvard Law Review*, Vol. LX (February, 1947), 368–69.

[17] *Spector Motor Service* v. *Walsh*, 139 F. (2d) 809, 814 (1944).

[18] *Ibid.*, 823.

ever there were precedents from the Supreme Court that gave direction for a case in his court, he yielded to that judgment. His conscientious effort to render opinions that would be supported by a higher court was clearly evident in his effort to draw from decisions of the Supreme Court some guidance for his decision in the Dennis case.[19] There he found no specific or direct precedent but sought to fit the controversy into what seemed to him to be a developing pattern of decisions.

In *National Labor Relations Board* v. *Federbush Co.*, Hand wrote an opinion accepting a ruling of the board even though he personally did not agree with it, thus demonstrating his willingness to abide by the decision of an official body which he understood had authority under the Constitution to make the determination. There he was faced with an action by the National Labor Relations Board limiting the freedom of employers to speak to their employees. After reciting the nature of some of the "unfair practices" found by the board, he said, "These appear to us trivial matters, but as the Board has seen fit to make them the occasion of an injunction, we cannot say that its order should not be enforced." Congress has authority to legislate concerning the right to speak freely, and ". . . the Board is vested with power to measure these . . . factors."[20] Subsequently the high court handed down a contrary decision in a similar case in which the board had found that the Virginia Electric and Power Company used coercion on its employees through a bulletin and a speech. The company had an anti-union history, but this fact was not elaborated upon in the record, and the Supreme Court did not find sufficient evidence in the material presented to sustain a finding of coercion which it reversed. Then Judge Hand's court was presented with another case, *National Labor Relations Board* v. *American Tube Bending Co.*, in which he said,

> Had it not been for the decision of the Supreme Court in *National Labor Relations Board* v. *Virginia Electric and Power Company*, 314 U.S. 469 . . . we might have considered some of that court's earlier decisions as requiring us to grant an enforcement order in the case at bar. . . . The only question here is therefore whether the respondent's letter and speech were different enough to count. . . . they appear to us to be substantially the same in their general tenor and purport. . . . It

---

19 *United States* v. *Dennis*, 183 F. (2d) 201 (1950).
20 *National Labor Relations Board* v. *Federbush Co.*, 121 F. (2d) 954, 956–57 (1941).

seems to us extremely undesirable, particularly in so highly charged a subject matter, to draw fine-spun distinctions between two situations so closely alike; any we could make would be insubstantial refinements without real significance; would promote controversy and exacerbate, where the purpose should be to assuage. If there was a basis for finding that such a presentation of the employer's side might be a covert threat to recalcitrants, there was as much basis in the Virginia case. If on the other hand the employer's interest in free speech in the Virginia case was thought to out-weigh an actual prejudice to the employees' right of collective bargaining, the employer's interest is the same in the case at bar and the employees' prejudice no greater. We can find no tenable distinction between the two.[21]

While Hand's original inclination was to support free speech, he acknowledged the power of the board to determine when it should not be privileged in *National Labor Relations Board* v. *Federbush Co.*; but when the Supreme Court reversed the board's judgment, he followed the lead of the superior court. His consistency rests in the fact that in both cases he was guided by official judgments he believed to be more authoritative than his own.

Where the relevance of the precedent to the case at hand was not clearly evident and the problem called for an exercise of judgment based on the facts of the case, he was not content to attempt to gather some solution from the mass of previous cases that might somehow be thought to be relevant. In *United States* v. *A. L. A. Schechter Poultry Corporation* he said:

It would be, I think, disingenuous to pretend that the ratio decidendi of such decisions is susceptible of statement in general principles. That no doubt might give a show of necessity to the conclusion, but it would be insincere and illusory, and appears formidable only in case the conclusion is surreptitiously introduced during the reasoning. The truth really is that where the border shall be fixed is a question of degree, dependent upon the consequences in each case.[22]

He thought that a court should either follow or explain why it did

[21] *National Labor Relations Board* v. *American Tube Bending Co.*, 134 F. (2d), 993, 994-95 (1943).

[22] *United States* v. *A. L. A. Schechter Poultry Corporation*, 76 F. (2d) 617, 625 (1935).

not follow opinions in cases that might reasonably be regarded as providing guidance in a case before it. He was particularly critical of the decision in *Brown* v. *Board of Education* for its failure to do so. The Dennis case seems to illustrate his own practice. When a particular precedent seemed ambiguous or a series of similar cases provided no discernible pattern, he did not feel bound, though he was careful to explain why. In this case also he distinguished between some prior cases and the one before him and explained why they offered no guidance.

It seemed to Learned Hand that in some important cases precedents once established had become so much a part of the American system that it would be almost impossible to upset them, although originally they might well have been decided differently. For instance, he thought that *Gibbons* v. *Ogden* could have been more wisely decided so that the court was not so clearly projected into the policy-making function in the area of interstate commerce, though it would not have occurred to him that in the light of historical development it should or could be reversed. Also in *Seelig* v. *Baldwin* he acknowledged that the precedent could have been different but was now thoroughly established. His conviction that once a decision had been made and become integrated into the fabric of society it should not be overruled by the court but altered through the political process was a fundamental element in his understanding of the judicial function. It was a primary factor in his criticism of the desegregation cases.

Learned Hand knew how difficult it was to achieve the goal of proper judgment to which he aspired. He sought guidance through the study of those judges who seemed most nearly to approach his ideal. His appraisal of the qualities which contribute substantially to the art of judging is interesting in view of his pragmatic understanding of the nature of man and appears to exemplify the very high standards and values Judge Hand chose for himself and as those appropriate for the democratic society in which he lived.

It was obvious to him that judges must be held to high standards of scholarship so that they might grasp the fine distinctions of a problem and analyze it carefully. He thought it important that judges have not only the technical legal training required of them but also a broad liberal education—an acquaintance with the great philosophers of history which helps free the spirit from provincialism. But, beyond these formal requirements, more important and certainly more rare are the high moral and ethical qualities which a man must bring to the bench. His almost exclusive attention to the matter of moral standards is interesting and even a little puzzling in light of his largely pragmatic assumptions about the nature of political life. The question must be raised, even if it cannot be answered satisfactorily, how his overriding concern for certain moral qualities in the nation's judges related to his total philosophy.

Hand accepted as true his own freely chosen moral standards on the basis of all knowledge available to him, and he supported his beliefs vigorously and ably. There was a certain personal morality which seemed to him to be not merely proper but necessary in the light of experience for persons engaged in public life and bearing great public responsibility. His concept of democracy was not egalitarian in the sense that all are equally fitted to govern. His description of the requirements for judges (and one may assume that the same ethical and moral requirements would be desirable if not absolutely essential for other public officers) makes it abundantly clear why he warned that the democratic system is precarious at best, for it is very difficult to achieve and maintain. It is suitable only for men who have progressed far along the path to humanity. It depends upon the consistent maintenance of detachment and tolerance by at least the dominant group in the society. If this capacity is tested too far or if for some reason it fails to endure, the system may be thrown into anarchy or autocracy. But since he regarded democracy as the system most appropriate to the highest development of man, it is worthy of whatever efforts man is capable of exerting, and Hand was willing to devote his best efforts to its achievement.

It may be reasonable to explain his devotion to the standards and moral values he found so necessary in American judges on the pragmatic basis that they are essential to the successful operation of democracy. However, if democracy is truly the way of life most suited to man and if these qualities are essential to the maintenance of democracy, there appears to be something objective or absolute in their value. This theory highlights what may be a fundamental dilemma in the pragmatic theory of relative values. Yet Judge Hand would have argued that certain qualities of personal morality are essential to a viable democratic sys-

97

tem, so far as human experience is complete, but knowledge to be achieved tomorrow may prove those standards to be inadequate.

This position appears to be legitimate if one accepts Hand's doctrine of the nature of man and the universe, of created values, of the necessity for freedom and tolerance, and of his pragmatic method for the discovery of truth. He would insist that it is inappropriate to apply the assumptions of relativity to the theory of pragmatism itself. If one reopens the question of the nature of man, he has reverted to fundamental assumptions for which there is no empirical proof and which are in the realm of metaphysics and speculation—the primary choice man makes as a matter of the will. Hand's theory of relative human values evolved out of his world view, which was chosen freely and was absolute for him. He did not consider seriously the possibility of any other philosophy regarding the nature of man. Relative values pertained only internally to the closed philosophic view that he held.

In Hand's view a well-educated judge with a fine mind can do much to clear away confusion, but he may not be constructive. First of all, he must be aware of the hazards and difficulties of judging.[23] Only this understanding will make him sufficiently cautious not to read more into the law than he finds in its words and will impel him to remember that the policy the law is intended to implement inheres in its limits as well as in its extent and to remind himself that the authors presumably said no more and no less than they intended. He must understand the law in its historical context and know the conflict which it sought to resolve:

[23] In discussing the need for judges to acknowledge the full extent of their powers and the potential dangers inherent in the "personal element" in their decisions, Jerome Frank wrote: "Some persons . . . have suggested that a judge, fully cognizant of the real nature of his powers and of the operation of the 'personal element' in his decisions, will necessarily be more prone to be arbitrary, knowing that he can effectively conceal his arbitrariness. That may be—it has been—a grave danger, when judges do not publicly admit that they have such powers. But contrast judges like, say, Marshall, Field and McReynolds, with those like, say Learned Hand and Rifkind: The former, I think, were not at all ignorant of their powers. But, concealing what they did under a show of complete 'objectivity,' they often ruthlessly decided in accordance with their personal predilections. Judges Hand and Rifkind, however, alive to, and avowing, the nature of the judging process, are far more demanding of themselves, far more given to critical self-scrutiny, far more cautious in the exericse of their authority." Jerome Frank, *Courts on Trial: Myths and Reality in American Justice,* 412.

But all this is only the beginning, for he must possess the far more exceptional power of divination which can peer into the purpose beyond its expression, and bring to fruition that which lay only in flower. Of the moral qualities necessary to this, before and beyond all he must purge his mind and will of those personal presuppositions and prejudices which almost inevitably invade all human judgments; he must approach his problems with as little preconception of what should be the outcome as it is given to men to have; in short, the prime condition of his success will be his capacity for detachment. There are those who insist that detachment is an illusion; that our conclusions, when their bases are sifted, always reveal a passional foundation. Even so; though they be throughout the creatures of past emotional experience, it does not follow that the experience can never predispose us to impartiality. A bias against bias may be as likely a result of some buried crisis, as any other bias. Be that as it may, we know that men do differ widely in this capacity; and the incredulity which seeks to discredit that knowledge is a part of the crusade against reason from which we have already so bitterly suffered.[24]

Some detachment from one's immediate and compelling personal interests must be present in any democratic society if man is to overcome the basic impulse to satisfy his own needs or desires at all costs. Hand believed that it is the one condition more than any other that is essential to a proper functioning of a system of independent courts. One of his colleagues on the bench said of him that "as nearly as any mortal can be, he is passionately dispassionate."[25]

Unlike some modern theorists who find no necessity for such a standard when democracy is viewed as the process of conflict resolution according to predetermined rules, Learned Hand believed that unabashed self-interest must be modified. Although the legislative process culminates in a compromise among interest groups and often the more powerful or the more wealthy prevail without reference to reasoned debate, he denied that the judges of the nation's courts can respond to these pressures and continue to fulfill the traditional function of judging. He believed that man—or at least certain men—are capable of

[24] Learned Hand, "Thomas Walter Swan," *Yale Law Journal*, Vol. LVII (December, 1947), as reprinted in *The Spirit of Liberty* (3d ed.), 217–18.
[25] Frank, "Some Reflections on Judge Learned Hand," *Chicago Law Review*, Vol. XXIV (1957), 680.

judging without bias or, as he said, of developing a bias against bias. The assumption that the spirit of detachment is not outside the realm of human possibility came from his belief in the power of man to reason and to distinguish between emotional attitudes or desires and the more objective elements in a case. While it is obvious in the end he must judge, it is crucial whether this decision is based on desire, passion and self-interest or on a reasoned analysis of the facts.

Hand was concerned not merely with the detachment from one's material self-interest but primarily with the intellectual capacity to encompass other points of view and to include all of those which appeared to be relevant in a given case. Intellectual detachment from one's most cherished and deeply held beliefs is far more rare than even the ability to keep one's material or economic interest in some proper perspective. This quality so essential to the capacity to judge comes most often from a liberal education which teaches that many ideas are worthy of respect and consideration and that there is more often than not a measure of truth in each of them. This openness of mind is rare since it tends to strip its holder of the comforting assurance that his own faith is absolute and eternal and opens the door to the relativity and tentativeness of all human understanding. Thus not only is it difficult to achieve but once the idea is caught it is often resisted, for the prospect of freedom from constraint is, as Hand understood, a frightening thing for most people. It is the uncommon men who can achieve this quality and maintain it with composure that he would select for the nation's judges. The glowing tribute he wrote at the death of Justice Benjamin M. Cardozo is a statement of his own ideal. He wrote:

> I have not told you what qualities made it possible for him to find just that compromise between the letter and the spirit that so constantly guided him to safety . . . because I do not know. . . . One ingredient I think I do know: the wise man is the detached man. By that I mean more than detached from his grosser interests—his advancement and his gain. Many of us can be that—I dare to believe that most judges can be, and are. I am thinking of something far more subtly interfused. Our convictions, our outlook, the whole make-up of our thinking, which we cannot help bringing to the decision of every question, is the creature of our past; and into our past have been woven all sorts of frustrated

ambitions with their envies, and of hopes of preferment with their corruptions, which, long since forgotten, still determine our conclusions. A wise man is one exempt from the handicap of such a past; he is a runner stripped for the race; he can weigh the conflicting factors of his problem without always finding himself in one scale or the other. Cardozo was such a man; his gentle nature had in it no acquisitiveness; he did not use himself as a measure of value. . . . Yet from this self-effacement came a power greater than the power of him who ruleth a city. He was wise because his spirit was uncontaminated, because he knew no violence, or hatred, or envy, or jealousy, or ill-will. I believe that it was this purity that chiefly made him the judge we so much revere; more than his learning, his acuteness, and his fabulous industry.[26]

To fill the role of a judge as Learned Hand defined it is a rigorous undertaking. There must be long years of study in which one develops an understanding of man and the world in which he lives; of his history, his triumphs, and his failures; and of the kind of society in which he may seek to achieve his highest potentiality. He must learn to understand the nature of law and the purpose it serves in society, and he must of course understand that particular law which he will be called upon to interpret. He must develop the proper moral and ethical qualities, as well as the intellectual ones. Even if all this is achieved, there are long hours of patient drudgery, much bickering, and many obstructions which distract and frustrate him. But there is also, in the calling of a judge, that most precious opportunity for man—the opportunity to create and to impress oneself upon the material before him. It is apparent that Hand found it a worthy and stimulating occupation and that in the pursuit of the law he found satisfaction as a human being. He said:

> But there is something else that makes it—anyway to those curious creatures who persist in it—a delectable calling. For when the case is all in, and the turmoil stops, and after he is left alone, things begin to take form. From his pen or in his head, slowly or swiftly as his capacities admit, out of the murk the pattern emerges, his pattern, the expression of what he has seen and what he has therefor made, the impress of his

[26] Learned Hand, "Mr. Justice Cardozo," *Harvard Law Review*, Vol. LII (January, 1939), as reprinted in *The Spirit of Liberty* (3d ed.), 131–33.

self upon the not-self, upon the hitherto formless material of which he was once but a part and over which he has now become the master. That is a pleasure which nobody who has felt it will be likely to underrate.[27]

[27] Learned Hand, "The Preservation of Personality," *Bryn Mawr Alumnae Bulletin,* October, 1927, as reprinted in *The Spirit of Liberty* (3d ed.), 43.

CHAPTER VI : *A Strict Argument for Judicial Review*

In analyzing the function of the federal courts, Judge Learned Hand distinguished between different types of law and the approach appropriate to each. First, there is constitutional law which allocates powers between state and nation and among the legislative, executive, and judicial branches. Second, there is constitutional law which is concerned with the interpretation and application of the Bill of Rights. Finally, there is statutory law.

Hand maintained that a judge properly assumes a different responsibility and attitude toward each of these kinds of law and interprets or applies each in a somewhat different manner. These different approaches emerge from his understanding of the proper function of the court as defined by the constitutional allocation of power. Thus his analysis of the role of the judiciary in questions regarding the distribution of functions is fundamental for it suggests the primary responsibility of the court as it relates to other levels and departments of government and provides the limiting framework within which a judge interprets the Bill of Rights and statutory law.

The extent of the power of judicial review has, over the years, created as many controversies as its exercise has settled. It is derived from the requirements of a written constitution which allocates functions and requires a definition of the specific role each institution of the system is to fulfill.

Judge Hand's understanding of the power of judicial review was drawn from his conceptions of democracy as a process and of law as the resolution of conflict by a formal declaration and from his historical interpretation. For him law was a solution one group is able to impose upon others, who accept it as authoritative until some opposing interest becomes powerful enough to alter it in the specific way society recognizes as legitimate. In the United States the Congress is the agency primarily responsible for enunciating law since all interests may be represented there. In the case of constitutional amendments the states and Congress act jointly in altering the basic law.

Since Hand believed that there is no divine will or natural law which provides sanctions for human law, he regarded the Constitution simply as an expression of the will of the state conventions that ratified it. Its authority was and is dependent upon the human sanctions available to enforce it, and its meaning can be gathered only from the words it contains, read in the historical setting in which it was created. Political power emanates from the people. The federal government and each branch of that government derived all their powers directly from the people according to the constitutional allocation. The departments were independent and equal, responsible to the whole people but without mutual dependence. The Constitution provided no explicit guidance on how one branch should act when in the exercise of its own authority it had to consider the validity of an act of another department. The second department was theoretically free to choose whether it would be guided by the judgment of the first department, make its own interpretation independent of the first, or accept as binding the decision of the courts in cases of constitutional interpretation. Hand believed that the third alternative denied the equality of the three branches and the principle of separation of powers and was thus inconsistent with that basic provision of the Constitution.

Learned Hand did not believe that the Supremacy Clause could be regarded as a justification for judicial review of congressional action. On the contrary, he understood it to mean that some express grant of power was necessary if courts were to have power to declare a law invalid because it conflicted with the Constitution. The Supremacy Clause did require state judges to follow federal laws and the Constitution when there was a conflict between them and state laws or constitutions. A state court may have to determine whether a federal law is constitutional when it is in conflict with a state law or constitution. The Judiciary Act of 1789 provides that on some occasions the Supreme Court may decide whether or not a state court has properly construed the Constitution in determining the validity of a federal or state law. But the Supremacy Clause itself was directed specifically to states and was designed to prevent them from usurping the powers they had delegated or failing to obey the limits they had accepted upon their own powers. It cannot be read as an authorization to pass upon other issues in which the legislative body might be in conflict with the Constitution.[1] In expounding a position similar to that taken by Hand, Alexander Bickel suggested that, while there is reason for involving the federal courts in questions regarding the constitutionality of state law, the same necessity does not prevail in matters of federal statutes. This assumption rests upon the fact that the court could accept as final the judgment of Congress and the President regarding the constitutionality of statutes or executive action and thus satisfy the needs of uniformity and the ultimate supremacy of federal authority. It does not answer the argument that, since the Constitution is law, it is the responsibility of the courts to interpret and judge in accordance with it.

In Hand's view the fact that Hamilton's argument in *The Federalist*, No. 78, and Justice John Marshall's reasoning in *Marbury v. Madison* did not make greater or more specific claims for the Constitution as the authority for judicial review supported his contention that the power is not provided for in the text. There is, moreover, historical support both for the position that the founders of the Constitution did assume the power of judicial review and for the contrary position that they did not.

It is clearly the responsibility of the court to determine what a given statute means and, when two laws seem to be in conflict, to determine which shall prevail. It is a very different thing when a court goes beyond the interpretation of a statute and determines that it is contrary to the Constitution and strikes it down: "When a court declares that a constitution does not authorize a statute, it reviews and reverses an earlier decision of the legislature; and, however well based its authority to do so may be, it does not follow from what it does in the other instances in which the same question does not arise."[2]

Although there is no explicit constitutional grant of the power of judicial review and the practice does invade the principle of the separation of powers, Judge Hand believed that there are good and sufficient

---

1 Alexander M. Bickel, *The Least Dangerous Branch*, 11–12.
2 Hand, *The Bill of Rights*, 10.

reasons for inferring this power. The legitimacy of judicial review is to be found in the practical necessity for the function to be fulfilled. The primary purpose a constitution serves is to allocate political power, and it is necessary for some agency to have authority to declare when the allocation has been disturbed. If the judicial branch had not assumed this power it is likely either that the legislative branch would have absorbed all power or that inconsistencies would have developed as each branch made independent judgments, so that coherent government would have been impossible. Thus, on the basis of experience and necessity, the power is justified. Furthermore, historically it has been considered proper when interpreting to interpolate provisions which, though unexpressed, are essential to the purpose intended. This is especially true of constitutions since they are general in nature and must cover a great number of situations which cannot be foreseen.

Perhaps the fundamental justification of judicial review is to be found in the nature of law itself (and constitutions which are but basic laws) as described by Aristotle whom Hand quoted with approval. Aristotle said in his *Ethics*:

> ... all law is universal but about some things it is not possible to make a universal statement which shall be correct. In those cases, then, in which it is necessary to speak universally, but not possible to do so correctly, the law takes the usual case, though it is not ignorant of the possibility of error. And it is none the less correct; for the error is not in the law nor in the legislator but in the nature of the thing.... When the law speaks universally, then, and a case arises on it which is not covered by the universal statement, then it is right, where the legislator fails us and has erred by over-simplicity, to correct the omission—to say what the legislator himself would have ... put into this law, if he had known.[3]

Hand understood by this that the nature of law makes it necessary for someone to supply the details of what must be a general rule. He thought it not only plausible but necessary and proper that in the American system the courts should serve this function insofar as they demarcate the limits of authority of the various departments of government.

[3] Aristotle, "Nicomachean Ethics," *The Basic Works of Aristotle* (Ed. by Richard McKeon), 1020.

Since the power of judicial review was not expressly granted by the Constitution but was based on necessity, Judge Hand believed that the court should use it with great restraint. He said:

> However, since this power is not a logical deduction from the structure of the Constitution but only a practical condition upon its successful operation, it need not be exercised whenever a court sees, or thinks that it sees, an invasion of the Constitution. It is always a preliminary question how importunately the occasion demands an answer. It may be better to leave the issue to be worked out without authoritative solution; or perhaps the only solution available is one that the court has no adequate means to enforce. As we all know, the Supreme Court has steadfastly refused to decide constitutional issues that it deems to involve "political questions"—a term it has never tried to define.[4]

According to Hand's view, the determination of certain questions of constitutionality are clearly within the province of other departments, and he believed that the Supreme Court had acknowledged this fact by standing aloof in such issues as those which relate to whether a state has a republican form of government, to constitutional amendments, to the identity of bills which have passed both houses of Congress, to explicit rulings on the validity of executive agreements having the force of a treaty, to matters of extradition, and to the right of executive officers to withhold information from Congress. In the years since his retirement from the bench the Supreme Court has involved itself in a number of major substantive issues which he believed to be within the delegated powers of Congress. This involvement does not damage the theoretical validity of his interpretation of judicial function. His position of extreme restraint with regard to the use of judicial power to review substantive issues is frequently challenged. It is often argued that his interpretation failed to provide sufficient protection for the personal rights and freedoms upon which democracy depends. Many democrats believe that there must be some institution which protects individuals against the majority will and view the courts as best able to serve this purpose.

Judge Hand recognized this point of view and thought that the most persuasive argument for the power of the courts to review the

[4] Hand, *The Bill of Rights*, 15.

merits of legislation arises in connection with the protection of free speech. The most serious invasions of this freedom occur when a majority of the people are hostile to the minority against which such a restraining law is directed, and it is true that legislatures are more ready than courts to repress what ought to be free. Even though the period of hysteria which gives rise to such laws is generally short, serious damage may be done to individuals for which there is no restitution. This fact seemed to him to be a strong argument for substantive judicial review. In other areas the issue did not seem so clear. While it is often argued that judges tend more than others to take the long view of things, this view varies greatly with individuals and is at best uncertain.

Learned Hand did not accept the preferred-position theory. He regarded the sum of the arguments for restricting the scope of judicial review as more impressive than those for liberal use of power in substantive matters. A crucial consideration for him was that, once it becomes the accepted pattern for judges to take sides on political issues, their political predispositions will be an important factor in their appointment. This view appears to have been borne out in recent nominations to the Supreme Court. Political factors have always been involved in judicial appointment to a certain extent, but to establish them as legitimate and usual criteria would, he thought, seriously impair the important judicial functions of the courts:

> In very much the greater part of a judge's duties he is charged with freeing himself as far as he can from all personal preferences, and that becomes difficult in proportion as these are strong. The degree to which he will secure compliance with his commands depends in large measure upon how far the community believes him to be the mouthpiece of a public will, conceived as the resultant of many conflicting strains that have come, at least provisionally, to a consensus. This sanction disappears in so far as it is supposed permissible for him covertly to smuggle into his decisions his personal notions of what is desirable.
>
> This consideration becomes especially important in appellate courts. It is often hard to secure unanimity about the borders of legislative power. . . . This is disastrous because disunity cancels the impact of monolithic solidarity on which the authority of a bench of judges so largely depends.[5]

---

[5] *Ibid.*, 71–72. Carl Swisher supported this view when he wrote: ". . . to the extent

Disagreement among the judges tends to free the people from the sense of the compulsion of the law. The impact upon the public of a split decision is to produce the belief that the case might have been decided either way—which is usually true in those cases where the courts pass upon the merits of legislation. It is contrary to democratic processes to vest in a group of men who are not responsible to the people the power to strike down a statute simply because they do not agree with it. A basic and perpetual problem of a free society is how much authority the will of the currently prevailing majority should have. Hand granted that some restraining organ might be necessary but, if so, that the Court should not serve as this third chamber, for it does not exercise a suspensive veto which requires additional deliberation. It forbids a statute by making a different evaluation of the values which is the essence of legislation and in fact removes the issue from further legislative consideration. Furthermore, he believed that this function would threaten the Court's capacity for fair adjudication because it would necessarily require an orientation to political matters.

The argument is frequently heard that the courts, through their review of legislation, may serve as teachers of society. While Learned Hand was unimpressed by this argument, he did accept responsibility for providing clear, intelligible, and compelling explanations for his decisions. It was precisely his concern that they must be completely justifiable and convincing to rational men that prompted him to decline the role of political mentor. He thought that on large questions of value no opinion, however eloquent or reasonable, could be convincing to those who chose other values as a matter of will.

When Hand took cognizance of the activity of the Supreme Court especially in cases dealing wth the First Amendment and the Due Process Clause, he acknowledged that in practice the Supreme Court did not limit itself in the manner he thought appropriate and necessary. His purpose was not to describe the power actually exercised by the Court nor to say how much its decisions have extended the scope of this power. He was trying to express the degree of judicial intervention that is implicit in the Constitution. He did not regard these deviations

of the inability of justices to agree on decisions and on statements of the law, the Court as a whole has failed to complete the performance of its ideal function." Carl B. Swisher, *The Supreme Court in Modern Role,* 181.

from the Constitution as insignificant even though the extension of the power had proceeded gradually and was often explained in terms of the organic growth of a functioning system. He knew that the modification sought to protect basic privileges through an institution removed from the immediate pressures of popular hysteria, panic, and greed, but he preferred to rely upon the substantial checks and balances incorporated explicitly in the Constitution by the Founding Fathers.

Judge Hand's emphasis on the desirability of judicial restraint in the exercise of the power of judicial review was an attempt to take into account the complexity and diversity of the national community. His pragmatism was evident in his insistence that only by trial and error can wise decisions be found and that it is thus necessary to allow legislatures to experiment freely within the framework of their constitutional power. His position was consistent with his whole political and legal philosophy and was not determined by a liberal or conservative view of the specific issues involved. Its foundation was an abiding confidence in the vital capacity of a free society to find its own solutions more successfully if it is not constricted by judicial intervention.

CHAPTER VII : *The Last Word on Allocation of Power*

Learned Hand's interpretation of the courts' right to exercise the power of judicial review is unique, but it is the implications he drew from this interpretation which are of special interest. He knew that the separation of power according to function was not absolute but believed that it denied any branch a claim to ultimate control over another. Only the necessity to prevent the failure of the Union justified allowing the courts to make final decisions in some cases. It was "no doubt a dangerous liberty, . . . but it was justified, ... for the need was compelling. On the other hand it was absolutely essential to confine the power to the need that evoked it; that is, it was and always had been necessary to distinguish between the frontiers of another 'Department's' authority and the propriety of its choices within those frontiers."[1] To Hand the distinction between the frontiers and propriety of choice was critical and must be adhered to rigorously if a basic tenet of American government, separation of powers, was to be preserved. The scope of the courts' power to review a statute for constitutionality was limited to the determination of the boundaries of legislation and was not to be extended to the correction of any abuses in the exercise of that power.

Laws result from discontent with the status quo and the need for some satisfactory substitute. The legislative branch seeks to overcome the displeasure by understanding its source and then offering some new measure that it hopes will be adequate for this purpose. Difficult as this procedure is, it is not nearly as hazardous as seeking to determine whether or not the change will be beneficial to society, for this decision involves a choice depending upon one's appraisal of the benefits and sacrifices that may be anticipated as a result of the proposed measure.

[1] Hand, *The Bill of Rights*, 29–30.

Benefits and sacrifices are incommensurables since they are made up of elements not common to each other. Thus, when this choice must be made for others, especially large numbers of persons each of whom has his own scale of values, the problem is incredibly difficult. Nevertheless, the function of the legislative branch is precisely to make these choices for society. It is the representative institution in which the interests of all may be pressed and the full impact felt by public officials, both through the activities of interest groups and through the ballot. It seemed impossible to Judge Hand for the court to invalidate the resulting laws without substituting the court's own scale of values for that already expressed by the legislature. Regardless of the rationalization offered, the process is the same that gave rise to the statute initially.

Hand believed that when the court engages in this kind of legislative supervision it clearly runs counter to the distinction between the function of legislating, which is assigned to the legislature, and that of interpreting, which was given to the courts. If the concept of separation can be supported on any basis, it must be the existence of a difference between legislating and interpreting that is one of kind and not simply of degree. He was certain that, while there may be many cases in which the delineation between them is difficult, they are in fact two different functions and are properly separated in the American system.

In his opinions Judge Hand sought to avoid substituting his own preferences for those of the legislature. Only in the Schechter case did he hold a major application of the federal law unconstitutional, and upon close analysis even this does not appear to be an exception to his self-restraint, though the opinion does limit the powers of Congress.[2] Here he was not dealing with an act of Congress which explicitly sought to bring the local working conditions in the poultry market in New York within the province of the national interest and thus subject to federal regulation. Punishment for violation of the codes promulgated under the National Industrial Recovery Act was dependent upon the finding that the transaction was one in or affecting interstate or foreign commerce. Since there was no congressional determination that wages and hours in the situation described in this case were in fact a part of interstate commerce, there was no occasion for the presumption of

---

[2] Wyzanski, "Judge Learned Hand's Contribution to Public Law," *Harvard Law Review*, Vol. LX (February, 1947), 351.

constitutionality which normally follows a specific act of Congress. Judge Charles Wyzanski argued that Congress invited judicial review of presidential determination regarding what constituted interstate commerce.

Hand thought the court properly involved, for the case concerned the definition of interstate commerce, and this question had become germane to the preservation of the boundaries established in the Constitution between state and national power. Even so, his sense of restraint is evident. He prefaced his reasoning with the following statement:

> It is always a serious thing to declare any act of Congress unconstitutional, and especially in a case where it is a part of a comprehensive plan for the rehabilitation of the nation as a whole. With the wisdom of that plan we have nothing whatever to do; and were only the Fifth Amendment involved I should be prepared to read the powers of Congress in the broadest possible way.[3]

But since the allocation of power between state and nation was also involved, the power of Congress to legislate had to be viewed by the court in light of state power.

Hand thought an additional argument against having courts assume legislative responsibilities was that it tends to weaken the popular branch and render it incapable of performing its function. A community learns best by living with and correcting its own mistakes, and it is deprived of this opportunity when the courts assume the role of "Platonic Guardians."

Writing about the powers of Congress and the courts under the Due Process Clause, Hand noted that there may be many abuses which the courts cannot properly relieve because the only remedy is popular sentiment brought to bear upon the legislature:

> The Constitution does not create the courts as certain safeguards from all legislative injustice, but only to keep the legislature within its proper powers. It may use those powers unwisely or unjustly, and the courts have no right to interfere. In this case [*United States* v. *Delaware and Hudson Company*, 164 Fed. 215 (1908)] the evil may be in fact exaggerated, the necessity for so stringent a remedy may not exist, the statute may bear unequally, and much damage may be done to innocent

---

[3] *United States* v. *A. L. A. Schechter Poultry Corporation*, 76 F. (2d) 617, 624 (1935).

HUNT LIBRARY
CARNEGIE-MELLON UNIVERSITY

persons. Not all these considerations together have any proper weight with a court, and none of them lends any actual weight to the argument against the act's validity.[4]

Judge Hand distinguished between the invalidation of a statute when it constituted an improper delegation of power and when it commanded something contrary to the Constitution. In the former the court

> overrules a decision of the legislature as to its powers; but there appears to me a tenable distinction between that situation and one where a court overrules the actual exercise of legislative authority; for the delegation of authority is *pro tanto* the abdication of authority over the subject matter by a transfer to others of authority that the legislature alone may exercise.[5]

This insistence that the function of legislating be performed by or under direction of Congress is compatible with strict construction of the constitutional allocation of powers. This part of the Constitution carries with it a kind of absolute command whose intention he understood to be sufficiently clear to guide the court in fulfilling the necessary task of review. Nonetheless, he did believe that Congress had much freedom in delegation and supported not only the act of delegation but also gave great weight to subsequent official determination as long as it could be justified in terms of the original allocation of power by the Constitution. This attitude was especially evident in *Republic Aviation Corp.* v. *National Labor Relations Board,* in which he said, ". . . we are certainly not called upon, nor should indeed be justified, to consider the question of law: *i.e.* the priority to be awarded between the conflicting interests. . . . We should still have to give presumptive validity to the Board's decision."[6] Hand believed it was the court's function to determine what agency was entitled to make the authoritative judgment and then abide by that decision. The real measure of his discomfort with the judicial role of the regulatory commissions was revealed when he said that they

[4] Learned Hand, "The Commodities Clause and the Fifth Amendment," *Harvard Law Review,* Vol. XXII, No. 4 (February, 1909), 262.

[5] Hand, *The Bill of Rights,* 49.

[6] *Republic Aviation Corporation* v. *National Labor Relations Board,* 142 F. (2d) 196 (1944).

get an expertness from familiarity with the subject matter that judges cannot possibly have. The thing that teases me most—and I confess seems to be insoluble as far as I have been able to judge—is at what point in the procedure should courts intervene and how far should they be allowed to go. I am satisfied that somewhere along the line they must intervene; you cannot leave the last word with the administrative tribunal. But, how can the judges, who have no specialized acquaintance with the subject, know when and where to do it? I wish I had some light on it.[7]

His sense of restraint and frustration reached perhaps its highest point in *Brooklyn National Corporation* v. *Commissioner of Internal Revenue*, where the issue was the power of the court to review decisions of the Tax Court. Hand's court had previously reversed a holding of the Board of Tax Appeals. Subsequently the Tax Court held that the reversal was wrong and refused to follow it. In this case Hand was concerned with whether the court should yield to the Tax Court's refusal to accept the court's ruling. If further reasoning of the Tax Court had convinced the Court of Appeals that its judgment had been in error, there would have been no problem, but this was not the case, and a similar appeal from a district court would have been reversed a second time. Hand noted, however, that

> the Supreme Court has repeatedly admonished us (in so many decisions that it would be idle to repeat them), that our power to review a ruling of the Tax Court is very much more limited than in the case of a district court. . . . although personally we are of the same mind as before, we think that we should yield to the insistence of the Tax Court, which within these limits is really the court of last appeal. . . . Our prior decision was then wrong. . . . because . . . by assuming jurisdiction to consider the question at all, we invaded the prerogative of the Tax Court and disregarded the finality of its orders. That finality depends, as we understand, upon the added competency which inevitably follows from concentration in a special field. Why if that be so, we—or indeed even the Supreme Court itself—should be competent to fix the measure of the Tax Court's competence, and why we should ever declare that it is

[7] Learned Hand, "Morals in Public Life," as reprinted in *The Spirit of Liberty* (3d ed.), 242.

115

wrong, is indeed an interesting inquiry, which happily it is not necessary for us to pursue.[8]

Determination of the proper relationship of the courts to administrative interpretation is not limited to the major regulatory agencies to which Congress has delegated broad discretion but also involves the interpretation of officials charged with administering laws. In *Fishgold v. Sullivan Drydock and Repair Corporation*, Judge Hand dealt with a case in which the plaintiff argued that, regardless of the original scope of the sections of the law on which he was basing his claim, they "have . . . by administrative interpretation and by later legislation, taken on the meaning which he claims."[9] In this instance Hand found that the legislation had been given contrary interpretation by officials in different agencies, and so there was no consistent ruling to which the court should yield its judgment, but, in any event, the court itself must determine the proper interpretation, for "upon the courts rests the ultimate responsibility of declaring what a statute means."[10]

Judge Hand supported the ultimate authority of the courts to interpret statutes by calling attention to a serious weakness in viewing administrative interpretations as authoritative. Under many laws the position of the officer charged with administration is not supposed to be wholly impartial. To Hand his capacity is different from that of one who must settle a dispute. Whenever an official charged with the administration but not final interpretation of a law has honest doubts about its meaning, he appropriately presses the case for the side he represents and leaves the decision to the courts who have that responsibility. For, "if he surrenders a plausible construction, it will, at least it may be surrendered forever; and yet it may be right. Since such rulings need not have the detachment of a judicial, or semi-judicial decision, and may properly carry a bias, it would seem that they should not be . . . authoritative."[11]

Society requires both stability and change. Hand believed that the separation of powers made the legislature responsible for change and

[8] *Brooklyn National Corporation* v. *Commissioner of Internal Revenue*, 157 F. (2d) 450, 452 (1946).
[9] *Fishgold* v. *Sullivan Drydock and Repair Corporation*, 154 F. (2d) 785, 799 (1946).
[10] *Ibid.*, 790.
[11] *Ibid.*, 789.

the court the guardian of continuity and stability. His own role he understood to be circumscribed by what Justice Holmes meant when he said: "That [to do justice] is not my job. My job is to play the game according to the rules."[12] In spite of the problems posed by the division of functions, Hand thought that the operation of this principle had been an important factor in the achievement of the ends of a liberal democracy and should be maintained. He said:

> In our country we have always been extremely jealous of mixing the different processes of government, especially that of making law, with that of saying what it is after it has been made. This distinction, if I am right, cannot be rigidly enforced; but like most of those ideas, which the men who made our constitutions believed in, it has a very sound basis as a guide, provided one does not try to make it into an absolute rule.[13]

The practice of judicial review relates not only to the separation of powers between different branches of the federal government but also to the allocation of power between the state and national governments. The issue involved here is not the usurpation of power by one of three equal departments but the delicate relationship established in the Constitution between national and state powers. Judge Hand insisted upon judicial restraint in this relationship also, since the need for a supreme power which might exercise its authority on occasion did not destroy the necessity for the states as well as the other departments to be free from interference by the courts in carrying out their functions.

As Hand understood it, the Supremacy Clause of the Constitution requires state courts to judge the validity of state laws and state constitutions in accordance with the federal Constitution. So that the power granted to the national government by the Constitution would be secure, in the Judiciary Act of 1789, Congress authorized the Supreme Court to review decisions of the highest state court qualified to rule in cases where (1) the decision was against the validity of a federal law or treaty that had been "drawn in question," (2) the decision favored a state statute that had been challenged as "repugnant to the constitution,

---

[12] Learned Hand, "A Personal Confession," as reprinted in *The Spirit of Liberty* (3d ed.), 307.

[13] Hand, "How Far Is a Judge Free in Rendering a Decision?" as reprinted in *The Spirit of Liberty* (3d ed.), 108.

treaties or laws of the United States," and (3) a part of the Constitution, treaty, statute, or commission held under the United States was drawn into question, and the decision was "against the title, right, privilege or exemption specifically set up or claimed by either party."[14] The underlying principle of this provision is that if the Constitution, laws, and treaties of the United States are to be observed by the states the Supreme Court must have the authority to review cases in which the state court rulings are adverse to federal rights which have been asserted.

The relationship of state to national power under the Commerce Clause is an example of problems of this kind, and of it Judge Hand said:

> It is impossible to avoid all such occasions, but it was a daring expedient to meet them with judges, deliberately put beyond the reach of popular pressure. And yet, granted the necessity of some such authority, probably independent judges were the most likely to do the job well. Besides, the strains that decisions on these questions set up are not ordinarily dangerous to the social structure.[15]

The suggestion is implicit that the judicial process of the United States, being relatively independent of public pressures, is appropriate only for those decisions which do not place severe strains upon society or attempt to resolve the most fundamental cleavages.

Hand believed that the courts handled the problems arising under the Commerce Clause well and without serious threat to the system because these matters are generally narrow in scope and do not raise serious problems of judicial power in relation to the democratic process, as do more widely controversial issues. Most Commerce Clause cases are concerned with procedure and structure rather than substance and usually do not completely foreclose the achievement of any public purpose. They tend to proscribe methods rather than goals, so that when some state regulation is invalidated under the Commerce Clause, another way is often found to accomplish much the same end.

While such decisions do not concern the fundamental conflicts in society, they are of vital concern on another basis—that of preserving the spheres of activity proper to each level of government. This has

[14] 1 U.S., *Statutes at Large*, 85–86, quoted in Walter F. Murphy and C. Herman Pritchett, *Courts, Judges and Politics: An Introduction to the Judicial Process*, 176.

[15] Learned Hand, "The Contribution of an Independent Judiciary to Civilization," as reprinted in *The Spirit of Liberty* (3d ed.), 160.

become a function of the courts under judicial review. In the Schechter case Judge Hand said:

> . . . the extent of the power of Congress to regulate interstate commerce . . . goes to the very root of any federal system at all. . . . To protect that framework there must be some tribunal which can authoritatively apportion the powers of government, and traditionally this is the duty of courts. It may indeed follow that the nation cannot as a unit meet any of the great crises of its existence except war . . . but that to some extent at any rate is implicit in any federation, and the resulting weaknesses have not hitherto been thought to outweigh the dangers of a completely centralized government. If the American people have come to believe otherwise, Congress is not the accredited organ to express their will to change.[16]

Hand's view of American democracy is apparent here: the Constitution with its amendments is the last expression by the people of a basic law, and until the people make a new expression in the manner specified in the Constitution, it must remain the fundamental law of the land.

Although some agency must have ultimate authority to settle disputes regarding the allocation of powers by the Constitution, it does not necessarily follow that this institution must always be the courts. The Constitution clearly gives Congress the power to regulate interstate and foreign commerce. It follows from Hand's view of judicial review and the Judiciary Act that the necessity for federal judicial involvement does not occur until a state court has decided in favor of state action against a claim made on behalf of some federal power.

Hand believed that the doctrine evolved from Marshall's ambiguous opinion in *Gibbons* v. *Ogden* came very close to denying the state effective legislative jurisdiction over interstate commerce even in areas where Congress had not acted. On its face the doctrine of concurrent powers which was urged in this case by the state of New York would have been satisfactory. He thought it reasonable to assume that the Supreme Court had not accepted this construction because it was fearful that if commerce among the states was left open to state regulation a tangled network of vested interests might be developed which would

---

[16] *United States* v. *A. L. A. Schechter Poultry Corporation,* 76 F. (2d) 617, 624 (1935).

threaten the national structure or impede future exercise of its power by Congress.

Aside from this possibility, Hand saw no compelling reason for judicial intervention in view of the constitutional allocation of powers. The concurrent-powers doctrine would have protected the ultimate authority of Congress because it could always legislate to substitute national regulation for whatever pattern of interstate commerce had developed among the states. This position, which was explicitly denied by Marshall, would have fitted nicely into Hand's view of constitutional separation of powers, which permitted maximum freedom of each branch to decide issues within its own sphere. Congress, not the courts, would have been responsible for preventing state action from interfering with the purpose of the Commerce Clause, which was to provide for a free national economy. This doctrine would have permitted the states to retain the full measure of their power over interstate commerce that was consistent with their original grant to Congress.

As a matter of fact, the Court has played a crucial part in the elaboration of the Commerce Clause. This is true because, although the Constitution clearly grants to Congress the power to regulate commerce,

> Congress gives its attention to commerce only sporadically, whereas the Court is continuously on tap. For a century since *Cooley* it has consistently performed the role of umpire, enforcing the laws of Congress against conflicting state laws, invalidating state statutes discriminating against commerce, and determining whether the states are entering fields belonging to the national government under the Constitution.[17]

Thus the judiciary has become the institution through which most of the solutions to interstate-commerce issues are sought. The decisions have often lacked consistency (Hand believed that this was a powerful argument against Court determination of such issues) because, as Justice Wiley B. Rutledge acknowledged, they have resulted from "not logic alone, but large choices of policy,"[18] which are not always related to the establishment of a free national market but are motivated by the justices' attitude regarding the amount of economic regulation which it is appropriate for government, either state or federal, to exercise.

[17] C. Herman Pritchett, *The American Constitution*, 264–65.
[18] *Prudential Insurance Co. v. Benjamin*, 328 U.S. 418 (1946).

The most obvious voluntary involvement of the courts in the commerce power relates to state regulation in areas where there is no federal legislation. Here the alleged conflict is directly with the Constitution, and the Supreme Court decides whether the state law is compatible with its understanding of a free national economy. Hand believed that this unnecessarily put the courts in the center of the political decision-making process.

In *Seelig v. Baldwin*, Hand said that the Constitution might have been interpreted to permit the state freedom to regulate all commerce, except for taxation of imports and exports (prohibited by Article I, Section 10), until Congress acted. However, his decision in that case held invalid a part of a law forbidding sale in New York of milk produced in New Jersey under conditions less favorable to farmers than those required in New York. While he thus limited state power to regulate interstate commerce in the absence of congressional action, his reasoning reaffirmed his obedience to precedent rather than the appropriateness of substituting the court's judgment for that of the state legislature. He said: "It might have been held that this [taxation of imports and exports] was the measure of the states' incapacity until Congress chose to act. But the contrary is now . . . thoroughly established."[19] Since the practice was well established, he felt compelled to follow the tradition and lead of the higher court, although he was critical of it.

Spector Motor Service, Inc. v. Walsh is a similar case in which Hand's dissenting opinion would have denied Connecticut the power to levy a franchise tax on foreign corporations engaged exclusively in interstate commerce. His position was based not on a belief that the Constitution requires this prohibition but on his deference to the Supreme Court's ruling. In this case he explicitly disassociated himself from the view that his opinion, following precedent, supported:

> If I were to start afresh, I should not myself make that distinction. . . .
> I think it a barren way to treat the distribution of power in a federation like ours to say that, if a state can tax a national activity, it follows that it must have the power to cripple or frustrate it. If I could, I should hold that, while Congress had a paramount power to prevent just that—or while in plain cases possibly the courts might themselves intervene— in ordinary situations the states were free to tax all activities within

[19] *Seelig v. Baldwin*, 7 F. Supp. 776, 778 (1934).

their borders provided they did so equitably. . . . the Supreme Court may eventually hold that. . . . But it seems to me clear that, whatever the future may hold, it has not done so yet; but that, on the contrary, it still adheres to the old distinction.[20]

Many cases involved a nice discrimination in judging what does and does not fall within the authority of the power in question. When the conflict is by its nature concerned with the boundaries of congressional power rather than its wisdom, the courts may legitimately intervene. In the Schechter case he said:

> In an industrial society bound together by means of transport and communication as rapid and certain as ours, it is idle to seek for any transaction, however apparently isolated, which may not have an effect somewhere; such a society is an elastic medium which transmits all tremors throughout its territory; the only question is of their size . . . in regard to what properly may come under the federal authority of the commerce clause . . . the regulation of the hours and wages of all local employees, who turn the fowls into merchantable poultry after they have become a part of the domestic stock of goods, seems to be so different in degree as to be beyond the line.[21]

Another area in which it seems necessary for the federal courts to make determinations related to allocation of powers is that of due process. Interpretation of this clause has changed radically within the last century. Since it has been extended to include substantive due process, it relates to the constitutional allocation of power both between nation and states and among the departments of the federal government. Judge Hand's understanding of this evolution of due process is worth recounting briefly. When the term "due process" first appeared about a hundred and fifty years after the signing of the Magna Carta, it merely meant customary legal procedure, and it was not until Sir Edward Coke's gloss upon it in Bonham's case that its extension began. Coke said, "When an Act of Parliament is against common right and reason, or repugnant, or impossible to be performed, the common law will control it and adjudge such Act to be void."[22] This was obviously an

---

[20] *Spector Motor Service, Inc.* v. *Walsh*, 139 F. (2d) 809, 823 (1944).
[21] *United States* v. *A. L. A. Schechter Poultry Corporation*, 76 F. (2d) 617, 625 (1935).
[22] *Coke*, 8 Rep. 118a, quoted in Hand, *The Bill of Rights*, 35.

expression of limitation upon legislative or executive power. Yet in *Murray's Lessee* v. *Hoboken Land and Improvement Co.* the Supreme Court spoke as though due process concerned only those customary legal steps necessary to invoke forcible sanctions when it said, "We must look to those settled usages and modes of proceeding existing in the common and statute law of England before the emigration of our ancestors and which are shown not to have been unsuited to their civil and political condition by having been acted on after the settlement of this country."[23] Just one year later, in *Dred Scott* v. *Sanford*, Chief Justice Roger B. Taney interpreted the clause as a limit upon the power of Congress to confiscate property, regardless of the procedure prescribed, and introduced the idea of substantive due process which has become a doctrine of paramount importance in the process of judicial review.

Hand regarded the shift from procedural to substantive due process as a fundamental deviation from the original function of the courts. They were authorized by the Constitution and were competent to ensure the maintenance of customary or accepted legal procedures, but the evaluation of the substance of legislation was an entirely different matter. It involved balancing incommensurable values, which was the specific province of the legislatures, state and federal.

Substantive due process came into vogue in the 1880's as a means of invalidating state laws regulating business. The charge was made that the new laws invaded those rights which the Constitution had been designed to protect, and they did invade rights traditionally defended as constitutional. It is not surprising that the judges, steeped in traditional law and belonging to the group seeking the continuing protection of the Constitution, should in good faith determine that the new laws contravened the fundamental presuppositions of society which the Bill of Rights was intended to protect.

The states defended their action in terms of their police power. The broad interpretation given both these concepts (due process and police power) by the courts made conflicts between them inevitable. The expansive interpretation of the police power by Taney in the license cases and by Samuel F. Miller in the slaughterhouse cases led

[23] *Murray's Lessee* v. *Hoboken Land and Improvement Co.*, 18 Howard 272, 277 (1856).

subsequent courts to try to limit it so that it would not be in constant conflict with due process. Judge Hand suggested that Justice Henry B. Brown's attempt in *Lawton* v. *Steele* was typical of these efforts. The case concerned a state law which provided for confiscation of nets and other equipment of fishermen who invaded the state's waters. The opinion held that the police power of the state would

> include everything essential to public safety, health and morals. . . . the State may interfere whenever the public interests demand it and in particular a large discretion is necessarily vested in the legislature to determine, not only what the interests of the public require but what measures are necessary for the protection of such interests.[24]

But then Brown turned his attention to the conditions which would justify a judicial veto. It must appear,

> first, that the interests of the public generally, as distinguished from those of a particular class, require such interference; and, second, that the means are reasonably necessary for the accomplishment of the purpose, and not unduly oppressive upon individuals. The legislature may not under guise of protecting the public interests, arbitrarily interfere with private business, or impose unusual and unnecessary restrictions upon lawful occupations. In other words, its determination as to what is proper exercise of its police powers is not final or conclusive, but is subject to the supervision of the courts.[25]

Judge Hand's reaction to this definition was clear—it regards the court as a third branch of the legislature, and the reasons are obvious. How does the court determine when the "interests of the public generally" make it necessary to interfere with those of a particular class? What is "reasonably necessary" and not "unduly oppressive"? When has a legislature "arbitrarily interfered," and what precisely is an "unusual and unnecessary restriction?" What "supervision" is it that the courts are authorized to exercise over the legislative judgment?

In 1908, Learned Hand expressed his view regarding the confusing relationship that had developed between due process and state powers over the public safety, health, welfare, and morals. The problem had arisen, he said, when the court began to "examine the expediency of the

---

[24] *Lawton* v. *Steele*, 152 U.S. 133, 156 (1894).
[25] *Ibid.*, 157.

measure and to determine whether it had in fact in their judgment any relation to the purposes and objects which it was designed to effect."[26] He believed, however, that even though the court examined the expediency of legislation it did not necessarily have to be concerned with the whole problem as the legislature had been. A judge may personally disapprove of an act and yet find it to be within the permissible bounds of legislative power. Only if it is obvious that the law is the result of passion, ignorance, or folly can the court say that it fails to meet the requirements of due process of law. The act meets the test if it may reasonably be thought to contribute to any purpose that a reasonable man may think desirable for the public welfare.

Public reaction to judicial interference grew with the increasing demand for social regulation. The application of substantive due process in the interest of property rights brought forth opposition from members of the bar, the bench, and the law schools, as well as from groups instrumental in securing the passage of the laws being struck down:

> These men believed that democracy was a political contrivance by which the group conflicts inevitable in all society should find a relatively harmless outlet in the give and take of legislative compromise after the contending groups had had a chance to measure their relative strength . . . . They had no illusion that the outcome would necessarily be the best obtainable, certainly not that which they might themselves have personally chosen; but the political stability of such a system, and the possible enlightenment which the battle itself might bring, were worth the price. . . . that statutes were not to be held invalid, so long as anyone could find a reasonable basis for not ascribing them purely to envy or greed.[27]

Supporters of substantive due process fought a losing battle but continued to maintain their position logically and firmly. The argument was almost exclusively centered around property rights, and although the ultimate outcome of the conflict was revolutionary and ended in the virtual demise of economic due process, Hand thought that it had

[26] Learned Hand, "Due Process of Law and the Eight-Hour Day," *Harvard Law Review*, Vol. XXI, No. 7 (May, 1908), 499.

[27] Learned Hand, "Chief Justice Stone's Concept of the Judicial Function," *Columbia Law Review*, Vol. LVII (September, 1946), as reprinted in *The Spirit of Liberty* (1st ed.), 204.

not greatly exceeded the prevailing consensus. Formal enunciation of changes already wrought in society appeared to him a proper function of the court. Supporters of economic due process insisted that

> if all it [due process] forbade were statutes or administrative excesses which were so utterly outrageous that nobody could give any rational support, it was an idle gesture, for it is nearly always possible to find a plausible justification for any measure that has commanded enough popular support to get itself enacted. . . . [their opponents] answered that, however that might be, it was apparent that any more stringent doctrine than they were willing to admit made the courts a third camera —in fact final arbiters in disputes in which everybody agreed they should have no part. Unless they abstained, the whole system would fall apart; or, if it did not, certainly the judges must be made sensitive and responsive to the shifting pressures of political sentiment, a corrective which few were prepared to accept. Therefore, they argued, theirs was the only possible canon, let political logic find in it what flaws it would.[28]

Thus far it is apparent Hand's sympathies were with those who urged judicial restraint in economic matters, the position generally expressed by a majority of Supreme Court justices in recent years. He noted that their decisions had been sprinkled with protestations that they were not sitting as a superlegislature and that there had been increasing restraint in most cases of economic regulation. Robert G. McCloskey affirmed this view when he suggested that, if the whole series of economic due process cases were taken together, "there could be little doubt as to the practical result: no claim of substantive economic rights would now be sustained by the Supreme Court. The judiciary had abdicated the field."[29] For practical purposes it appears as though the decline of economic due process is virtually complete, but an occasional ambivalence of the Supreme Court seems to support Hand's position that many decisions depend upon the justices' individual appraisals regarding the wisdom of legislative determinations.

Almost simultaneously with the movement away from economic due process, the Supreme Court began to use due process as a major

[28] *Ibid.*, 205.

[29] Robert G. McCloskey, "Economic Due Process and the Supreme Court: An Exhumation and Reburial," *The Supreme Court Review, 1962* (Ed. by Philip B. Kurland), 38.

check on substantive legislation dealing with individual liberties. As Hand approved the movement away from the former, he deplored the rise of the latter.

One rationalization for this new use of substantive due process is that due process itself is not an adequate standard by which the Court may reasonably limit legislation but that when the "liberty" of the Due Process Clause is understood to embody the First Amendment the standard becomes adequate. This permits some members of the Court to use substantive due process in civil-liberties cases and to deny its validity in economic problems.

Justification for substantive due process in civil-liberties cases in terms of incorporation is challenged by others who question that it provides adequate protection for the newer democratic values which have grown up in recent years and are thus not included specifically in the Bill of Rights. Herman Pritchett suggested, for example, that it deprives the Court of a constitutional basis for dealing with such matters as sterilization legislation, as illustrated by *Buck v. Bell*, and leaves only procedural protection for individuals who are publicly branded by the government as "security risks" or naturalized citizens who are threatened with denaturalization. Thus, it seems to Pritchett, substantive due process itself is a valuable concept which will endure, although its use will be selective and depend upon the judgment of the courts.[30]

In 1962, McCloskey regretfully noted that while the Court had made a radical shift in its use of substantive due process within the previous thirty years, it had failed to provide a rationalization for the change. In the absence of such a clarification, he attempted to discover whether or not there was a valid explanation for the abolition of economic due process and the simultaneous rise of substantive due process in the field of individual liberties.

It can be argued, he said, that acts which impinge upon individual freedom of expression are more destructive of the human personality than restrictions on economic freedom, and thus the Court is justified in exerting its authority more rigorously in the area of individual liberties. Without disagreeing with this judgment about the relative values

[30] Pritchett, *The American Constitution*, 590–91.

of the two kinds of freedom, he questioned whether it provides a justification for denying all protection to economic rights.[31]

Another argument revolves around the democratic necessity for a free trade in ideas and the protection of all in their right to participate in the political process. But this argument does not justify a downgrading of economic rights or other freedoms in the name of political freedom. This view overlooks the difficulty of "discrete and insular minorities,"[32] who can have no realistic hope of persuading the majority to rescind the law that harms them. McCloskey argued further that there is no rationalization for restricting protection to ethnic or religious minorities who may at least have advantages of cohesiveness that scattered individuals subjected to economic discrimination may not enjoy.[33] According to Hand's view all such groups or individuals are simply dependent upon the moderation and toleration inherent in a democratic society.

While McCloskey believed that there are good and adequate arguments for the use of substantive due process in both economic and individual-liberty problems, and Hand regarded the whole doctrine as pernicious, they were in agreement that the Court had not provided an acceptable justification for its abandonment in one case and its persistent use in another. McCloskey noted:

> the arguments against judicial intervention in economic affairs become arguments against intervention in the policy sphere generally. Learned Hand of course was ready to accept this implication. . . . But it is certainly not the dominant doctrine of the modern Court, which has fairly consistently held to the "dual standard" enunciated by Stone in the *Carolene Products* case. So we are left with a judicial policy which rejects supervision over economic matters and asserts supervision over "personal rights"; and with a rationale, so far as the written opinions go, that might support withdrawal from both fields but does not adequately justify the discrimination between them.[34]

Consistency in application was of paramount importance to

[31] McCloskey, "Economic Due Process and The Supreme Court: An Exhumation and Reburial," *The Supreme Court Review*, 1962, 45–46.

[32] *Minersville School District v. Gobitis*, 310 U.S. 586, 606, (1940).

[33] McCloskey, "Economic Due Process and The Supreme Court: An Exhumation and Reburial," *The Supreme Court Review*, 1962, 50.

Learned Hand, for to intervene selectively in cases involving personal or property rights seemed to leave the function of judging to the personal whim of the individual judges. While he thoroughly disapproved judicial intervention on behalf of property rights and clearly regarded any judicial legislation as contrary to the legitimate exercise of judicial review, it appears he could accept the Court's involvement in both areas better than the selective intervention he saw becoming the practice. He thought that the Court suffered loss of public confidence and support for its decisions and that society suffered confusion and uncertainty because of judicial intrusion into the political arena through substantive due process. His position was that the whole concept of substantive due process was a judicial fabrication. In this view he was joined by Justice Louis D. Brandeis, who said, "Despite arguments to the contrary which had seemed to me persuasive, it is settled that the due process clause of the Fourteenth Amendment applies to matters of substantive law as well as to matters of procedure."[35] There seems to be little doubt that Hand's insistence upon judicial restraint reached its ultimate in cases dealing with the substantive interpretation of due process as applied to both economic problems and individual liberties.

[34] *Ibid.*, 44–45.
[35] *Whitney v. People of the State of California*, 274 U.S. 357, 373 (1927).

CHAPTER VIII : *Judicial Review and the Bill of Rights*

Judge Hand believed that judicial interpretation of the Bill of Rights is a special kind of constitutional interpretation and must be fulfilled in a way which accords and does not interfere with the more general work of judges. This view arose from his unique understanding of the Bill of Rights. He believed that constitutions are primarily instruments for the distribution of powers, but that American constitutions go further:

> ... they assume to lay down general principles to insure the just exercise of these powers. . . . It is true that the logic which has treated these like other provisions of a constitution seems on its face unanswerable. Are they not parts in the same document? Did they not originally have a meaning? Why should not that meaning be found in the same way as that of the rest of the instrument? Nevertheless there are vital differences. Here history is only a feeble light, for these rubrics were meant to answer future problems unimagined and unimaginable. Nothing which by the utmost liberality can be called interpretation describes the process by which they must be applied. Indeed if law be a command for specific conduct, they are not law at all; they are cautionary warnings against the intemperance of faction and the first approaches of despotism. The answers to the questions which they raise demand the appraisal and balancing of human values which there are no scales to weigh.[1]

The very sharp distinction that he made between what he regarded as the primary function of a constitution—the distribution of powers—and the general principles designed to ensure the just exercise of those

---

[1] Hand, "The Contribution of an Independent Judiciary to Civilization," as reprinted in *The Spirit of Liberty* (3d ed.), 160–61.

powers permitted his view that the latter are less amenable to judicial interpretation. His view that constitutions are primarily instruments for the distribution of powers is not supported by the evidence, for historically principles of justice are included more often than not.

The Holmes Lectures reveal his basis for this distinction. There he recalled that the Bill of Rights was originally understood to embody the same political postulates that had been suggested if not fully articulated in the Declaration of Independence. But these postulates—"self-evident" and "unalienable rights" with which all men "are endowed by their Creator" and among which are "life, liberty and the pursuit of happiness"—clearly depend upon a natural-rights doctrine. Since he did not accept this doctrine, the Bill of Rights had for him only the meaning of the words themselves and whatever "feeble light" history provides.

Hand believed that the fundamental political conflicts suggested by the Bill of Rights must be resolved by the legislative branch. By what standard can the courts determine that the contributions of one group in a society do or do not entitle it to special advantages? Or the degree to which society is willing to permit the strong, capable, or shrewd to exploit their powers? Or when speech partakes more of action than of thought? Or how far the state may justify intervening in the rearing of children? These problems are not solved by reason or some abstract wisdom but by the legislative evaluation of popular choice insofar as it can be assessed. There is no other basis on which these issues may be determined, for values are not commensurable. Hand referred to the general principles enshrined in the Bill of Rights as "stately admonitions" which are beyond analysis. They merely reflect the resolution of old conflicts that have been stated in universal terms but have lost their specific historical significance and now have only the content provided by each new generation. Determining this content seemed to him more nearly akin to lawmaking than to interpretation. He argued that these general principles are significantly different from the allocation of powers. The latter are specific; the intent remains clear and understandable today and continues to provide an adequate basis for legally enforceable restraints on government.

Hand suggested that the limitations imposed by the Bill of Rights may be interpreted in three different ways. They may be thought to perpetuate the limitations current at the time it was written and understood in the light of historical development. This interpretation would give it a more or less specific content. It may be read as the embodiment of natural law or unalienable rights, and as such it would be imperative upon all of government. Judge Hand rejected these two concepts and chose the third, which permits the Bill of Rights to be read as "admonitory or hortatory, not definite enough to be guides on concrete occasions, prescribing no more than that temper of detachment, impartiality, and an absence of self-directed bias that is the whole content of justice."[2]

These admonitions do not deny legislative action on the issues to which they refer. This was clear in *Masses Publishing Co. v. Patten*, a case involving an alleged violation of the Espionage Act of 1917, which made it an offense willfully to make false reports with intent to interfere with the operations of the armed forces or willfully to obstruct recruiting or enlistment. The postmaster general ruled that an issue of the *Masses* was non-mailable because it violated this provision. In Hand's opinion he denied the ruling, but in so doing he narrowed the issue before the court when he held that "no question arises touching the war powers of Congress. . . . Here is presented solely the question of how far Congress after much discussion has up to the present time seen fit to exercise a power."[3]

Hand thought that through the Bill of Rights the Founding Fathers were calling attention to areas that are particularly delicate and urging that great caution and care be exercised in dealing with them. This is especially true of the First Amendment, but it applies in some measure to all of them. Legislators as well as judges are bound by the Constitution, and the overwhelming majority of legislative determinations which relate to the Bill of Rights should stand unchallenged by the courts. It is theoretically possible that the courts might on rare occasions intervene, not because the legislature has appraised the values incorrectly but because they failed to do so at all, a condition that would almost never arise. The courts might also be involved if the legislature has given them some responsibility because of the nature of

[2] Hand, *The Bill of Rights*, 34.
[3] *Masses Publishing Co. v. Patten*, 244 Fed. 535, 538 (1917).

the problem and by necessity if the legislature has exceeded its constitutional grant of powers.

When a First Amendment case arises under a law specifically covering the occasion, Hand believed that the standard set by the law should be controlling unless the court is convinced that it did not result from an effort to settle the conflicting interests fairly. If the occasion is not explicitly covered by the statutory standard, the court must, of course, first interpret the law as he did in the *Masses* case. While this case is famous primarily because it represented great courage in sustaining individual liberties against the mood of the times, it is also a significant illustration of Judge Hand's attitude toward the restraints placed on Congress by the Bill of Rights. Congress has power to deal with problems relating to willful interference with the military effort, and he saw as the only real question the interpretation of the law and determination as to whether the text and cartoons in the *Masses* came within the statutory language. Hand agreed that such publications discourage the people of the United States and encourage its enemies and thereby have an adverse effect upon the success of the war effort, but that was not the paramount question. Rather, it was, Does the language of the publication come within the specific limitations of the law? In finding that the speech in question remained privileged under the Espionage Act, he made the now-famous distinction between words that are privileged and those that are not:

> Words are not only the keys of persuasion, but the triggers of action, and those which have no purport but to counsel the violation of law cannot by any latitude of interpretation be a part of that public opinion which is the final source of government in a democratic state. . . . If one stops short of urging upon others that it is their duty or their interest to resist the law, it seems to me one should not be held to have attempted to cause its violation.[4]

Once the legislature has acted, Hand was willing to interpret the statute as best he could, for there is almost always a discernible purpose behind legislation to guide the court. It seemed to him very different to attempt to divine through the Bill of Rights purposes that would provide adequate guidance in specific cases. His reluctance to apply the

[4] *Ibid.*, 540.

Bill of Rights directly to particular problems stems from his belief that to do so comes precariously close to judicial legislation and from his knowledge that judicial interpretations of the Constitution can be overruled only by amendment, while the legislature may always correct what it deems to be a faulty interpretation of legislative action. He felt much more freedom in the interpretation of statutes or matters of common law than general constitutional principles.

Questions arising under the Bill of Rights invariably relate to policy and choice. The usual interpretation reads into them the dominant political assumptions of the time, but with concern for the protection of the individual from the excesses of faction. Another theory holds that the solution to differences of popular opinion is experimentation and that almost any experiment is less dangerous than its suppression. This view accords with the pragmatic temper of Hand's philosophical outlook and is the one he sought to follow. Thus his opinions do not reflect his personal beliefs so much as his understanding that the Constitution did not provide for a tricameral system and that there are many matters in which a judge may not properly intervene.

Judge Hand's opinion in *United States* v. *Dennis* indicates the way he thought the courts may properly proceed in determining the constitutionality of a statute which is challenged as a violation of the Bill of Rights. This case grew out of the 1940 Smith Act, the first peacetime sedition act since 1798. The act makes it unlawful to advocate or teach the doctrine of violent overthrow of government in the the United States; to print, publish, or distribute any material advocating revolutionary violence with intent to destroy government in the United States; or to help to organize a group which teaches, advocates, or encourages overthrow of government by violence. It also makes conspiracy to accomplish these ends punishable.

Speaking for the court, Hand found the Smith Act to be a legitimate exercise of congressional power as it was interpreted and applied. The act itself is unconditional and forbids "advocacy or teaching of such a violent overthrow at any time and by anyone, weak or strong; literally, they make criminal the fulminations of a half crazy zealot on a soap box, calling for an immediate march upon Washington."[5] As interpreted by the court, the evils which Congress may prevent

[5] *United States* v. *Dennis*, 183 F. (2d) 201, 214 (1950).

are limited to those which are "probable." The defendants argued that the court may not so limit the statute through interpretation in order to preserve it but must determine its validity as stated by Congress. Hand denied the claim on the basis that the Supreme Court often limits general words of a statute in order to make it conform to the Constitution. Whenever a court does this it runs the risk of assuming that Congress would have enacted the limited form had it known that the wider scope would be invalid. But

> we have no such problem here, because there can be no doubt as to the intent; Congress has explicitly declared that it wished the words to govern all cases which they constitutionally could. Nor do we think that, so limited, the Act becomes too vague to stand up. . . . it is to be observed that it would have been impracticable to provide against the evil and yet to define the forbidden conduct more definitely.[6]

Hand pointed out that it is the nature of law to speak in general terms, and so it is not possible to draft a statute which provides a specific rule for each instance which properly comes under it. While deliberating the constitutionality of the Smith Act, he distinguished the choices appropriate to the legislature and those which the courts can legitimately make. Existence of a

> "clear and present danger" depends upon whether the mischief of the repression is greater than the gravity of the evil, discounted by its improbability; and it is of course true that the degree of probability that the utterance will bring about the evil is a question of fact. On the other hand, to compare the repression with the evil, when discounted, is not a question of fact at all; for it depends upon a choice between conflicting interests. Ordinarily such choices are for a legislature, whose chief function it is indeed to make them, since a legislature is best qualified to represent the divergent interests of society. However, . . . it is at times impracticable to make such choices in general propositions, because the occasions which will arise within the ambit of the general purpose, are multiform. . . . When the dispute does involve interests of high moment, and Congress, thinking it impracticable to deal with them specifically, makes the courts its surrogate, the choices so delegated must be treated as questions of law.[7]

[6] *Ibid.*
[7] *Ibid.*, 215–16.

The responsibility of judges in cases arising under statutes relating to First Amendment freedoms does not differ from their duty to "legislate" in other areas when the wording of a statute delegates to them the task of filling in the gaps in necessarily general laws. In such cases Judge Hand knowingly legislated.

The due-process clauses of the Fifth and Fourteenth Amendments have traditionally afforded individuals procedural protections through the courts against arbitrary governmental infringement upon life, liberty, and property. This is the specific meaning that Hand believed these clauses bore and insofar as they imply more they simply express a mood, an admonition to fairness in the application of the law without which justice is impossible.

Judge Hand had applauded the movement away from economic due process, but as this doctrine was being destroyed, there developed a dual meaning to the clause, depending upon whether it applied to personal or to property rights, though

> just why property itself was not a 'personal right' nobody took the time to explain; and perhaps the inquiry would have been regarded as captious and invidious anyway; but the fact remained that in the name of the Bill of Rights the courts were upsetting statutes which were plainly compromises between conflicting interests, each of which had more than a merely plausible support in reason.[8]

This dual interpretation arose when the prohibitions of the First Amendment were absorbed into the Fourteenth Amendment beginning with the Gitlow case. The Supreme Court became more willing to reverse legislative choice when the conflicting values involved were "personal" as defined by the First Amendment and gave new emphasis to the due-process clauses in the protection of individual liberties. Since Hand regarded the First Amendment as simply admonitory, it follows that he did not regard the incorporation doctrine as adequate justification for the increasing intervention of the court on behalf of individual liberties at both the state and national levels.

Support for this new judicial activism often took the form of the

[8] Hand, "Chief Justice Stone's Concept of the Judicial Function," *Columbia Law Review*, Vol. LVII (September, 1946), as reprinted in *The Spirit of Liberty* (1st ed.), 206.

preferred-position doctrine, which held that, while the reasonable man test may be appropriate for determining the constitutionality of legislation in other areas, it is not adequate when the fundamental freedoms of the First Amendment are at stake. In these cases the Court must hold itself and the legislatures to higher standards because of the "preferred position" which the Constitution gives these liberties.[9] The people acting through their legislatures should be permitted to make laws with considerable freedom provided that all are protected in their rights to participate in the political process and advocate their opinions. According to the preferred-position doctrine the government is required to justify statutes restricting First Amendment freedoms by showing that a major interest of the state would be immediately and substantially injured if the liberty were permitted. The requirement for constitutionality became indispensability rather than reasonableness.

Learned Hand did not approve of this doctrine. He was not at all certain that the Constitution did give preference to some liberties over others. He said:

> I cannot help thinking that it would have seemed a strange anomaly to those who penned the words in the Fifth to learn that they constituted severer restrictions as to Liberty than Property, especially now that Liberty not only includes freedom from personal restraint, but enough economic security to allow its possessor the enjoyment of a satisfactory life. I can see no more persuasive reason for supposing that a legislature is *a priori* less qualified to choose between "personal" than between economic values; and there have been strong protests, to me unanswerable, that there is no constitutional basis for asserting a larger measure of judicial supervision over the first than the second.[10]

Learned Hand believed that acceptance of his conception of the Bill of Rights would greatly limit the fundamentally disrupting conflicts the courts would seek to settle. It would protect their institutional integrity and leave the basic conflicts to other organs of government

[9] "Black and Douglas [argue] . . . that it is the Constitution itself which has set up this preference. For, while the Fourth Amendment offers protection only against 'unreasonable' searches and seizures, and the Fifth Amendment only prohibits a taking of life, liberty, or property 'without due process of law,' the First Amendment is literally absolute in its terms: 'Congress shall make no law . . . .'" Murphy and Pritchett, *Courts, Judges and Politics: An Introduction to the Judicial Process*, 627.
[10] Hand, *The Bill of Rights*, 50–51.

which are better equipped to measure and evaluate the possible solutions and are directly subject to popular reaction when they fail to appraise the problem properly. In matters of fundamental importance where there is substantial disagreement within the society, the courts cannot afford to assume responsibility for disappointing large numbers of persons, an inevitable outcome when issues of this kind are authoritatively resolved. The proper way for the courts to protect their power is to withdraw from such controversies.

Learned Hand raised a different question about the controversial segregation cases (he believed that the difference between the due-process and the equal-protection clauses was almost negligible). Did the court intend, he asked, to reverse legislative judgments of the values involved by a substitution of their own appraisal? Or do the decisions imply that the Fourteenth Amendment exempts the value of racial equality from legislative consideration because it must prevail against any contrary interest? The first, which he believed to be more likely, involved the court in judicial legislation. The second assumed that the Constitution gives racial equality such a high value that it can never be subject to legislative evaluation. Since for him all values were relative and subject to compromise in a democratic society, the idea of the absolute supremacy of racial equality was inconceivable. Nonetheless, he thought the opinion ambiguous regarding the basis of the decision.

Judicial encroachment upon legislative prerogative in segregation decisions appeared to Hand to be directly contrary to the intent of the Fourteenth Amendment, which gives Congress power to enforce it through appropriate legislation. The Supreme Court ignored this provision and assumed the responsibility allocated to Congress by the Constitution. His conviction that it is not the role of the court to elaborate such admonitions "from its own bosom" guided his own behavior as a judge, for in 1947, toward the end of Hand's long career, Judge Wyzanski reported that Hand had never invalidated a statute on the ground that it did not satisfy due process.[11] Any attempt by judges to interject themselves into the delineation of the general constitutional principles embodied in the Bill of Rights is hazardous, for almost any solution in such a conflict seems unfair to one or both

[11] Wyzanski, "Judge Learned Hand's Contribution to Public Law." *Harvard Law Review*, Vol. LX (February, 1947), 354.

parties. There is no hedonistic rod by which pleasures and pains may be measured:

> If an independent judiciary seeks to fill them [the "stately admonitions" of the Bill of Rights] from its own bosom, in the end it will cease to be independent. And its independence will be well lost, for that bosom is not ample enough for the hopes and fears of all sorts and conditions of men, nor will its answers be theirs; it must be content to stand aside from these fateful battles.
>
> . . . I believe that for by far the greater part of their work it is a condition upon the success of our system that the judges should be independent; and I do not believe that their independence should be impaired because of their constitutional function. But the price of this immunity, I insist, is that they should not have the last word in those basic conflicts of "right and wrong—between whose endless jar justice resides." You may ask what then will become of the fundamental principles of equity and fair play which our constitutions enshrine; and whether I seriously believe that unsupported they will serve merely as counsels of moderation. I do not think that anyone can say what will be left of those principles . . . but this much I think I do know—that a society so riven that the spirit of moderation is gone, no court *can* save, that a society where that spirit flourishes, no court *need* save.[12]

There appears to be some tension between Hand's apparent agreement with Hamilton's assertion in *The Federalist*, No. 78, that the Constitution is law to be interpreted by the courts and Hand's assertion that the Bill of Rights is "admonitory," "hortatory," and "not definite enough to be guides on concrete occasions." If the Bill of Rights is part of a basic law (and he did assume that the parts of the Constitution which dealt with allocation of powers were basic law), it would seem that the courts should have the same obligation to interpret and enforce it as they have for the main body of the Constitution.

Jerome Frank provided a perceptive criticism of Hand's position. He pointed out that Hand admitted that the Constitution might not have been ratified without the promise of the Bill of Rights and that the people believed that it embodied mandates against which "no statute should prevail." Frank regarded this position as historically accurate and raised the question:

[12] Hand, "The Contribution of an Independent Judiciary to Civilization," as reprinted in *The Spirit of Liberty* (3d ed.), 163–64.

Why . . . should not the courts respect that history which discloses that the First Amendment was intended to be a legal "mandate" and note solely a "moral adjuration?"

Judge Hand thinks it folly to believe that the courts can save democracy. Of course, they cannot. But it seems to me that here, most uncharacteristically, Judge Hand indulges in a judgment far too sweeping, one which rests on a too-sharp either-or, all or nothing, dichotomy. . . . Obviously, the courts cannot do the whole job. But, just as obviously, they can sometimes help to arrest evil popular trends in their inception.[13]

Nevertheless, it is very clear that Learned Hand did not believe that the due-process and equal-protection clauses should be interpreted to extend judicial protection for individual liberties. He thought it inappropriate to distinguish between judicial scrutiny of governmental action challenged under these and other parts of the Constitution. The task of the court was the same in either case: to ascertain whether the action was within the scope of constitutional power.

It is in his interpretation of the Bill of Rights as "admonitions" against excess that the true measure of Learned Hand's sanguineness about American democracy is most apparent. He had no illusions about the difficulty of preserving democracy, and yet he possessed a high hope and a certain faith in its endurance. His view that trial and error and experimentation are the only paths to truth accounts for his willingness to permit the legislature freedom to experiment within the boundaries established by the Constitution. The problems of man are great and their human solutions uncertain and inadequate, but he was convinced that compromises must be worked out through the democratic process if the country is to remain free:

If they [the resolutions of conflict] are to be upset under cover of the majestic sententiousness of the Bill of Rights, they are likely to become centres of frictions undreamed of by those who avail themselves of this facile opportunity to enforce their will. . . . I submit that it is well for us to pause and consider how important in the days ahead may be his attempt to keep alive . . . the tradition of detachment and aloofness without which, I am persuaded, courts and judges will fail. And make no

[13] Frank, "Some Reflections on Judge Learned Hand," *Chicago Law Review*, Vol. XXIV (1957), 697-98.

mistake, that tradition is under attack, even if it be not a frontal attack.[14]

Judge Hand's opinion in *United States* v. *Dennis*, which dealt with a case arising under the First Amendment, was written during his last years on the bench. His Holmes Lectures provide more recent insights to his understanding of First Amendment issues. In the Dennis case he sought to discover those interests which the amendment was intended to protect and the assumptions upon which it rested. His interpretation reflected his personal philosophy. He said that the First Amendment

> rests upon a skepticism as to all political orthodoxy, upon a belief that there are no impregnable political absolutes, and that a flux of tentative doctrines is preferable to any authoritative creed. It rests upon a premise as yet unproved, and perhaps incompatible with men's impatience of a suspended judgment when the stakes are high. However, it concerns beliefs alone, not actions, except in so far as a change of belief is a condition upon action.[15]

The First Amendment seeks to protect tolerance and moderation, those values essential to liberty. It includes willingness to submit ideas and values to experimentation—to trial and error—and to accept change when new ideas prove to be more workable than the old ones which, after all, were only tentative. It appears to embody the essential conditions of democracy and the aspirations of the community and to state its highest ideal. According to Learned Hand, support for it, as well as support for democratic society itself, must come primarily from a spirit of liberty in the hearts and minds of the people—from the tolerance and moderation that comes to man slowly and is quickly lost.

Nevertheless, the First Amendment does make freedom of expression a legal question, as well as a political issue in the United States. Traditionally the courts have determined not only whether an expression comes under the law but also whether the law is a valid exercise of legislative power under the Constitution. The weighing of values arising under this amendment is, as Hand understood it, primarily the function of the legislature. However, some statutes, for example, the

[14] Hand, "Chief Justice Stone's Concept of the Judicial Function," as reprinted in *The Spirit of Liberty* (1st ed.), 207.
[15] *United States* v. *Dennis,* 183 F. (2d) 207 (1950).

Smith Act, delegate to the courts the responsibility for making specific choices that arise within the framework of the law. Hand considered this delegation necessary since the great variety of situations that may arise under such a statute preclude more specificity on behalf of the legislature. Furthermore, he noted that in *American Communications Association, C.I.O. v. Douds* the Supreme Court held that "when particular conduct is regulated in the interest of public order, and the regulation results in an indirect, conditional, partial abridgment of speech, the duty of the courts is to determine which of these two conflicting interests demands the greater protection under the particular circumstances presented."[16]

A fascinating part of the record of the United States courts is the search for adequate concepts that may serve as tests or measuring rods against which specific acts or laws can be judged in their relationships to the Constitution. In the area of individual liberties perhaps no other concept has created so much discussion and difference of opinion as "clear and present danger," which was first enunciated by Justice Holmes in *Schenck v. United States.*

In *United States v. Dennis,* Judge Hand analyzed the case law with "scrupulousness and simplicity,"[17] found the clear-and-present-danger test inadequate, and provided a major reinterpretation of it. His view was repeated in the official opinion of the Supreme Court but was probably not accepted by a majority of the justices, and the doctrine has subsequently fallen into disuse. Hand's lengthy review, which spelled out the manifold interpretations to which it was amenable, doubtless contributed to its demise.

In both the Dennis and Masses cases Hand assumed that the First Amendment sought to preserve freedom of belief and speech because it is essential to the survival of democracy. But the demands of communal life require that action be distinguished from speech. He believed the amendment provides no protection for speech when it partakes more of action than of belief, but the doubt begins

> when the utterance is at once an effort to affect the hearers' beliefs and a call upon them to act when they have been convinced. As a new

[16] *American Communications Association, C.I.O. v. Douds,* 339 U.S. 382, 399 (1950).
[17] Wyzanski "Learned Hand," *The Atlantic,* Vol. CCVIII, No. 6 (December, 1961), 56.

question it might have been held that the Amendment did not protect utterances, when they had this double aspect: i.e., when persuasion and instigation were inseparably confused. In that view the Amendment would give protection to all utterances designed to convince, but its protection would be conditional upon their not being part of, or coupled with, provocation to unlawful conduct, whether that was remote or immediate.[18]

If this view had prevailed, the speech of the Communists would have been protected insofar as they sought to convince others but would have lost that protection because their speech was also coupled with advocacy of unlawful means. But precedent has given another interpretation to this amendment so that the question in the case was "what limits, if any, the advocacy of illegal means imposes upon the privilege which the aims or purpose of the utterer would otherwise enjoy."[19]

The test alluded to in the Dennis case is precisely the one Hand offered in his opinion in the Masses case. He thus reaffirmed his approval of the standard he had applied over thirty years earlier and implied that he believed it would have been as adequate as those actually used. In the earlier case he found that the normal test for the limits of free speech is not the justice of its substance or the decency and propriety of its temper but the strong danger that it will cause injurious acts. He saw no justification for revising this national policy unless Congress had clearly intended to do so in the Espionage Act of 1917. Hand, always concerned with the purpose of Congress in interpreting statutes, found no such intent. The portions of the *Masses* cited by the postmaster general in support of its exclusion from the mails did not actually advocate violence, and the court held that he had no right to suppress the magazine

upon the doctrine that the general tenor and animus of the paper as a whole were subversive to authority and seditious in effect. . . . [for] The tradition of English-speaking freedom has depended in no small part upon the merely procedural requirement that the state point with exactness to just that conduct which violates the law.[20]

[18] *United States* v. *Dennis*, 183 F. (2d) 207 (1950).
[19] *Ibid.*
[20] *Masses Publishing Co.* v. *Patten*, 244 Fed. 535, 542–53 (1917).

He would deny protection to those who counsel others to violate existing laws, for this is not a part of the public debate which is essential in a democracy.

Hand acknowledged that any discussion of error in existing laws may result in their violation, but one should not be held to have sought to cause illegal conduct if he has not actually urged that it is the duty of others or in their interest to resist the law. He found no justification in the language of the law to go further. He provided an objective test— the nature of the words used—by which criminality under the 1917 Espionage Act could be determined. He did not attempt to spell out the maximum power of Congress but held simply that this statute sought only to punish dangerous acts and speech, which has all the effect of such acts, because they could have no other purpose than the direct and dangerous interference with the war.[21] The advantages of this test for criminality under the law were its objectivity, clearness, and the consistency with which it could be applied. It provided the jury with a concrete problem to consider—the nature of the words themselves and the threat they posed of interference with the armed forces. Since Hand was free from the obligation of a substantial body of precedent from the Supreme Court in this case, we may accept his statement here as a reflection of his own position:

> Political agitation, by the passions it arouses or the convictions it engenders, may in fact stimulate men to the violation of law. Detestation of existing policies is easily transformed into forcible resistance of the authority which puts them in execution, and it would be folly to disregard the causal relation between the two. Yet to assimilate agitation, legitimate as such, with direct incitement to violent resistance, is to disregard the tolerance of all methods of political agitation which in normal times is a safeguard of free government. The distinction is not a scholastic subterfuge, but a hard-bought acquisition in the fight for freedom.[22]

Judge Hand's decision was reversed by a holding that the postmaster general's decision must stand unless it was clearly wrong.

After World War I the Supreme Court sought to formulate a test by which sedition could be identified and drew on Hand's reasoning

[21] Zechariah Chafee, Jr., *Free Speech in the United States*, 44–45.
[22] *Masses Publishing Co. v. Patten*, 244 Fed. 535, 540 (1917).

in the Masses case. The Espionage Act of 1917 made it illegal to make false statements intended to obstruct the war effort, including attempts to hinder recruitment or cause insubordination in the armed forces. The issue in the Schenck case was whether or not the circulation among men of military age of material declaring the conscription unconstitutional and encouraging them to exert their rights against it was protected by the First Amendment. Holmes, speaking for a unanimous Court, set forth the criteria for determining when such acts of expression came under the protection of the First Amendment:

> The question in every case is whether the words used are used in such circumstances and are of such a nature as to create a clear and present danger that they will bring about the substantive evils that Congress has a right to prevent. It is a question of proximity and degree. ... We admit that in many places and in ordinary times the defendants in saying all that was said in the circular would have been within their constitutional rights. But the character of every act depends upon the circumstances in which it is done.[23]

Congress may make speech or publication a criminal offense, for the words themselves may become a substantive evil. The words must be in close proximity to action. However, the circumstances surrounding the expression determine whether or not it is so construed, and thus the criterion loses the preciseness of the objective test offered in the Masses case—that is, urging others to illegal action. The Court in this case supported, if it did not precisely follow, Hand's opinion.

In *Abrams* v. *United States* a majority upheld a conviction under the Espionage Act on the basis that the alleged crime (printing and circulating pamphlets attacking the government's action in sending troops to Russia in the summer of 1918 and calling for a general strike of munitions workers) constituted a dangerous tendency. Judge Hand observed that the Court found it sufficient that the accused had as his purpose a substantive evil and did not raise the question of gravity or imminence, and so this opinion was not helpful in the Dennis case.

Gitlow v. *New York* provided the first systematic development of the dangerous-tendency doctrine in the Supreme Court. Justice Edward T. Sanford held that

[23] *Schenck v. United States*, 249 U.S. 47, 52 (1919).

The State cannot reasonably be required to measure the danger from every such utterance in the nice balance of a jeweler's scale. . . . It cannot reasonably be required to defer the adoption of measures for its own peace and safety until the revolutionary utterances lead to actual disturbances of the public peace or imminent and immediate danger of its own destruction; but it may, in the exercise of its judgment, suppress the threatened danger in its incipiency.[24]

The majority did not ignore the clear and present danger test but said that it did not apply. The opinion held that the role of the Court was to judge whether the law was a "reasonable" determination of the danger and the action necessary to prevent it. The reasonable man test supported by the doctrine of presumed validity, for the Court also said, "Every presumption is to be indulged in favor of the validity of the statute."[25] The same reasoning was used by the majority in *Whitney* v. *People of the State of California.*

Brandeis' concurring opinion in Whitney rejected the idea of presumptive validity and made more specific and more difficult the finding of a danger sufficient to suppress speech:

. . . no danger flowing from speech can be deemed clear and present, unless the incidence of the evil apprehended is so imminent that it may befall before there is opportunity for full discussion. If there be time to expose through discussion the falsehood and fallacies, to avert the evil by the processes of education, the remedy to be applied is more speech, not enforced silence. Only an emergency can justify repression.[26]

In the Dennis case Hand interpreted this opinion as follows:

. . . here too the reasoning should be remembered for it was that delay in execution would give opportunity for the corrective of public discussion. It does not follow that he would have been of the same opinion, if the conspirators had sought to mask their purposes by fair words, as they did in the case at bar.[27]

Thus Hand concluded that when the purpose of the speech was not to engage in honest discussion but to achieve goals under false pretenses

[24] *Gitlow* v. *New York*, 268 U.S. 625, 669 (1925).
[25] *Ibid.*, 668.
[26] *Whitney* v. *People of the State of California*, 274 U.S. 357, 377 (1927).
[27] *United States* v. *Dennis*, 183 F. (2d) 201, 208 (1950).

there could be no corrective public discussion and so the solution of "more speech" is irrelevant to the problem.

In his continuing review of possible precedents in the Dennis case Hand noted, that although the conviction was reversed in *Stromberg* v. *People of the State of California* because the statute was judged to be too vague to serve as a guide for conduct, the opinion specifically acknowledged that the state had power to legislate in this area when it did so properly. The opinion further held that there is no constitutional protection for speech which incites to the violent overthrow of government. In *Herndon* v. *State of Georgia* the court did not reach the constitutional question, but Hand thought that subsequent cases followed precedent already established which he understood to be that the legislature may limit the First Amendment guarantee of free speech when in its judgment this privilege is used to oppose a vital function of government. This power is necessary if society is to protect itself. The courts must determine whether the cases arising under the statutes do in fact come within the meaning of the law. He regarded this entire series of opinions as relevant to the Dennis case, for they, like it, were concerned with threats to the vital interest of society in maintaining itself.

In fact there are indications that had he felt free to choose, Hand would have used Gitlow as a precedent for the Dennis case. He found, for instance, parts of the New York statute which were so similar to the Smith Act that the former might have been the model for the latter. In his Dennis opinion he noted that a majority in Gitlow held it sufficient that the pamphlet, broadcast by the accused, "advocates and urges in fervent language mass action which shall . . . overthrow and destroy organized parliamentary government" and used the "language of direct incitement."[28] Furthermore, he noted that the case had been cited often during the subsequent twenty-five years, "never with disapproval and frequently as authoritative."[29] The dissent, he found, would have made immediacy of the evil a condition of unlawfulness but also emphasized that the efforts which gave rise to this case were so paltry that they could never effect their purposes within any time the court could reasonably conceive.

[28] *Ibid.*, quoting *Gitlow* v. *The People of the State of New York*, 268 U.S. 652, 665 (1925).
[29] *United States* v. *Dennis*, 183 F. (2d) 201, 208 (1950).

The tests used to determine constitutionality in Gitlow were reasonableness of the statute supported by the doctrine of presumed validity of legislative action, both of which are compatible with Hand's concept of judicial review. Judge Samuel Chase urged in his concurring opinion that Gitlow should have been the precedent for the Dennis opinion. The question remains, then, what were Judge Hand's reasons for not using it and resorting to the clear-and-present-danger standard which he clearly thought of limited value. The answer seems once more to be found in his conviction that it is the duty of a lower court to render opinions as its appellate court would decide if the case were appealed. It must have been apparent to him that this was the test the Supreme Court would apply.[30] Furthermore, the Douds case provided the opportunity to reinterpret clear and present danger in a way that was compatible with his own reasoning.[31]

Hand surveyed the use of the clear-and-present-danger test in several subsequent series of cases but found that for one reason or another the decisions were not helpful in finding a solution to the Dennis case. He did, however, find the opinion in *American Communication Association, C.I.O.* v. *Douds* relevant for, though it was not a precedent in a strict sense, it shed some light on the reasoning of the Supreme Court. In this case the majority upheld a requirement of the Labor-Management Act (159 [h], Title 29 U.S.C.A.) that union officers take a non-Communist oath if their union is to receive any benefits of the act. The significant thing for him in this case was that the test applied was the

[30] Chief Justice Vinson specifically pointed this out in *Dennis* v. *United States*, 341 U.S. 494 (1951): "Although no case subsequent to *Whitney* and *Gitlow* has expressly overruled the majority opinions in those cases, there is little doubt that subsequent opinions have inclined toward the Holmes-Brandeis rationale." *Ibid.*, 507. Judge Wyzanski says of Hand's decision in Dennis: "The majority of the Supreme Court, of the bar, and of the public have agreed with Judge Hand. He made the choice which was not merely vindicated by contemporary opinion but was consistent with his deepest conviction of the subordinate role of the judiciary as only the disinterested interpreter of the stated will of the dominant forces in society. Not a few critics says this puts too low the creative, ethical, and spiritual possibilities of the Judge." Wyzanski, "Learned Hand," *Atlantic Monthly*, Vol. CCVIII, No. 6 (December, 1961), 56.

[31] "When the effect of a statute or ordinance upon the exercise of First Amendment freedoms is relatively small and the public interest to be protected is substantial it is obvious that a rigid test requiring a showing of imminent danger to the security of the Nation is an absurdity." *American Communications* v. *Douds*, 339 U.S. 382, 397 (1950).

same as in the case of a criminal prosecution for utterances threatening the stability of the government; *i.e.* "clear and present danger;" and because this was used to weigh the danger to commerce considering its gravity and proximity, against the repression of political activity involved —indeed a minority included even repression of political belief. The danger in that case included "political" strikes, and the danger to commerce from such strikes is closer than the danger to the existence of the government is to the teachings of the defendants; but the second danger is vastly graver if it be realized. We do not pretend that the decision is authoritative here. . . . What we do say is that no longer can there be any doubt, if indeed there was before, that the phrase, "clear and present danger," is not a slogan or a shibboleth to be applied as though it carried its own meaning; but that it involves in every case a comparison between interests which are to be appraised qualitatively.[32]

The obvious suggestion is that if the Court permitted the closeness of a lesser danger to commerce to constitute sufficient necessity to curtail political liberties it would surely accept a much graver danger to government, though admittedly less close, as a valid limit upon this freedom. Thus Hand concluded from the analysis of Supreme Court precedents:

The same utterance may be unprotected, if it be a bare appeal to action, which the Amendment will cover, if it be accompanied by, or incorporated into, utterances addressed to the understanding and seeking to persuade. The phrase, "clear and present danger," has come to be used as a shorthand statement. . . . It is a way to describe a penumbra of occasions, even the outskirts of which are indefinable, but within which, as is so often the case, the courts must find their way as they can. In each case they must ask whether the gravity of the "evil," discounted by its improbability, justifies such invasion of free speech as is necessary to avoid the danger. We have purposely substituted "improbability" for "remoteness," because that must be the right interpretation. Given the same probability, it would be wholly irrational to condone future evils which we should prevent if they were immediate; that could be reconciled only by an indifference to those who come after us. It is only because a substantial intervening period between the utterance and its realization may check its effect and change its importance, that its immediacy is important.[33]

[32] *United States* v. *Dennis*, 183 F. (2d) 201, 211–12 (1950).
[33] *Ibid.*, 212.

The emphasis on probability rather than immediacy is clearly based on Hand's understanding that the Communist effort is not to persuade through political dialogue which is protected by the First Amendment but to entrench itself in the structure of society by camouflaging its real purpose until the time is ripe for it to seize control of the government by whatever means are available including force and violence.[34] Thus the probability of clear and present danger is not decreased by time because Communism will never offer itself to the free market of ideas.

Hand knew that where the danger is not serious it is a sign of the confidence of a society to permit its malcontents to vent their animus without restraint. But the case before him was something very different —here the American Communist Party,

> of which the defendants are the controlling spirits, is a highly articulated, well contrived, far spread organization, numbering thousands of adherents, rigidly and ruthlessly disciplined, many of whom are infused with a passionate Utopian faith that is to redeem mankind. . . . The violent capture of all existing governments is one article of the creed of that faith, which abjures the possibility of success by lawful means. . . . Our democracy . . . must meet that faith [Communism] and that creed on the merits, or it will perish; and we must not flinch at the challenge. Nevertheless, we may insist that the rules of the game be observed, and the rules confine the conflict to weapons drawn from the universe of discourse.[35]

Hand believed that when the Communist challenge exists within the borders of the United States it is possible to establish the rules and the weapons with which the battle will be waged. These rules must conform to the spirit of democracy and liberty upon which the country is based and are embodied in what Hand understood to be the democratic process. Weapons available in international conflict are not necessarily available to the Communist conspiracy when it invades a democratic community. The protection of speech in the First Amend-

---

[34] "Budenz's . . . testimony was that there were certain passages in the Communist Constitution, which were innocent upon their face, but which were understood by the initiate to be only a cover—'window-dressing'—for the violent methods advocated and taught. This was so patently competent testimony that it needs no discussion." *Ibid.*, 229.

[35] *Ibid.*, 212–13.

ment is a protection of the dialogue related to political life. When speech passes beyond this and seeks to alter the political life of the society by advocacy of violent overthrow, there is no longer the same measure of protection.

Hand believed that any teaching or advocacy of constitutional change would be protected no matter how revolutionary it might be but that there is no "right" to violent revolution. This is a contradiction of terms,

> for a society which acknowledged it, could not stop at tolerating conspiracies to overthrow it, but must include their execution. The question before us, and the only one, is how long a government, having discovered such a conspiracy, must wait. When does the conspiracy become a "present danger?"[36]

This determination is the responsibility of the courts. Hand denied that the First Amendment protects the right to plan and plot the destruction of freedom so that society can only await the Communists' choice of the moment when they will strike the fatal blow. Hand's commitment to the tradition which protects freedom of speech remained firm, however, for he said that even such a well-organized confederation as the one the Communists presented might not always be regarded as a "present danger." The real question was how much of a threat to society it constituted in 1948, when the indictment was found. After an evaluation of the progress of the Communist conspiracy on the worldwide front in the thirty years ending in 1948, he concluded:

> We do not understand how one could ask for a more probable danger, unless we must wait till the actual eve of hostilities. The only justification which can be suggested is that in spite of their efforts to mask their purposes, so far as they can do so consistently with the spread of the gospel, discussion and publicity may so weaken their power that it will have ceased to be dangerous when the moment may come. That may be a proper enough antidote in ordinary times and for less redoubtable combinations; but certainly it does not apply to this one.[37]

[36] *Ibid.*, 213. Compare this with Justice Sanford's opinion in *Gitlow v. The People of the State of New York*, 268 U.S. 652 (1925).
[37] *Ibid.*

Hand did not find this an easy choice and warned that the country must remain sensitive to the dangers inherent in any such constraint upon liberty. But a choice had to be made, and in this case the loss of freedom for those convicted under the act seemed to him the lesser of two evils. It would be folly, he believed, not to recognize the threat that Communism poses to all freedom and liberty.

Judge Hand argued that the devious character of the Communist conspiracy removed it from the protection of the First Amendment and the Dennis decision was not incompatible with Brandeis' Whitney dissent. Nevertheless, his position that the danger need be only probable and not immediate is regarded as a withdrawal from the strongest statement of the clear-and-present-danger doctrine. Likelihood and immediacy of success are here balanced against the interest the government is trying to protect, and when that interest is sufficiently great, the danger need not be immediate. If the advocacy to overthrow the government by violence and force is now, with intent to bring it about some time in the indefinite future, it may still come under the law for there is no right to revolt.

Chief Justice Fred H. Vinson, speaking for four justices, relied on Judge Hand's reasoning and interpretation of clear and present danger in the majority opinion of the Supreme Court. He said:

> In this case we are squarely presented with the application of the "clear and present danger" test, and must decide what that phrase imports. We first note that many of the cases in which this Court has reversed convictions by use of this or similar tests have been based on the fact that the interest which the State was attempting to protect was itself too insubstantial to warrant restriction of speech. . . . Overthrow of the Government by force and violence is certainly a substantial enough interest for the Government to limit speech. . . .
>
> Obviously, the words cannot mean that before the Government may act, it must wait until the *putsch* is about to be executed.
>
> Chief Judge Learned Hand, writing for the majority below, interpreted the phrase as follows: "In each case [courts] must ask whether the gravity of the 'evil,' discounted by its improbability, justifies such invasion of free speech as is necessary to avoid the danger." . . . We adopt this statement of the rule. As articulated by Chief Judge Hand, it is as succinct and inclusive as any other we might devise at this time. It takes

into consideration those factors which we deem relevant, and relates their significances. More we cannot expect from words.[38]

But Chief Justice Vinson further modified the standard when he said, "Certainly an attempt to overthrow the Government by force, even though doomed from the outset because of inadequate numbers or power of the revolutionists, is a sufficient evil for Congress to prevent."[39] Hand had made it clear that the conviction depended upon "how imminent" and "how probable of execution" it was when the indictment was found.

Learned Hand's belief that the clear-and-present-danger doctrine is merely a shorthand term for the process of judging the specific values and facts in each case as it comes before a court was emphasized in his Holmes Lectures in which he quoted with approval Freund's comment:

> "The truth is that the clear-and-present-danger test is an over-simplified judgment unless it takes account also of a number of other factors: the relative seriousness of the danger in comparison with the value of the occasion for speech or political activity; the availability of more moderate controls than those which the state has imposed; and perhaps the specific intent with which the speech or activity is launched. No matter how rapidly we utter the phrase 'clear and present danger,' or how closely we hyphenate the words, they are not a substitute for the weighing of values. They tend to convey a delusion of certainty when what is most certain is the complexity of the strands in the web of freedom that the judge must disentangle."[40]

Learned Hand thought it proper to apply the same standard of constitutionality to all laws relating to the First Amendment, the due-process and equal-protection clauses: Has the legislature made a sincere attempt to evaluate the competing values involved? When the matter touched upon moral problems, he noted, publications which generally arouse lascivious emotions were regarded as criminal under common law.[41] Obscenity had long been punished under state and federal laws,

---

[38] *Dennis v. United States*, 341 U.S. 508–10 (1951).

[39] *Ibid.*, 509.

[40] Paul Freund, *On Understanding the Supreme Court*, 27–28, as quoted in Hand, *The Bill of Rights*, 60–61.

[41] This was a common assumption, but Harry Kalven, Jr., suggests that most of these cases arose before the development of the constitutional doctrines of free speech ex-

and reviewing courts had assumed their constitutionality. The problem was finding an adequate basis for determining what was obscene. The test provided in the English case *Regina* v. *Hicklin* was widely accepted in the United States. The Hicklin decision sustained statutes designed to protect the young, immature, ignorant, or sensually inclined rather than mature people of high intelligence, and under it any book which contained a single passage which might excite lustful or sensual desires in the minds of those into whose hands it might fall was condemned.

Although the Hicklin doctrine was never clearly affirmed by the United States Supreme Court, it became so thoroughly established that in 1913 Hand felt constrained to be guided by it even though he personally rejected it. However, his opinion in *United States* v. *Kennerley* provided the beginning of the movement away from the old doctrine. He said:

> I hope it is not improper for me to say that the rule as laid down, however consonant it may be with mid-Victorian morals, does not seem to me to answer to the understanding and morality of the present time. . . . I question whether in the end men will regard that as obscene which is honestly relevant to the adequate expression of innocent ideas, and whether they will not believe that truth and beauty are too precious to society at large to be mutilated in the interests of those most likely to pervert them to base uses.[42]

He then offered what he considered a more suitable test: that

> the word "obscene" be allowed to indicate the present critical point in the compromise between candor and shame at which the community may have arrived here and now. . . . To put thought in a leash to the average conscience of the time is perhaps tolerable, but to fetter it by the necessities of the lowest and least capable seems a fatal policy.[43]

This was the first indication that a proper test might be the current

---

pounded by the Supreme Court beginning with *Schenck* and so may have lost their relevance. "Thus, the law of obscenity regulation seems to have had a kind of 'sleeper' development, outside the main stream of decisions dealing with the problems of freedom of speech, until recently." Harry Kalven, Jr., "The Metaphysics of the Law of Obscenity," *The Supreme Court Review*, 1960, 2.

[42] *United States* v. *Kennerley*, 209 Fed. 110, 120–21 (1913).
[43] *Ibid.*, 121.

moral standards of the community. Nevertheless, Hand felt bound by the large body of prevailing precedent and sustained the conviction. A higher court decided that the book in question, *Hagar Revelly*, was not obscene even under the old doctrine, and so it did not consider the standard offered by Judge Hand. It was not until the 1930's that two decisions by the Second Circuit Court of Appeals overruled the Hicklin doctrine.[44]

Hand approved this action and affirmed it in *United States* v. *Levine*. In rejecting the Hicklin test he said:

> This earlier doctrine necessarily presupposed that the evil against which the statute is directed so much outweighs all interests of art, letters or science, that they must yield to the mere possibility that some prurient person may get a sensual gratification from reading or seeing what to most people is innocent and may be delightful or enlightening.[45]

His objection to the old doctrine—that the evil of obscenity so far outweighs other possible values that it approaches the absolute—forecast his concern that the segregation decisions raised the value of equality to an absolute which may not be subjected to legislative compromise. In the Levine case he affirmed his understanding that Congress has authority to deal with all issues arising under the First Amendment. The proper judgment must rely upon the sense of the community which in this instance is best drawn from the jury:

> As so often happens, the problem is to find a passable compromise between opposing interests, whose relative importance, like that of all social or personal values, is incommensurable. We impose such a duty upon a jury (Rosen v. U.S., supra, 161 U.S. 29, 42, 16 S. Ct. 434, 480, 40 L. Ed. 606), because the standard they fix is likely to be an acceptable mesne, and because in such matters a mesne most nearly satisfies the moral demands of the community. There can never be constitutive principles for such judgments, or indeed more than cautions to avoid the personal aberrations of the jurors. We mentioned some of these in *United States* v. *One Book Entitled Ulysses*, supra, 72 F. (2d) 705; the work must be taken as a whole, its merits weighed against its defects (Konda v. U.S. [C.C.A. 7] 166 F. 91, 22 L.R.A. [N.S.] 304);

[44] *United States* v. *Dennett*, 39 F. (2d) 564 (1930), and *United States* v. *One Book Entitled Ulysses*, 72 F. (2d) 705 (1934).
[45] *United States* v. *Levine*, 83 F. (2d) 156, 157 (1936).

if it is old, its accepted place in the arts must be regarded; if new, the opinions of competent critics in published reviews or the like may be considered; what counts is its effect, not upon any particular class, but upon all those whom it is likely to reach. Thus "obscenity" is a function of many variables, and the verdict of the jury is not the conclusion of a syllogism of which they are to find the minor premise, but really a small bit of legislation ad hoc, like the standard of care.[46]

This comment conforms to Hand's statement of the proper role of the jury in judging values in the Dennis case, and the opinion itself is in accord with his whole political philosophy.

In his opinion in *Roth* v. *United States*, Justice Harlan specifically objected to permitting the trial judge or jury to determine what was obscene and insisted that the Court itself cope with this difficult question. Harlan feared that under the majority opinion

the classification as obscene, which . . . is decisive of the constitutional question, will be made by the original trier of fact and deferred to, thus encouraging the state and federal reviewing courts "to rely on easy labelling and jury verdicts as a substitute for facing up to the tough individual problems of constitutional judgment involved in every obscenity case."[47]

But after careful consideration of the efforts made by the courts to find a more apt solution, Kalven wrote, "Finally, I wonder whether the only experts on the issue at hand are not the jury, as Judge Learned Hand suggested years ago."[48]

There now appear to be two kinds of constitutional problems regarding obscenity. One is concerned with the ambiguity of the term itself, and the second derives from the application of the clear-and-present-danger test to this issue.[49] The problem of the relationship of obscenity to the clear-and-present-danger test appeared after Judge Hand had retired from the bench, and he was clearly concerned only with the definition of the term. What is particularly striking about his handling of the two cases which came to him (*United States* v. *Ken-*

[46] *Ibid.*
[47] *Roth* v. *United States*, 354 U.S. 476, 498 (1957).
[48] Kalven, "The Metaphysics of the Law of Obscenity," *The Supreme Court Review*, 1960, 39–40.
[49] *Ibid.*, 2–3.

nerly, 209 Fed. 110 [1913] and *United States* v. *Levine,* 83 F. [2d] 156 1936]) is the frequency with which they are cited and quoted with approval and respect even after so many intervening attempts to deal more fully with the issue.

In Levine, Hand said that, even if statutes regulating obscenity "may be a menace to the free development of the arts, it is a risk which Congress has seen fit to impose, and which we cannot gainsay, even if we would."[50] He noted approvingly that the Supreme Court in *Winters* v. *New York* determined that when a "legislative body concludes that the mores of the community call for an extension of the impermissible limits, an enactment aimed at the evil is plainly within its power, if it does not transgress the boundaries fixed by the Constitution for freedom of expression."[51] Hand commented, "I know of no such boundaries other than that there shall have been an honest effort to weigh the values according to the prevalent mores."[52]

In *Butler* v. *Michigan* the Court appeared to affirm Hand's dictum in Kennerley that the appropriate audience test was the average adult audience rather than the young and vulnerable. When Hand delivered the Holmes Lectures, *Roth* v. *United States* was the most recent Supreme Court decision in this area. There the Court upheld both a federal and a state statute charged with violating the First Amendment. He approved the decision for it affirmed his contention that "it is for the legislature to determine what are the not 'impermissible limits' by balancing the evil of those lustful emotions that the language may excite against depriving the author and his audience of the benefit of what he has to say."[53] The standard used in the majority opinion was taken from that recommended by the American Law Institute, which is similar to Hand's proposal in Kennerley. Justice William J. Brennan said that the question was "whether to the average person, applying contemporary community standards, the dominant theme of the material taken as a whole appeals to prurient interest."[54]

Hand's reference to the obscenity cases in his Holmes Lectures was an attempt not to analyze the problems but merely to illustrate

[50] *United States* v. *Levine,* 83 F. (2d) 158 (1936).
[51] *Winters* v. *New York,* 333 U.S. 507, 515 (1948).
[52] Hand, *The Bill of Rights,* 61–62.
[53] *Ibid.,* 63.
[54] *Roth* v. *United States,* 354 U.S. 489 (1957).

his understanding that the Bill of Rights was an admonition to the legislature. He did not deal with the increasingly difficult problem of an adequate definition of obscenity or whether it should be confined to what is currently referred to as "hard-core pornography." He was not called upon to comment upon the increasingly complex and subtle issues growing out of the multiopinion cases coming from the Court. He would have insisted that when the justices are so lacking in unanimity that each case brings forth a whole series of separate opinions the Court is trying to resolve conflicts over values in society which are incommensurable and that it is not authorized to declare such a compromise nor is it a suitable institution for doing so.

In 1964, Justice Brennan quoted at length from Hand's opinion in Kennerley in an effort to clarify what appeared to be confusion about the concept of contemporary community standards. He said:

> It seems clear that . . . Judge Hand was referring not to state and local 'communities,' but rather to "the community" in the sense of "society at large; . . . the public, or people in general." Thus, he recognized that under his standard the concept of obscenity would have a "varying meaning from time to time—not from county to county, or town to town."[55]

It should also be noted, however, that Judge Learned Hand's urbane resignation, his acceptance of legislative judgment and the common conscience of the community about what is and what is not permissible speech, is completely unacceptable to those who, like Justice William O. Douglas and Hugo Black, read the First Amendment as providing equal protection for all kinds of speech. This standard is also rejected by Justice John Marshall Harlan and by Edmond Cahn, who insisted (as Hand also acknowledged) that it is very difficult for a judge to find the prevalent "common conscience" and, furthermore, that a judge who relies on this standard (assuming that he can determine what it is), shirks his duty by shifting his responsibility to the community. Cahn has written, "What the community needs most is the moral leadership of such a man as Learned Hand and the full benefit of his mature and chastened wisdom."[56]

[55] *Jacobellis* v. *Ohio*, 378 U.S. 184, 193 (1964).
[56] Edmond Cahn, *The Moral Decision: Right and Wrong in the Light of American Law*, 310.

In *Ginzburg* v. *United States,* Justice Brennan again turned to one of Hand's opinions, *United States* v. *Rebhuhn.* One of the three publications Ginzburg was charged with improperly sending through the mail was *The Housewife's Handbook on Selective Promiscuity,* which was purported to have some medical or scientific value. In Rebhuhn, Hand had held that the works had been written by men who were either proved to have or could be assumed to have scientific standing and that "most of the Books could lawfully have passed through the mails, if directed to those who would be likely to use them for the purposes for which they were written."[57] However, after reviewing the "enterprise as a whole" in which the defendants were engaged, he held that even though "the books were not obscene per se [and] had a proper use, ... the defendants woefully misused them, and it was that misuse which constituted the gravamen of the crime."[58] He had also insisted, "It was the books that offended, if offense there was,"[59] because the circulars advertising the books had been sent at random and not to a select clientele which might have made appropriate medical or scientific use of them.

In upholding the charge against Ginzburg, Brennan quoted the Rebhuhn opinion as follows:

[T]he works themselves had a place, though a limited one, in anthropology and in psychotherapy. They might also have been lawfully sold to laymen who wished seriously to study the sexual practices of savage or barbarous peoples, or sexual aberrations; in other words, most of them were not obscene per se. In several decisions we have held that the statute does not in all circumstances forbid the dissemination of such publications. . . . However, in the case at bar, the prosecution succeeded . . . when it showed that the defendants had indiscriminately flooded the mails with advertisements, plainly designed merely to catch the prurient, though under the guise of distributing works of scientific or literary merit. We do not mean that the distributor of such works is charged with a duty to insure that they shall reach only proper hands, nor need we say what care he must use, for these defendants exceeded any possible limit; the circulars were no more than appeals to the sala-

---

[57] *United States* v. *Rebhuhn,* 109 F. (2d) 512, 514 (1940).
[58] *Ibid.,* 515.
[59] *Ibid.,* 514.

ciously disposed, and no [fact finder] could have failed to pierce the fragile screen, set up to cover that purpose. 109 F. 2d 514–515.[60]

It appears that Brennan broadened Hand's opinion to include any material (not merely that which had a claim to medical or scientific value and when used for that purpose to escape the charge of obscenity) which may not, when standing alone, be regarded as obscene. With regard to all three publications Ginzburg was charged with distributing, Brennan said:

> We agree that the question of obscenity may include consideration of the setting in which the publications were presented as an aid to determining the question of obscenity, and assume without deciding that the prosecution could not have succeeded otherwise. . . . we view the publications against a background of commercial exploitation of erotica solely for the sake of their prurient appeal. The record in that regard amply supports the decision of the trial judge that the mailing of all three publications offended the statute.[61]

Justice Harlan in his dissent properly pointed to the problems of such a decision:

> Although it is not clear whether the majority views the panderer test as a statutory gloss or as constitutional doctrine, I read the opinion to be in the latter category. The First Amendment, in the obscenity area, no longer fully protects material on its face non-obscene, for such material must now also be examined in the light of the defendant's conduct, attitude, motives. . . . Were a State to enact a "panderer" statute under its police power, I have little doubt that—subject to clear drafting to avoid attacks on vagueness and equal protection grounds—such a statute would be constitutional. . . . What I fear the Court has done today is in effect to write a new statute, but without the sharply focused definitions and standards necessary in such a sensitive area. Casting such a dubious gloss over a straightforward 101-year-old statute (see 13 Stat. 507) is for me an astonishing piece of judicial improvisation.[62]

Hand did distinguish between the general principles set forth in

[60] *Ginzburg v. United States,* 86 S. Ct. 942 (1966).
[61] *Ibid.,* 944–45.
[62] *Ibid.,* 954.

the First Amendment, the due-process and equal-protection clauses, and the individual protections found in the remaining provisions of the Bill of Rights. The latter are pointed to specific problems and generally have no such broad scope as the former.

One group of protections arising under the Bill of Rights—those which are concerned with criminal proceedings—are to be distinguished, according to Judge Hand, because he believed that the courts have a major responsibility for securing them. These cases are concerned with matters clearly assigned to the judiciary by the constitutional allocation of power. In these areas judges are competent to weigh and measure conflicting interests under direct authority of the Constitution. There is no danger of encroaching upon the powers of another branch or of substituting the courts' judgment for a decision arrived at by some other department which has the constitutional authority to make it. Where the admonitions of the Bill of Rights relate to criminal proceedings, the court is clearly the appropriate institution to make the necessary discriminations.

The impact of the Bill of Rights remains the same. It urges fairness, honesty, and disinterestedness, which are essential to justice and provides a framework within which the courts seek to assure just decisions. When specific meaning can be drawn from these admonitions, it may supplement or elaborate the constitutional grant of powers to the federal judiciary.

In upholding the defendant's right against unreasonable search and seizure, Hand said of the Fourth Amendment:

> Such constitutional limitations arise from grievances, real or fancied, which their makers have suffered, and should go pari passu with the supposed evil. They withstand the winds of logic by the depth and toughness of their roots in the past. Nor should we forget that what seems fair enough against a squalid huckster of bad liquor may take on a very different face, if used by a government determined to suppress political opposition under the guise of sedition.[63]

But the Fourth Amendment does not carry within it its own specific standard—what is an "unreasonable" search and seizure and what is a "probable" cause? He was fully aware that, throughout government,

---

[63] *United States v. Kirschenblatt*, 16 F. (2d) 202, 203 (1926).

161

values are appraised and choices made. He did think it important that they be made by the properly constituted authority, which in this case is the judiciary. In response to an objection that one of his rulings (that the mere smell of fermenting mash did not justify a search for illegal liquor without a warrant) would make law enforcement difficult if not impossible, he observed simply, "Any community must choose between the impairment of its power to punish crime and such evils as arise from its uncontrolled prosecution."[64]

Hand found guidance in the historical meaning of these amendments. He said, upon denying an individual's request to be relieved of appearing before a grand jury, that it is

> the voice of the community accusing its members, and the only protection from such accusation is in the conscience of that tribunal. . . . A court shows no punctilious respect for the Constitution in regulating their conduct. We took the institution as we found it in our English inheritance, and he best serves the Constitution who most faithfully follows its historical significance.[65]

Here he showed his determination that the agency assigned a function in the Constitution be permitted to fulfill it unobstructed. History provided guidance for *Loubriel* v. *United States,* in which Hand insisted that when a person is committed for contempt, a distinction be made between punishing him and compelling him to testify. He said:

> If Loubriel was to be punished, his punishment must be fixed; if he was to be coerced, it might be only while the inquiry was on. . . . The reasons . . . go very deep into the past. Even when men did not wince at the most awful sanctions, the evidence procured was regarded with suspicion. A man, faced with perpetual imprisonment till he discloses his confederates, will in the end find confederates to disclose.[66]

Hand's interpretation of the courts' responsibility for the personal protections found in the Bill of Rights was based upon his understanding of the constitutional allocation of powers, which gave the courts authority in some of these areas but not in all. It is logical in light of his interpretation of the Bill of Rights and constitutional allocation of

---

[64] *United States* v. *Kaplan,* 89 F. (2d) 869 (1937).
[65] In re *Kittle,* 180 Fed. 946, 947 (1910).
[66] *Loubriel* v. *United States,* 9 F. (2d) 807, 809 (1926).

powers to distinguish between provisions directed specifically to judicial action and the more general constitutional principles and to define the role of the courts in regard to each. Furthermore, Hand's distinction between the more sweeping clauses of the Bill of Rights and those directed to more specific problems is not unique, though Herbert Wechsler commented that "the contrast . . . often implies an overstatement of the specificity or the immutability these other clauses really have—at least when problems under them arise."[67] He did point out, however, that there are many instances in which the court is called upon to interpret imaginatively those constitutional provisions which apply specifically to judicial action. Hand agreed that the courts should be engaged in the creative interpretation of these sections, for they are the special province of the judges and are so allocated by the Constitution. He did not shrink from balancing values, resolving conflicts, or applying general provisions to specific conflicts when in his judgment it was properly his responsibility.

[67] Herbert Wechsler, "Toward Neutral Principles of Constitutional Law," *Harvard Law Review*, Vol. LXXIII (November, 1959), 17.

CHAPTER IX : *Statutory Interpretation*

The complexities of contemporary American society and the speed with which they have multiplied since the beginning of the twentieth century have resulted in a sharp increase in public regulation of what had been regarded as private. The change has been accompanied by proliferation of statutory law and decline of the old common law, which no longer seems adequate. This shift in emphasis, together with an expansion of the democratic base of the political community, suggested to Judge Hand the growing inappropriateness of judge-made law in modern America. Law through legislative enactment has become a commonplace process, and judges no longer represent a governing elite. It is increasingly imperative that judges be thoughtful and self-conscious about their role and refrain whenever possible from policymaking decisions.

According to Hand's view "enacted law" is the command of the government prescribing the conduct sanctioned or required by society. Its authority comes from the democratic process by which it is spelled out in a legislature which represents all those who have a claim to representation. His approach to statutory interpretation was consistent with his philosophy and understanding of the extent and limits of the judicial function.

Democratic theory assumes that each man is the best judge of his own welfare and so all must have an opportunity to participate in common choices. Even so, as Hand pointed out many times, the correctness of man's purpose or choice depends upon his capacity to determine in advance the relative pleasures and pains of the alternatives available to him. He can never really know what he wants until he has realized through experience the implications of his choice, and

... although political controversy is poor makeshift, it is the best we can get in advance, and law must speak in futuro. These vague stirrings of mass feeling which many who pride themselves upon their democracy mistake for the popular will must always be made concrete before they can become law in any practical sense, and the process of definition is as important as the dumb energy which provokes it, perhaps more so.[1]

Law then is akin to a hypothesis, the actual testing or trial of which comes after enactment. Its elaboration, specification, and application are under the supervision of the courts. Learned Hand, with his pragmatic concern with experience and trial and error, understood this process to be of great importance in the life of the law. His appraisal of the role of the courts is one of high importance and significance. Law in its most general meaning has two aspects. It includes the initial statement by the legislature and the subsequent interpretation and testing by the courts. The participation of each branch through its unique function is essential to the rule of law.

Whether or not a statute fulfills the needs which gave rise to it may well depend upon the capacity of the judge to sense, to feel, to comprehend the mood of the community in its most subtle form, to understand the nice distinctions and discriminations implied in the purpose and intent of the law but not made explicit or spelled out to completion. The daily interpretation and application of the multitude of laws controlling the life of the community largely determine the measure of justice a society enjoys. In this aspect of a court's work disinterestedness, lack of bias, sense of fair play, and integrity of the judges are essential both to the success of the task and to the confidence of the people that justice will prevail.

The necessity for the judicial function to be performed and the problems it poses are timeless. Aristotle said that legislators sometimes,

> find themselves unable to define things exactly, and are obliged to legislate as if that held good always which in fact only holds good usually; or where it is not easy to complete, owing to the endless possible cases presented, such as the kinds and sizes of weapons that may be used to inflict wounds. . . . If, then, a precise statement is impossible and yet legislation is necessary, the law must be expressed in wide terms; and

[1] Hand, "The Contribution of an Independent Judiciary to Civilization," as reprinted in *The Spirit of Liberty* (3d ed.), 156.

so, if a man has no more than a finger-ring on his hand when he lifts to strike, or actually strikes, another man, he is guilty of a criminal act according to the written words of the law; but he is innocent really, and it is equity that declares him to be so.[2]

Hand's own language when he discussed this problem in the Dennis case is very similar. He said:

Obviously it would be impossible to draft a statute which should attempt to prescribe a rule for each occasion; and it follows, as we have said, either that the Act is definite enough as it stands, or that it is practically impossible to deal with such conduct in general terms. Such a consideration is relevant in judging the constitutionality of any statute.[3]

The legislature provides a solution by enacting a statute, but the law's capacity to satisfy the need which engendered it depends upon the incisiveness with which the courts spell it out and apply it. The law is an unknown quantity until it is given specific and final definition through application to individual cases.

A general law is normally understood to cover all the cases the language includes and assumes that in each instance arising under it a choice will necessarily be made between the satisfaction to be attained and the sacrifice to be accepted. It also presupposes that the general choice of values made in the law will not vary too greatly from the appraisals made in individual cases:

This assumption is not troublesome, so far as the values and sacrifices do not vary in the different settings in which they appear, but they do vary greatly, so that an occasion may arise that, although it is within the words used, imposes a choice between values and sacrifices altogether different from any that the legislators would have made if they could have foreseen the occasion.[4]

This problem can be met in two ways. Either the legislature may specify as precisely as language permits the cases in which the law will apply or it may trust interpreters to determine and decide upon the proliferation of purposes embodied in the law. The difficulties of the first choice are obvious, and the problems of the second no less so, for

[2] Aristotle, *Rhetoric*, ii. 13. 1374, 18–40; quoted in Hand, *The Bill of Rights*, 22–23.
[3] *United States v. Dennis*, 183 F. (2d) 210, 214 (1950).
[4] Hand, *The Bill of Rights*, 23.

it involves the interpreters in an "imaginative projection" of what was in the minds of the lawmakers. This sometimes appears as no more than a guess which serves as a cover for the substitution of the judges' choice of meaning. Nonetheless, it is a common practice to leave such matters to judges.

This delegation of choice to the courts, whether it be deliberate or careless, has been extended so far that judges at times ignore the actual words of the statute, even when they are unambiguous, in order to effectuate the equally obvious purpose of an act. Hand himself did this when the general purpose was evident but the specific words were for some reason contrary to it. He illustrated this necessity by the supposed acquittal of an Italian surgeon who had bled a patient in the face of a law prohibiting anyone from drawing blood in the streets of Bologna.

In *United States* v. *Associated Press*, Hand acknowledged that his opinion involved resolving conflicts within society, a function most often properly reserved to the legislative, but said,

> . . . it is a mistake to suppose that courts are never called upon . . . to appraise and balance the value of opposed interests and to enforce their preference. The law of torts is for the most part the result of exactly that process, and the law of torts has been judge-made, especially in this very branch. Besides, even though we had more scruples than we do, we have a legislative warrant, because Congress has incorporated into the Anti-Trust Acts the changing standards of the common law, and by so doing has delegated to the courts the duty of fixing the standard for each case.[5]

Congress had, he thought, under the antitrust laws, left these particular controversies to the courts. He knew that judges must sometimes make choices on policy grounds and that a judge is required to exercise more than skill in manipulating legal techniques. As Judge Jerome Frank said, ". . . he is required to display ripe wisdom and experience, together with a lively imagination and a capacity for empathy. All these things Hand can do and do superbly in his struggle to accomplish justice."[6]

Archibald Cox noted in his article "Judge Learned Hand and the

[5] *United States* v. *Associated Press*, 52 F. Supp. 362, 370 (1943).
[6] Frank, "Some Reflections on Judge Learned Hand," *Chicago Law Review*, Vol. XXIV (1957), 682.

Interpretation of Statutes" that the phrase "the intent of Congress" may carry several meanings. In one sense it connotes the purpose or general aim which the policy stated in the statute is intended to achieve. All intelligible legislation has some such meaning. Although individual congressmen may occasionally disagree even about the broad purposes to be achieved by the law, "their conflicting views may be fairly said to blend in a resultant, just as their differences regarding the words to be enacted are merged by the legislative process into a final product . . . [which] we metaphorically describe as the 'intent of Congress.' "[7]

The second understanding of the term is concerned with the specific, particular application which the law is "intended" to be given. The "general purpose" and "specific intent" may sometimes be almost identical, but that is not true for broad legislative actions, and so the distinction seems appropriate. The specific intent may also have two meanings. It may be that which the legislature consciously intended but failed to make explicit, or it may be the specific application which the judicial interpreter believes the legislature would have made if it had been faced with the specific controversy. Cox illustrated this progressive interpretation by reference to Hand's opinion in *Borella* v. *Borden Co.*:

> In enacting the Fair Labor Standards Act . . . it was the "purpose" of Congress to raise the standard of living of workers engaged in interstate commerce or in the production of goods for commerce. When it defined production to include "any process or occupation necessary to the production thereof," . . . Congress "intended" . . . to make the act applicable to maintenance workers in the executive offices of interstate producers.[8]

The process Judge Hand followed in finding intent in this case is worth quoting. He said:

> The case may, therefore, be further narrowed to whether the administrative agents and employees of a producing company are themselves "engaged . . . in the production of goods for commerce." . . . We can best reach the meaning here, as always, by recourse to the underlying purpose, and, with that as a guide, by trying to project upon the specific occasion how we think persons, actuated by such a purpose, would have dealt with it, if it had been presented to them at the time. To say that

[7] Cox, "Judge Learned Hand and the Interpretation of Statutes," *Harvard Law Review*, Vol. LX (February, 1947), 371.
[8] *Ibid.*

that is a hazardous process is indeed a truism, but we cannot escape it, once we abandon literal interpretation—a method far more unreliable.[9]

Relying upon precedent,[10] he then proceeded to reason that employees like the plaintiffs are "engaged in production" when they take care of the quarters of those who manufacture or handle goods, since the caretakers' work is necessary to the activity of production. In one sense the employees in Borella were closer to production than those in the controlling case because they were employed directly by the manufacturer, but in another sense they were further removed since they cared for the offices of administrative personnel rather than the shops of the producers. Hand disagreed with a decision of the Tenth Circuit Court that this distinction removed them from the protection of the law, for "it seems to us that the circumstance that administrative officials do not come in physical contact with the goods at any stage of their production, could not have been thought relevant to the object to be attained. We can conjure up no reason that could have induced Congress, having included employees who made tenantable the quarters of artisans and shipping clerks, to exclude those who made tenantable the quarters of the president, the managers, the cashiers, superintendents and the rest."[11]

Statutory interpretation depends upon both the general and the specific intent of Congress, and uncertainty with regard to purpose may cause difficulty in finding intent. For instance, the task of applying the specific intent of a law to a given situation is often complicated by the fact that the legislature seldom seeks to accomplish any single purpose or end fully at the expense of complete frustration of competing interests. The problem for the courts is then to discover the line that the legislature would have drawn between the conflicting interests represented in a specific case. When the law clearly left this issue to be resolved in the courts, Hand did not shrink from the responsibility.

The problem is immeasurably more complicated when intent is ambiguous or simply not apparent in a given case. This happens occasionally because legislators rarely think in terms of specific controversies as they draft legislation and also because new situations arise which they

[9] *Borella* v. *Borden*, 145 F. (2d) 63, 64–65 (1944).
[10] *A. B. Kirchbaum Co.* v. *Walling, Administrator*, 316 U.S. 517 (1942).
[11] *Borella* v. *Borden*, 145 F. (2d) 63, 65 (1944).

did not foresee. Learned Hand quoted one of his law teachers at Harvard regarding the problem when there was really no intent in the mind of the legislature that would apply to a question raised under a statute. He said:

> May I start with some words of my unforgettable master, John Chipman Gray. . . . "what the judges have to do is, not to determine what the legislature did mean on a point that was not present to its mind, but to guess what it would have intended on a point not present to its mind, had the point been present." I cannot believe that any of us would say that the "meaning" of an utterance is exhausted by the specific content of the utterer's mind at the moment.[12]

Of course, it is always necessary to ask, What did a legislature mean by the words of a statute? What were the points they had in mind, and even more difficult, did the majority that voted for it all have the same points, meaning, or common understanding—or were their understanings and intentions at variance with one another even then? Hand believed that for all practical purposes it is impossible to tell specifically what the legislators individually and collectively intended:

> All we know is that a majority has accepted the sequence of words in which the "law" has been couched, and that they expect the judges to decide whether an occasion before them is one of those that the words cover. That is an intricate process made up of many factors; perhaps the single most important one is the general purpose, declared in, or to be imputed to, the command. Gray calls the result a "guess" and indeed it is; but who are we that we should insist upon certainties in a world of no more at best than probabilities?[13]

Yet another situation a judge may face arises when the language of the law is not specific enough to be intelligible. In such cases the statute is not a law at all, for it is not a command that is understandable to those to whom it is addressed. In such cases the judge must necessarily dispose of the case and base his judgment on law of some sort. "However," Hand commented, "I cannot suppose that he must snatch a meaning from any gibberish that may emanate from a legislature. In our system at any rate a party asking relief must be able to satisfy the

---

[12] Hand, *The Bill of Rights*, 18–19.
[13] *Ibid.*, 19.

court that there is a command that he shall have it, and he loses if he fails to do so as much as though he failed in proving his facts."[14]

Perhaps the most striking feature of Learned Hand's approach to statutory interpretation was his overriding emphasis upon first determining the broad general purpose of the legislature in enacting a law. In some cases the purpose was easily apparent. In others he found it necessary to resort to the legislative history, to the words of the text, and, if all else failed, to "guess" as best he could what it was the legislators had in mind. Once he had fairly determined this purpose, he turned again to the legislative record, to textual analysis, to precedent, or to his own reason to determine what specific application was most nearly in accord with it. He was not inclined to permit technicalities, carelessness, or ambiguities to interfere with the spelling out of the law in accord with that purpose.

Hand's devotion to legislative purpose came from his understanding of the constitutional allocation of powers which gives the legislature the responsibility for announcing the laws by which the community will be governed. It conformed to his view that democracy is simply a process which permits all interests a voice in formulating policy through the legislature. It was compatible with his disavowal of any higher divine or natural law and his acceptance of law as the pragmatic resolution of conflict in society.

Hand repeatedly drew upon the clear purpose of a law to assist in its application to a specific case. In his dissent in *Commissioner of Internal Revenue* v. *Ickelheimer* he said:

> Compunctions about judicial legislation are right enough as long as we have any genuine doubt as to the breadth of the legislature's intent; and no doubt the most important single factor in ascertaining its intent is the words it employs. But the colloquial words of a statute have not the fixed and artificial content of scientific symbols; they have a penumbra, a dim fringe, a connotation, for they express an attitude of will, into which it is our duty to penetrate and which we must enforce ungrudgingly when we can ascertain it, regardless of imprecision in its expression. . . . Here we can have no doubt of the purpose of what Congress was aiming at; and that, I submit, we truncate, if we do not

[14] *Ibid.*, 49. See *Fire Companies Bldg. Corp.* v. *Commissioner of Internal Revenue*, 54 F. (2d) 488 (1931).

include transactions by which, in accordance with a preexisting design, property passes by whatever combination of moves at a substantially unchanged price from one member to the other of any of the specified pairs.[15]

Although the purpose of a statute is transmitted to the public and to the courts through the words it contains, Hand rejected a literal or dictionary interpretation. He understood that law must be intelligible to the people and thus expressed in common parlance. Even if it were possible to coin a technical language of the law which would provide greater precision, it would be foreign and incomprehensible to those to whom it would be addressed and thus inappropriate.

Hand was a leader in the movement away from literal interpretation from his earliest days on the bench, long before the broader view was in vogue. The definition of the term "employee" was understood to have an ordinary meaning that was clear to all in 1914. According to the conservative tradition which prevailed at the time, legislatures were assumed to use the term in this sense, and the test of whether social legislation designed to protect employees covered an individual was whether or not the person could be regarded as a servant or independent contractor under the law of torts. The Lehigh Valley Coal Company made contracts with individuals to mine coal and sell it to the company at a fixed price per ton in an apparent attempt to cause miners to be classified as independent contractors rather than employees. The plaintiff in *Lehigh Valley Coal Co. v. Yensavage* was injured in the mines and brought suit under a state employers' liability act, which required companies to provide safe working conditions for their employees. The company claimed that the plaintiff was an independent contractor and thus not covered by the law. Although the case presented by the company had great weight in precedent, Hand rejected it and maintained that the method of payment was irrelevant in the light of the purposes of the act under which the term "employee" had to be given meaning. He said:

> This [the company's interpretation] misses the whole purpose of such statutes, which are meant to protect those at an economic disadvantage.
> It is true that the statute uses the word "employed," but it must

---

[15] *Commissioner of Internal Revenue v. Ickelheimer*, 172 F. (2d) 660, 661 (1943).

be understood with reference to the purpose of the act, and where all the conditions of the relation require protection, protection ought to be given. It is absurd to class such a miner as an independent contractor in the only sense in which that phrase is here relevant. He has no capital, no financial responsibility. He is himself as dependent upon the conditions of his employment as the company fixes them as are his helpers. By him alone is carried on the company's only business; he is their "hand," if any one is. Because of the method of his pay one should not class him as though he came to do an adjunctive work, not the business of the company, something whose conduct and management they had not undertaken.[16]

Judge Hand did not always expand the literal meaning of a statute by examining its purpose, for the purpose of legislation is found in its limits as well as its authorization. When in *RCA Manufacturing Co. v. Whiteman* he was urged to expand the protection of the law to include a purpose which was not evident, Hand declined on the familiar ground that the legislature was the proper institution to conclude conflicts of interest. In this case, which involved the use of records for broadcasting which were labeled "not for broadcast," he held the restrictions invalid. He reasoned that a copyright is a monopoly which prevents others from reproducing the work copyrighted. The records had not been copied but merely used, and the copyright does not protect the use of the works. Restrictions upon goods once they are absolutely sold are prima facie invalid and must be justified by some exceptional reason which was not present in this case. He found nothing to justify the continued control over the use of the records claimed by Paul Whiteman and said:

> We are adjured that courts must adjust themselves to new conditions, and that in the case at bar justice clearly points the way to some relief. We cannot agree; no doubt we should be jealous to execute all reasonable implications of established doctrines; but we should be equally jealous not to undertake the composition of substantial conflicts of interests, between which neither the common-law, nor the statute, has given any clue to its preference. We cannot know how Congress would solve this issue; we can guess—and our guess is that it would refuse relief as we are refusing it—but if our guess were the opposite, we should have no right to enforce it.[17]

16 *Lehigh Valley Coal Co. v. Yensavage*, 218 Fed. 547, 552–53 (1914).
17 *RCA Manufacturing Co. v. Whiteman*, 114 F. (2d) 86, 89–90 (1940).

Gradually the literal interpretation of statutes yielded to a more imaginative understanding. The new approach was based partly upon the increasing volume of legislative and administrative materials used in discovering legislative intent. This new source of understanding has generally been widely acclaimed, but as Archibald Cox noted:

> . . . there is danger that these new techniques . . . will serve merely to increase the arsenals of advocates—both on and off the bench—without advancing the search for justice according to law. The opinions of Judge Hand have had significant influence both in breaking down the restrictions imposed by the dry literalism of conservative tradition and in showing how to use with sympathetic understanding the information afforded by the legislative and administrative processes.[18]

The courts have never been reluctant to seek out committee reports and the record of legislative debates when in doubt about the major purpose of a statute. It has always been believed that they provide an appreciation of the problem, the general conditions which gave rise to the legislation, and an understanding of the aspirations the laws sought to satisfy. Today such historical data are considered even when the words of the statute are not ambiguous. The courts are often so overwhelmed by arguments from legislative history that it is a problem simply to evaluate and separate the relevant and valid material from the useless. When applied to the understanding of the general purpose, these aids may help a judge establish empathy with the need which gave rise to the law. Further use of such material is subject to greater hazards. The legislative record is not unambiguous and may not be representative of legislative consensus. It may have been prepared in the original instance specifically for its future effect upon the courts, or the reports may have been drafted hastily and carelessly without thought of their implications beyond the legislature.

While Learned Hand rejected the literal interpretations of the words of a statute, he was careful and judicious in his use of legislative history. He regarded it as useful but, like the specific words of the act, necessarily subordinate to the sympathetic understanding of the full intent of the congressional purpose. Cox said that "one of the striking

[18] Cox, "Judge Learned Hand and the Interpretation of Statutes," *Harvard Law Review*, Vol. LX (February, 1947), 370.

characteristics of Judge Hand's opinions construing federal legislation is the regularity with which he first reasons out what disposition of the controversy would best conform to the apparent purposes of Congress and only then turns to the legislative history to verify his conclusions."[19]

In *Fleming* v. *Arsenal Building Corporation*, Hand was concerned with whether or not employees of the owner of a building who leased space to tenants primarily engaged in interstate commerce were covered by the overtime-pay provisions of the Fair Labor Standards Act of 1938. In writing the court's opinion, he reasoned by logical analysis from the purpose of the act that the employees should be covered by the statute. Then, turning to the text of the law itself, he found that it contained no limiting words and so the court was free to assume that Congress had not intended to draw a line. He then turned to the legislative history of the act and found there also confirmation of his original analysis.

Judge Hand occasionally turned to legislative history when the point in question was relatively minor and the statute provided no specific guide. Then, by following the development of the act through the legislature, he often discovered that the ambiguity resulted from an error, an oversight, or some carelessness through which an amendment failed to take into account all sections of the act. Once understood, such discoveries gave some guidance in interpretation. Legislative history, when used in this way,

> may reliably explain a choice of words which on their face seem meaningless, or inconsistent with the general purpose. It may reveal, for example, a deliberate truncation of the purpose, in which event the words must govern; or it may show that the choice of words resulted from some decision quite unrelated to the point at hand and so permit taking otherwise objectionable liberties with the normal meaning of the words.[20]

In *Guiseppi* v. *Walling*, Hand's concurring opinion was concerned with an instance in which the words of a statute if literally applied would appear to make unintelligible the purpose of an administrative regulation issued under the Fair Labor Standards Act of 1938. The administrator had issued a far-reaching order establishing minimum

[19] *Ibid.*, 382.
[20] *Ibid.*

wages in the embroidery industry, together with regulations designed to ensure complicance. There was evidence which supported his authority to do so. However, the law distinguished between wages fixed by statute and those determined by advisory committees. The administrator appeared to be authorized to proclaim this drastic measure with regard to those fixed by advisory committees but not those determined by law, and Hand thought it inappropriate to permit it in one case and not the other. If Congress had in fact intended the distinction, he had serious doubts that there was sufficient basis to permit such a regulation controlling committee wages. He said:

> I should have not had any trouble as to §8 (f), had it applied to all wages—those fixed by statute as well as those fixed by "advisory committees"—indeed, I am not sure that the Administrator would have needed any express grant of power to promulgate the regulation which he did, had the Act been silent. . . . But, since the power is in terms limited to what I may call "committee," as opposed to "statutory," wages, I have had some doubts whether we should construe it to comprise so drastic an exercise as is here in question . . . for in that event the purpose we should have to ascribe to Congress would be nothing short of absurd.
>
> Not only does every consideration which can support so heroic a remedy apply equally to "statutory" wages, but their exclusion so mutilates the only purpose that could have actuated the regulation, as to leave no intelligible purpose at all.
>
> Even so, I should have had the utmost compunction in disregarding the explicit language with which the section begins, were it not for its legislative history.[21]

His examination of the legislative record revealed that the grant of power to the administrator which was in question was included in the original Senate bill, where it was a part of the plan entirely different from that contained in the statute. In the intervening action amendments were passed in the Senate and a whole new scheme was introduced in the House. In conference a compromise was worked out which provided for the two kinds of wages, and Section 8, which made an explicit grant of power to the administrator, was reintroduced as it had originally been introduced in the Senate version, under which all labor

[21] *Giuseppi* v. *Walling*, 144 F. (2d) 608, 623-24 (1944).

standards were to have been fixed by a board. Hand commented that Section 8,

> having had its origin in a plan which allowed wages to be fixed ad hoc . . . took its place in that part of the act which still allowed them to be so fixed, though within limits. It was entirely natural that, when so introduced, the power should be thought of as limited to "committee" wages, forgetting its capricious and egregious incidence, if that were done. It does not therefore seem to me an undue liberty to give the section as a whole the meaning it must have had, in spite of the clause with which it begins. . . . There is no surer way to misread any document than to read it literally. . . . As nearly as we can, we must put ourselves in the place of those who uttered the words, and try to divine how they would have dealt with the unforeseen situation; and, although their words are by far the most decisive evidence of what they would have done, they are by no means final.[22]

Hand quoted with approval Edmund Plowden's note on *Eyston* v. *Studd*, in which Plowden described the process by which the judge seeks to understand the meaning of a statute as the legislator understood it even though the specific intent is not clear. Plowden said:

> In order to form a right judgment when the letter of a statute is restrained, and when enlarged by equity, it is a good way, when you peruse a statute, to suppose that the law-maker is present, and that you have passed him the question you want to know touching the equity, then you must give yourself such an answer as you may imagine he would have done, if he had been present. . . . And if the law-maker would have followed the equity, notwithstanding the words of the law (as Aristotle says he would . . .) you may safely do the like, for while you do no more than the law-maker would have done, you do not act contrary to the law, but in conformity to it.[23]

In composing his response for the legislator, a judge may appropriately take into account any specific projections the members of the legislature may have made in discussion of the law. While these projections often represent the concepts of the individuals or small groups of men who worked to draft or review the legislation in committee, they are likely to conform to the conceptions of a majority of Congress as

[22] *Ibid.*, 624.
[23] 2 *Plowden* 459, quoted in Hand, *The Bill of Rights*, 20–21.

well. These men understood the background and cause of the statutes and felt the temper of the times and the pressures of conflicting interests which are inaccessible to judges. Since, in Judge Hand's view, it is a most important task for the judge to determine what the basic accord was—what purpose or end the law was intended to serve—he would be remiss to disregard this evidence. It is not necessarily obligatory, but should be considered along with the text of the law, other evidence available to the courts, and the judge's own reasoning about the relationship of the law to a particular instance which arises under it.

Cox suggested that Judge Hand's opinion in *Lenroot v. Western Union Telegraph Co.* was an outstanding example of this kind of analysis of the projection of the specific intent of members of the Congress and that the reversal by the Supreme Court through an analysis of the text emphasized the advantage of Hand's position.

The case arose under the Fair Labor Standards Act, which forbids any producer to "ship . . . in commerce any goods produced in an establishment . . . in or about which within thirty days prior to the removal of such goods therefrom any oppressive child labor has been employed."[24] Children were being used by Western Union under conditions that clearly came under the statute, but the question remained whether or not Section 12 of the law applied to sending telegrams from one state to another. On one side, Section 2 of the law defined "goods" and "produced" in such a way that the activities of Western Union were covered. On the other side, there was some evidence in the text that Section 12 applied only to production of goods for commerce and that it did not apply to Western Union since it was engaged in "commerce." The textual analysis thus produced arguments of about equal strength for both parties in the dispute, and a unanimous court of appeals, through Hand's opinion, made the general purpose of Congress the deciding factor in ruling that Western Union was controlled by the act.[25]

According to Hand's reasoning, it was the will of Congress to use the full measure of its constitutional power to eliminate substandard working conditions for children. There was no limiting language in the

[24] *Fair Labor Standards Act*, 52 Stat. 1067 (1938), 29 U.S.C. § 212 (1940).
[25] Cox, "Judge Learned Hand and the Interpretation of Statutes," *Harvard Law Review*, Vol. LX (February, 1947), 386.

statute, and he thought that Congress would not seek to control employment of children in the production of goods for interstate commerce and leave unregulated the employment of children directly engaged in interstate commerce. At that time the power of Congress over working conditions relating to production for commerce was still unclear, but it had always had power to regulate the commerce itself. To seek to control the former and not the latter would appear irrational, so reason suggested that the act applied. Judge Hand then turned to the legislative history and found that the apparent textual differences were not the result of congressional intent but were the accidental result of amendments in conference committee which caused the ambiguity in the words of the law. Once the differences were accounted for on a basis other than the deliberate choice of Congress to control conditions of child labor in production for commerce but not for those engaged in commerce, he was free to let his initial reasoning prevail. He did not rely upon the legislative record as conclusive but interpreted it as an explanation of the verbal difficulties of the law which left the court free to implement the broader intention of the law in the face of some confusion in the words of the law itself.

In a five-to-four decision which relied upon textual analysis, the Supreme Court reversed Judge Hand's reasoning in an opinion by Justice Robert Jackson because he found no definite policy explicitly spelled out in the law itself, which would guide the Court. He specifically denied any attempt to look beyond the words of the law for legislative purpose when he said for the Court, "We take the Act as Congress gave it to us, without attempting to conform it to any notions of what Congress would have done if the circumstances of this case had been put before it."[26]

Learned Hand sought to spell out as clearly as he could this distinction between judicial legislation and interpretation. It may be a matter about which it is impossible to make a statement so precise that it serves as a practical standard rather than an indication of spirit or philosophy with which a judge approaches his task. In defining the function of judges as seeking the intent of Congress, he stated an ideal. Certainly he did not mean that judges do nothing but voice the meaning—either explicit or implicit—of the legislature. The feeling of satis-

[26] *Western Union Co. v. Lenroot,* 323 U.S. 490, 501 (1945).

faction and creativity that he experienced as a judge implies more than routine application. But he did insist that the creativity of a judge be carried on within a certain limiting framework.

He knew that it was not possible for judges to separate completely their personal views of right and wrong from their appraisal of acts of the legislature. He did not deny that in a small way a judge must make law if he is to fulfill his own function. How then, is it possible to distinguish Learned Hand's position that a judge properly interprets law from the view that the judge makes law? The answer seems to come from his spirit, his frame of mind, his philosophy of law, and his understanding of the society in which he lived and worked.

While in a strict sense the dilemma of a judge may be insoluble, there are profound differences in the approaches judges take to the application of law. There are different ways of finding a solution, which often depend upon the judge's understanding of his own role or function in the process of government. Cox emphasized the difference in approaches when he said:

> While those who say the court must recognize that it is making law have done the necessary work of teaching the profession the importance of this aspect of deciding cases, they sometimes come too quickly to a point at which they cease to search for the legislature's meaning and either restrict the statute, deciding the case according to judicial precedent, or else make their own adjustment of the interests, extending the enactment into fields the legislature did not enter. . . . [Judge Hand's position] asserts another point of view, requiring the court as best it can to submerge individual notions to that which was determined in another forum; commanding it to manifest the legislative purposes in their completeness and there to stop, remembering that the policy of a statute inheres as much in its limitations as in its affirmations.[27]

Hand believed that judges must remember the pragmatic origin of the law which they seek to interpret, and, while they must not go contrary to it and cannot legitimately go beyond it, they must be a party to its growth and development so that it continues to represent an

---

[27] Cox, "Judge Learned Hand and the Interpretation of Statutes," Vol. LX (December, 1947), 375. This is almost precisely the language Hand himself used; for example: ". . . the notion that the 'policy of a statute' does not inhere as much in its limitations as in its affirmations, is untenable." *Borella* v. *Borden*, 145 F. (2d) 63, 65 (1944).

acceptable solution to the conflict it temporarily concluded. It is not the responsibility of the judges to accommodate the law to a radical shift in political power. When the old law with its accumulated inter-pretation is no longer acceptable to a majority of the community, those who have achieved the new preponderance of power must seek by the prescribed and legitimate means to change the law. It is the role of the judge to develop the law along the lines set forth through some expres-sion of the government. He may perhaps, within limits, extend its application to problems which clearly seem to be implied by the original expression. He may refine and further define it in accordance with its intention, for no law is ever so completely elaborated that it may be applied routinely. "It is not as the priest of a completed revelation that the living successors of past lawmakers can most truly show their reverence or continue the traditions which they affect to regard."[28]

[28] Hand, "The Speech of Justice," *Harvard Law Review*, Vol. XXIX (April, 1916), as reprinted in *The Spirit of Liberty* (3d ed.), 16.

PART IV : *What Philosophy of Democracy?*

CHAPTER X : *American Political Thought*

Judge Learned Hand was a product of the radical reorientation in political thought which followed the scientific revolution and occurred about the beginning of the twentieth century.[1] His philosophical assumptions were typical of this contemporary thought, and he sought to translate them into terms that were significant for the functioning of the American political system. It appears relevant to consider briefly the nature of the subtle but substantive changes that occurred in American political thought before attempting to examine Hand's understanding of the democratic society in which he lived and worked.

It is true that there has never been a monolithic American philosophy. It can be argued that opposing views were held by the men who framed the Constitution, as well as by those who have elaborated it in the twentieth century. Nevertheless, it is possible to identify the fundamental intellectual assumptions which dominated eighteenth- and nineteenth-century America with the natural-law tradition.

This philosophy included a belief in the natural rights of man and was a part of the natural-law theories in which law established the framework for human society and was above both ruler and ruled. Sir

[1] Brecht, *Political Theory: The Foundations of Twentieth Century Political Thought,* 3–7. Walter Lippmann referred to this change as "the loss of the public philosophy." It is what William Barrett calls "the general pattern of philosophical development which is a turning away from idealism. . . . in America it is pragmatism." William Barrett and Henry Aiken, *Philosophy in the Twentieth Century,* 136. Daniel Boorstin, who denies that there has ever been a public philosophy in America, also noted a significant change about the turn of the twentieth century: "Some of the bewilderment in which we find ourselves is due to the fact that, while belief . . . in destiny has been growing, the belief in 'giveness' has declined. . . . More than ever we feel that we are cast in a great role, but, for the first time, we begin to wonder if we ourselves may not have some responsibility for composing the plot." Daniel J. Boorstin, *The Genius of American Politics,* 163.

Ernest Barker described the long continuity of this political thought which prevailed in Europe since the time of the Stoics:

> the rational faculty of man was conceived as producing a common conception of law and order which possessed a universal validity. . . . this common conception . . . [has] formed a European set of ideas for over two thousand years. . . . spoken through the mouth of Locke, [it justified] the English Revolution of 1688, and . . . served to inspire the American Revolution of 1776. . . . They were ideas of the proper conduct of states and governments in the area of internal affairs. They were ideas of the natural rights of man—of liberty, political and civic, with sovereignty residing essentially in the nation, and with free communication of thoughts and opinions; of equality before the law, and the equal repartition of public expenses among all the members of the public.[2]

Edward S. Corwin noted that "the conveyance of natural law ideas into American constitutional theory was the work pre-eminently—though by no means exclusively—of John Locke's *Second Treatise on Civil Government*."[3] Walter Lippmann believed that the founders of America were adherents to the higher-law philosophy but that a fundamental change evolved in American political thought which permitted "public agnosticism and practical neutrality in ultimate issues."[4]

As early as 1930, in *The Revival of Natural Law Concepts*, Haines pointed out the tremendous influence of these doctrines upon American life and emphasized the impact they had on concepts of law and all legal thinking in the United States. He noted, however, that the orthodox legal view had become one in which "there is no case in which the courts have held an act invalid or refused to enforce a law because regarded as contrary to natural law, except when such a law was in conflict with an express constitutional provision,"[5] and as far as the legal profession is concerned the traditional natural-law doctrine had become largely a matter of history.

The belief that there was originally in America a basic agreement upon fundamental philosophical assumptions is attested to by the way

[2] Sir Ernest Barker, *Traditions of Civility*, 10–11.
[3] Edward S. Corwin, *The "Higher Law" Background of American Constitutional Law*, 61.
[4] Walter Lippmann, *The Public Philosophy*, 79.
[5] Charles Grove Haines, *The Revival of Natural Law Concepts*, 75.

political ideas were presented and supported for the first hundred years after the Constitution was adopted. In the Declaration of Independence, Jefferson's reference to the Creator in traditional terms indicated his understanding of a popularly held belief in divine law. The specific use of the idea of natural right coming from John Locke also implied a general acceptance of some higher law. The "right" to rebel (which Hand specifically denied) came directly from Locke's understanding of the inherent rights of man. Thus, while the specific nature or source of the superior law may be ambiguous, it seems clear that belief in such a law was dominant during the constitutional period and permeated the entire society.

Political thinkers oriented to the natural-law concept were concerned with the best end of the state and the proper means to that end— with good and evil, worthy and unworthy, valuable and useless. They supported their beliefs by recourse to first principles, which came from religion, nature, history, or self-evident postulates. These various political theories and the answers they provided were regarded as contributions to the knowledge of man and were assumed to be on the same level as scientific findings.

At the beginning of the twentieth century political philosophers became acutely conscious of the limits of scientific discovery based strictly upon the tools of science, such as observation, measurement, and logical reasoning. Anything not proved by the scientific method came to be regarded as simply personal opinion, religious dogmas, or tentative assumptions to be tested. The potential implication for political life and theory was revolutionary. Devotion to science precluded scholars from determining in absolute terms the superiority of any ends or purposes. Scientists could only examine their relative superiority in terms of other further, more ultimate ends. Arnold Brecht wrote,

> ... what occurred was more than a mere shift in emphasis of scholarly work; the new methods if strictly observed compelled scientists to withdraw *completely* from all statements that expressed evaluations and preferences in absolute terms and thus from all those questions that had played a dominant role in former writings—the "best" form, the "proper" ends and means of government, right and wrong, good and evil, just and unjust.[6]

[6] Brecht, *Political Theory*, 6.

Brecht emphasized that these negative aspects of the new philosophy were scarcely recognized for the first quarter of the century because there was still broad general agreement on basic values and principles in the Western world. These principles included, among others, the natural rights of man, respect for human dignity, freedom of thought and belief, equality before the law, and abolition of slavery and torture. It did not seem particularly significant then that scientific investigation could not prove the validity of these basic values. They were simply assumed by most of the Western world to be the essential elements of justice in human society.

It was only after World War I that the practical consequences of this new perspective—that agreement on fundamental principles was no longer scientifically necessary—came to be understood. These principles were then being challenged and abandoned by Communism and Fascism. The concepts that had prevailed throughout much of the Western world were simultaneously deprived of scientific and philosophical support and practical agreement.

There was no scientific proof of the validity of any of the totalitarian doctrines, but neither was there disproof, since science cannot verify ultimate principles of right and wrong. The twentieth-century philosophers were able to suggest implications of such systems and to predict that they would not lead to happiness, but they could not legitimately condemn them as immoral, unjust, or evil.

It is a vulgarized version of Pragmatic philosophy which seems most descriptive of the direction toward which American political thought is becoming oriented. Learned Hand's views were more self-conscious and thoughtfully and lucidly expressed than those of most of his fellow citizens. It is not possible to assert with certainty that his philosophic assumptions are those which dominate American thought. Although any sampling of contemporary political literature would support this contention, it is often in the intellectual world that fashions of political thought are established, and there is always a substantial lag and often a distortion between the inception of an idea and its popularization. It is not unreasonable, however, to assume that the philosophical assumptions Judge Hand typified will prevail in some form in the foreseeable future and that an understanding of their relationship to the American democratic system may illuminate some contemporary political problems.

The disagreement between the old and new theories about ultimate values and purposes is fundamental for political life. One looks toward and seeks to achieve some ultimate ideal which it accepts as authoritative, while the other is intent upon finding a viable solution to an immediate problem. The practical consequences of these two views may be of overwhelming importance, and the record is not clear which will contribute most to man's happiness and well-being, either immediately or in the ages to come.

The history of man is strewn with atrocities committed in the name of some higher law. Yet men devoted to this concept have also achieved great heights in human development, judged not only by the standards of the natural law tradition but also by modern humanistic philosophies. On the other hand, loosening of the restraints of traditional concepts has opened whole new avenues for human achievement. Yet there is a frightening aspect of the modern view which was acknowledged by Learned Hand. It is that, since man is undetermined and absolutely free to choose according to his own desire, he may choose badly, and the ultimate destiny of man may be Nietzsche's last man or the absolute rule of the stronger.

Natural law was regarded as an ideal to which all just laws must conform. It was thought that if man constantly strives to attain an ideal he will necessarily move toward. it. This theory acknowledged that because of man's freedom and imperfection he may move in the opposite direction, for, while there is a proper end for man, he may not understand it, or he may choose to ignore it. Nonetheless, an imperative part of the natural-law tradition is belief in a human impulse toward the good which is objective and is at least theoretically knowable to man through his reason. The failure of the natural-law philosophers to discover purposes and goals upon which all men can agree is regarded as evidence of need for some new way of approaching human problems.

It was the teaching of John Locke that, since all men are born with certain "natural rights," they are the absolute and ultimate "goods" for man. No government may legitimately deprive him of these rights. Government was strictly circumscribed in its powers, and if it sought to infringe upon these rights, which were the limits provided by nature, the government was dissolved, or, as it is more popularly asserted, the people had a legitimate right to rebel against it. The standards by which a government will be judged in terms of good and evil, just and unjust, right and wrong are the rights to which man is entitled by the nature of his humanity. Belief in natural law implies a government limited either by the natural rights of man or by the restraints of a higher law which is above all human law and authority or by some combination of these.

The new philosophy which denies absolutes and allows each to select his own values provides no standard outside society by which government shall be judged or limited by the purposes of the dominant group in the community. If good and evil, just and unjust, right and wrong are determined by positive law, whatever that pronounces to be good, just, and right are that in fact. A society based on this point of view may be democratic or despotic depending upon whether the process for declaring the law rests in the hands of the many, few or one. Experience—the teacher the Pragmatists so often call upon—indicates that all are possible.

Learned Hand knew that it is difficult enough for each individual to establish his own ultimate goals and that to do so for a society composed of many millions of persons is an almost incomprehensible task. The difficulty of defining ultimate community goals accounts for the fact that those goals to which modern political thinkers generally refer are the more or less agreed-upon social needs of the community, or a set of hypothetical ends postulated by a political elite which are at least not rejected by the majority of citizens. The goals may be largely personal and sometimes unarticulated.

Hand was typically pragmatic in that he often spoke of the "good life" as the end of men but did not define it. His frequent references to it indicate that it is what each man determines and that man must be free in order to make this choice. Material well-being is important but appears to be a condition, not an element, of the good life. It seemed clear to him that in a democracy the content of the good life will be determined and defined by means of the democratic process. Insofar as the goals of society remain vague and unclear, it is difficult if not impossible to measure human progress or even to define what progress means. The difficulty of establishing explicit goals for the community may sometimes result in an apparent lack of concern for ultimate ends and an increasing interest in the selection of alternative solutions to immediate problems.[7]

In a society where there are no acknowledged natural limits or purposes, disagreements upon fundamental issues and goals are not only possible but likely. Conflict and dissent are not limited to the best means of achieving agreed-upon goals but extend to the very ends of the society itself. Since this view regards ultimate ends as arbitrary choices, there is no logical or rational way to select them. Hand believed that experience taught that the democratic process is the best method—that it does not pay to fight.[8] But ultimately each individual must determine for himself that it does not pay to fight. It is possible that some group in society which consistently loses through the democratic process may decide that experience has taught that it does, or at least may, pay to fight. Since Pragmatism legitimates and encourages diversity on the most basic assumptions held by the people in a society, it appears to invite conflict over goals, while the natural-law theories assume and seek to stress the commonality of ultimate ends and may suppress or ignore differences.

A vital part of Judge Hand's understanding of the American system was his concept of law as the formal resolution of a conflict which government will support. Stated thus, the legislative branch serves an almost instrumental but vital function of marking the point at which the resolution was reached and declaring that the government will enforce this agreement unless and until the whole process is repeated—the issue agitated and argued, its support measured, and the solution altered. Hand knew that legislatures do more than this—they can and do actively participate in finding an acceptable compromise,

[7] However, John E. Smith says that today there is "a new interest in goals and purposes and a more acute awareness of the limitations of the merely instrumental intelligence. Upheavals abroad and insecurites at home have served to bring into clearer focus questions about genuine values and worthwhile aims. Americans are not as sure as they once were that if questions of means can be solved, the ends will take care of themselves." John E. Smith, *The Spirit of American Philosophy*, 43–44.

[8] "Conflict is normal; we reach accommodations as wisdom may teach us that it does not pay to fight. And wisdom may; for wisdom comes as false assurance goes." Hand, "Democracy: Its Presumptions and Realities," *Federal Bar Journal*, Vol. 1, No. 2 (March, 1932), as reprinted in *The Spirit of Liberty* (3d ed.), 101.

but the status of the resulting law is not thereby altered. It remains the culmination of a contest among interests in the community waged in conformity with certain generally accepted rules of the game, more specifically known as the "democratic process." His high regard for the role of law in human society indicated his appreciation of the importance of the process and of the institution primarily responsible for its articulation.

This positivistic view is contrary to the natural-law theory, which anticipates that claims may be judged and conflicts may be resolved rationally in a way that is compatible with the superior law. Hand did not think that American legislatures operate in this fashion or that they should. Since he believed that there is no absolute standard to be discovered, to profess to seek and to find it would allow a choice on some undisclosed and unacknowledged basis under guise of eternal principles and thus the subversion of the democratic process. (This was his objection also to judicial decisions which are in fact legislative but which pose as interpretation of the general principles.) Legislators are not and need not be concerned with some ultimate good but with a choice among alternative actions—a solution which appraises as accurately as possible the weight of the interest on both sides and creates a minimum of dissatisfactions and a maximum of satisfactions. The values sought by the contending parties are incommensurable—there is no fixed hierarchy of values which can be brought to bear upon the solution—and a measuring of the interests expressed through the democratic process provides a peaceful solution.

Learned Hand had a profound belief in the diversity of human capacity and assumed that because of this difference some persons would have greater weight in public determinations than others. This was not a question of "justice" or "injustice" but simply a matter of fact. In some ways his position was akin to Aristotle's, who said that all "affirm that the will of the major part of the civic body should be sovereign."[9] But this leaves open the definition of the "major part." Hand thought that various factors, such as aggressiveness, persistence, wealth, and large numbers, would be relevant and that each group would moderate the power of the others.

The importance of Learned Hand's philosophy in terms of practi-

[9] Ernest Barker (trans.), *The Politics of Aristotle*, 261.

cal application to the courts lies generally in his view of the pragmatic origin of all law, but most specifically in his unique interpretation of the Bill of Rights. Understood as a declaration of the rights of man in accord with a higher law, it would impose a restraint upon the power of government and draw meaning from the natural-law tradition of which it was a part. This view was inconsistent with his denial of absolute standards and the belief that all purposes and values are created by men. Thus, in judging, he sought to distinguish between the general principles which were clearly drawn from a philosophy alien to his own and those parts of the Constitution which allocate powers. It must be noted that his interpretation of the general principles is based primarily on his personal philosophical assumptions. So, in an ultimate sense, his entire view of the system and the role of the judiciary is dependent upon this choice and is a product of his own will rather than merely an interpretation of the words of the Bill of Rights read in their historical context.

Judge Hand's approach to the Bill of Rights was internally consistent with the major assumptions of his philosophy, with his belief that tolerance is necessary to freedom, which in turn is essential for man's creativity, and it is suggestive of his more specific understanding regarding the American system. It permits the courts to exercise judicial review in the area he regarded as essential to the system while denying the power of judicial review in areas he thought dangerous both to society and to the integrity of the courts.

Hand's dual interpretation of the Constitution supported his democratic belief that all should have an opportunity to share in determining the basic laws under which they live, requiring only that the final determination be made in accord with the democratic process. It, as well as the federal structures which he supported, allows the maximum achievement, but it does not assume or require perfection. It is compatible with the assumption that man will be determined by what he chooses and permits him to move in any direction. This system provided by a constitutional framework of positive law seemed to him to be justified by successful experience.

Democracy as a process affords many interpretations, and Hand's position regarding the nature of the constitutional limits differs from other positive-law perspectives. Many, such as Justice Black, regard the

Bill of Rights as part of the fundamental positive law which provides substantive limits on government that must be enforced by the courts. Still others, who may not deny the reasonableness of Hand's interpretation, view the development of the system as having been so substantially different from his position regarding the way it should function that, while it may be theoretically interesting, it has little relevance for contemporary American life. Hand himself acknowledged through his judicial opinions that his view had not prevailed. As a judge he did not try to impose his view, but he thought that the questions raised by his interpretation suggested problems relevant to contemporary political life.

Edward S. Corwin explained the transition which took place in the American system with the decline of belief in natural law and why the change did not result in legislative supremacy as Hand thought it should:

> ... in the American written Constitution, higher law at last attained a form which made possible the attribution to it of an entirely new sort of validity, the validity of a statute *emanating from the sovereign people*. Once the binding force of higher law was transferred to this new basis, the notion of the sovereignty of the ordinary legislative organ disappeared automatically. . . . But . . . even statutory form could hardly have saved the higher law as a *recourse for individuals* had it not been backed up by *judicial review*. Invested with statutory form and implemented by judicial review, higher law, as with renewed youth, entered upon one of the great periods of its history, and juristically the most fruitful one since the days of Justinian.[10]

Haines held the same view: "Judicial review, then, as originally adopted, would have had relatively slight influence on the American government and politics, . . . but for the development of these implied restrictions arising from a revised version of natural law theories."[11] Haines added a further argument which may help to explain Judge Hand's great restraint in interpretation of the Due Process Clause: ". . . due process of law has come to be . . . the main provision through which natural law theories were made a part of current constitutional law."[12]

[10] Corwin, *The "Higher Law" Background*, 89.
[11] Haines, *The Revival of Natural Law Concepts*, 85.

Pragmatism and the whole range of twentieth-century political philosophies doubtless developed partly in response to an awareness of the problems that appear to inhere in a belief in natural law. Political life founded on new philosophical assumptions implies new problems, and attention may properly be focused on those which may evolve from the new perspective.

Harry Jaffa has suggested that people who prefer to define democracy as "process" rather than as the production and maintenance of a good society have an inadequate understanding of what was originally intended by democratic procedure. He regarded the procedure devised by the Constitution as a means of achieving a certain kind of society, not an end in itself. He emphasized that democratic procedure was intended to operate within the framework of a broad consensus about the fundamental philosophical assumptions upon which the institutions were based:

> If ... the citizens differ among themselves on questions concerning the very basis of society, they cannot, in a moral sense, be fellow-citizens. Without agreement on fundamentals there can be no trust, and without trust there is no basis for citizenship. Free government, properly so called, involves ruling and being ruled in turn. Men cannot confide into the hands of others their families, their property, or their religion, if they think those others are fundamentally hostile or indifferent to them. Majority rule presupposes an agreement, more or less unanimous, on the all-inclusive aims of life, as they may be touched by the action of government. It cannot create such agreement.[13]

If the issues at stake are the most fundamental assumptions the people hold, acquiescence in the majority choice appears to pose a dilemma. If the people readily accede to the relative character of these basic assumptions, the problem of the external defense of the democratic system against attacks from opposing systems is crucial. Learned Hand was very much conscious of this possibility, and it was Arnold Brecht's thesis that the major crisis in modern political thought is not the antithesis between totalitarianism and democracy but the loss by the Western democracies of the ability to defend their value system as supe-

[12] *Ibid.*, 104.
[13] Harry V. Jaffa, "The Nature and Origin of the American Party System," *Political Parties, U.S.A.* (ed. by Robert A. Goldwin), 67.

rior to all others—the theoretical position that no choice between ulti-mate values can be made.[14] On the other hand, if the citizens hold firmly to conflicting views about fundamental principles, the problem of exter-nal defense is that the people cannot "hang together and fight," and the democratic system itself is exposed to the problem of inadequate inter-nal support. Under scientific analysis democratic value systems become, like all others, merely dogma, ideology, or as R. M. MacIver called it, myth.[15] Those who claim scientific or absolute validity for any value system are simply in error.

Hand was aware of the problems posed by the necessity of resolving disagreements about basic values in society and argued that only the legislature should attempt to deal with them because of the potential danger to tranquillity or even continuance of the system. The courts, being nonrepresentative and nonresponsible, should leave these issues in the hands of the democratic branch. This argument does not answer the query how long the democratic process will endure or how effec-tively it will serve if it becomes an end in itself rather than a means to some generally accepted goals. Natural-law philosophers of the consti-tutional period assumed that man's strongest political attachment was to the rights of man according to nature and that all his political actions would be devoted to their protection. The institutions and procedures devised to provide the ways and means for the accomplishments of this purpose were secondary and would give way if they failed to satisfy the need which gave rise to them.

Learned Hand appeared to assume that man will be devoted to a process which permits him to retain a maximum of personal liberty consistent with life in society. This assumption seems to imply the necessity for man to be sufficiently rational to understand that his choices are arbitrary, personal, and relative; that the choices of his fellowmen have equal validity; and that it is better to live and let live on the basis of a democratic resolution of issues than to deny the democratic procedure in the name of some individually chosen purpose or end. This suggests a high degree of rationality—perhaps more than most Pragmatists would be willing to admit. It is, however, also possible to argue, as Thomas Hobbes did, that even instrumental rationality

14 Brecht, *Political Theory*, 9.
15 R. M. MacIver, *The Web of Government*, 51.

will lead to the understanding that peaceful accommodation is better than endless conflict. Again, Hand's position appears to be supported by his evaluation of the pragmatic view and usefulness of the democratic process.

Lippmann believed that, even though discussion of the public philosophy has been "tabled" in the liberal democracies today, there still remains "a body of positive principles and precepts which a good citizen cannot deny or ignore. . . . It does not have to be discovered or invented. It is known. But it does have to be revived and renewed."[16] The question that he, like Jaffa, posed for the liberal democracies is whether a society whose institutions are premised upon a natural-law philosophy can continue to function in a community that no longer adheres to that philosophy. He doubted that it is possible:

> Except on the premises of this [natural law] philosophy, it is impossible to reach intelligible and workable conceptions of popular election, majority rule, representative assemblies, free speech, loyalty, property, corporations and voluntary associations. The founders of these institutions, which the recently enfranchised democracies have inherited, were all of them adherents of some one of the various schools of natural law.
>
> In our time the institutions built upon the foundations of the public philosophy still stand. But they are used by a public who are not being taught, and no longer adhere to, the philosophy. Increasingly, the people are alienated from the inner principles of their institutions. The question is whether and how this alienation can be overcome, and the rupture of the traditions of civility repaired.[17]

Insofar as there continues to exist, even tacitly, a residue of basic consensus on fundamental principles, the democratic system as created and understood in Western liberal societies has not been sustained without a higher-law philosophy. Thus the capacity of a strictly relativist philosophy to sustain a democratic system over a period of time has not been tested and cannot be supported on the basis of the experience of the last half century. The pragmatic test may come if and when belief in relative values dominates society. Or, in the alternate the system itself may be gradually altered as the new perspective gains acceptance so that old institutions will be compatible with it. If this

16 Lippmann, *The Public Philosophy*, 79.
17 *Ibid.*, 79–80.

197

occurs, experience will then have provided practical evidence of the tremendous viability and stability of the democratic process in societies imbued with the Western traditions and of its capacity to accommodate to and successfully serve societies based on radically different philosophical assumptions.

The democratic process as originally understood is rational only as a means for achieving common goals or ends and loses this rationality in a society that denies the existence of such goals. However, it might continue to serve effectively as long as the satisfactions it produces sufficiently outweigh the dissatisfactions for the "major part" of the society. It can also be argued that there is a de facto interest in the United States in the peaceful settlement of disputes and that this interest will be sufficient to maintain a democratic process for the indeterminate future. Nevertheless, in such a society it is difficult to know what ultimately can sustain the agreement to abide by the democratic process. Hand himself argued that self-restraint and tolerance are the rarest of human qualities. What will convince a minority that feels itself consistently depressed that its own well-being is sustained by adherence to the democratic process?

Hand's theoretical view of the judicially enforceable limits imposed upon the system by constitutional prohibitions was an extreme one that is not shared by others who also deny natural-law standards. His position places the maximum stress upon the system in terms of fundamental disagreement about the basic issues in society. He offered no reassurance about the viability of such a system. He simply said that a democratic society can continue only as long as the spirit of toleration prevails in the hearts and minds of the people. Once that spirit is lost, nothing can save it.

The question, nevertheless, remains: Can a pluralistic society with many diverse values and tolerance for them all defend itself in an ideological struggle for men's minds? Belief in relative personally chosen values requires accepting any value honestly chosen or desired as legitimate. Is there something inherent in this belief that denies to its holder a capacity to defend his faith in the freedom for diverse values with adequate passion and dedication in the face of the challenger who has complete faith in absolute values? Must he not accept his adversary's absolute as legitimate and thus, perhaps even subconsciously, weaken his desire to combat it or deny his own faith by intolerance of those who hold other views? Does dedication to the proposition that there are no tables from Sinai to guide man in his determination of right and wrong force the advocate to accept as equally valid a concept which is substantively incompatible with his own relative faith or to deny that faith through intolerance for the contrary view? Either choice is inconsistent with tolerance and destructive of it.

This dilemma appears to inhere in all relative philosophies, and Hand did not suggest a solution. Nonetheless, in the final statement of his mature understanding of human values, he appeared to accept the position of Albert Einstein, a refugee from National Socialism, who wrote in 1940: "If someone approves as a goal, the extirpation of the human race from the earth, one cannot refute such a viewpoint on rational grounds."[18]

Learned Hand did not shrink from contemplating the possibility that democracy might fail. It might falter in the face of attack from abroad, or it might disintegrate from within because of human error, unsuccessful choices, excessive demands, or conflicting goals. While he had no doubt that it was the best kind of life for man, he believed that its future depended upon free choice and that there is no necessity that this choice will support a democratic system. Democracy's fate, as well as man's personal fate, is dependent upon his ability to choose well. His first impulse is toward intolerance; democracy demands tolerance and self-restraint. Man is imperfect, and so democracy will be also. According to his understanding of the American system, it provides no absolute guides for its citizens, and some may seek the comfort of certainty rather than the disconcerting uncertainty of relative and changing values:

> . . . make no mistake; these are the days of testing. It is just in such times of stress that wide horizons and a suspended judgment become least bearable; that men, not content to follow the lights they have, will reach out for other lights—warmer, rosier, more comforting. Indeed such other lights there are, whose consolations we may indeed envy their possessors: lights to which many are turning. Let us meet the issue squarely: ours is a stern creed, and we do not prophesy the outcome; we carry no passports to paradise; we accept the chance that it may prove

[18] Brecht, *Political Theory*, 9, quoting Albert Einstein, "Freedom and Science," in *Freedom, Its Meaning* (ed. by Ruth Anshen), 382.

a creed too Spartan for men to live by. Time's womb may be full of monsters; the salvation of mankind from complete liquefaction may turn out to demand infallible rulers, having absolute power, choosing their own successors and exempt from all control. Plato has not been alone in that belief. Granted that "all power corrupts, and absolute power corrupts absolutely"; absolute power must in the end be lodged somewhere.[19]

Democracy is inefficient and may be rejected in the name of expediency, but man's whole history is filled with the gross inefficiency of trial and error, success and failure, and this will inevitably be the nature of the democratic epoch which in the end will be judged by its consequences. It is possible, but not as evident as it might have seemed in the 1950's, that in the United States all groups can achieve enough satisfaction through the democratic process that they will continue to abide by it. As long as it remains an open society in which all ideas have an opportunity to be heard and all interests may be urged, Hand saw reason for optimism. Experience gained in almost two hundred years of experimentation has added to our knowledge of the ways and means to satisfy the multiplicity of man's desires and should contribute to the continued success of the system.

Learned Hand remained loyal to his pragmatic position while comprehending fully its implications for American democracy. He had firm convictions but knew that they were personal and relative and accepted the possibility that they might not prevail. Intellectually he conformed to his ideal of the detached, tolerant, democratic citizen. If, as A. A. Berle, Jr., suggested, he was not always so detached in practice, Hand might be expected to acknowledge that fact a bit ruefully but then reiterate that absolute detachment is an ideal which could destroy democracy if completely achieved at the expense of loyal devotion to freely accepted purposes and values.[20]

[19] Hand, "At Fourscore," *Harvard Alumni Bulletin*, Vol. LIV, No. 10 (February, 1952), as reprinted in *The Spirit of Liberty* (3d ed.), 259–60.

[20] "He opposes, vehemently, the idea that any eternal principles of justice exist. He does, also vehemently, insist that every society has fundamental attitudes. Those which our society has evolved, he treasures. Should they vanish, we will be in sad straits, he thinks. And today sometimes he apprehends that they may vanish, blown away in the current hurricanes of social intolerance. Nevertheless, it is one of his deepest convictions that judges cannot, and must not try—as judges—to save our people from their follies." Frank, "Some Reflections on Judge Learned Hand," *Chicago Law Review*, Vol. XXIV (1957), 701.

CHAPTER XI : *Judicial Restraint and the American Democratic System*

The political perspectives represented by Learned Hand make an impact upon the American democratic system at two levels. The first relates to the primary assumptions from which all subsequent political presuppositions are drawn. The broad differences between positive- and natural-law doctrines provide the basis for the most critical issues in American political life, but the differences between Hand and other contemporary thinkers have important implications for interpreting the system on a secondary level. When considered at this level, and with primary focus upon the debate about the proper role of the courts in the American system, the lack of uniformity in twentieth-century thought is striking. Both judicial restraint and activism can be justified in terms of historical data, and each has a long and venerable tradition. It seems useful to view this issue as it exists within a framework conditioned by twentieth-century philosophy.

The total impact of Judge Learned Hand's political philosophy, his conception of the American democratic system, and his understanding of the primary function of the national courts leads to judicial restraint in constitutional issues. His position was internally consistent, reasonable, and logical. On the continuum of restraint to activism it was extreme insofar as it related to judicial review of the Bill of Rights and favored restraint where the question involved the power of another department or agency of government. However, when the court was operating in what he regarded as its primary sphere, he was willing to exercise a full measure of judicial power. These areas included statutory interpretation; the amendments which are explicit enough to give guidance to the court in providing full rights to persons charged and standing trial for crime; the common law which is uniquely the responsibility for making judgments that might have otherwise been regarded as legislative (that is, antitrust, torts, patents, negligence, and care); and First Amendment cases which arise under statutory law.

In his introduction to Hand's *The Bill of Rights*, Charles E. Wyzanski, Jr., asserts that "Judge Hand's thesis has not yet been supported by a single eminent judge or professor."[1] It may be true that no other prominent jurist or scholar has simply affirmed his assertion that the Bill of Rights is merely an admonition to justice and that the courts properly have no responsibility for its interpretation except to satisfy themselves that the legislature has weighed the values implicit in the issue. It is not true that others have failed to argue with similar eloquence the case for judicial restraint. This position has been urged by a bevy of judicial giants, as well as by lesser members of the bench. Justices Holmes, Frankfurter, Jackson, and Harlan have fairly represented this position in the twentieth century.

It may be that in the evolution of the great institutions of government some periods are more critical than others—that their development, the context in which they operate, and the changing social, economic, and political forces combine to pose in sharp focus questions which have been largely dormant or submerged. It may be that such a time is at hand for the United States Supreme Court. The last half century has witnessed great shifts in the Court, and the contrast between the positions it assumed before 1937 and those it has taken since has caused even the unsophisticated to question what its role is and what it should be in the American system.

Two conflicting theories, representing differing though great traditions of American jurisprudence, may be characterized as "activist" and "restraint." Both have had powerful advocates in the Court, and it is possible that conflict between them may place the institution itself in danger. Wallace Mendelson has written: "Until we have a better understanding of the Supreme Court's real function, that institution will be in trouble. . . . Eventually, perhaps, we will have to choose between them [the two traditions]."[2] The idea of vital and vigorous controversy in and about the Court is a fascinating one, for it contrasts markedly with the outward appearance of reserve, dignity, tradition,

[1] Wyzanski, in his introduction to Hand, *The Bill of Rights*, viii.
[2] Wallace Mendelson, *Justices Black and Frankfurter: Conflict in the Court*, ix.

judicious weighing of the fine points of the law, and seeming insulation from pressures and conflict.

Appreciation of the significance of this issue is heightened by the fact that the Civil War was waged over constitutional doctrine. It is somewhat reassuring to remember that the Supreme Court has been the scene of controversy ever since Marshall's decision in *Marbury* v. *Madison.* The Dred Scott decision so angered the Republicans that Lincoln devoted a part of his first inaugural address to criticism of the Court. The Pollock case, in which the income-tax law was struck down, inspired William Jennings Bryan in his presidential campaign. Labor decisions early in the twentieth century were protested by Progressives Theodore Roosevelt and Robert M. La Follette, while Franklin D. Roosevelt openly attacked the Court in 1937. More recently cases dealing with national security, integration, and reapportionment have placed the question regarding the proper role of the Court in issue. All parties and groups have at different times both approved and criticized the use of judicial review, and none has consistently supported or challenged it.

Each time the issue is revived, the grounds are shifted perceptibly, and it is possible to argue that decisions which have given rise to the current problem are sufficiently unique to constitute a controversy that is different in kind from all previous ones. Insofar as this is true, it appears to stem from a new position of the activists that the court is the prime defender of all democratic processes, principles, and institutions, as expressed in the following statement:

> One of the central responsibilities of the judiciary in exercising its constitutional power is to help keep the other arms of government democratic in their procedures. The Constitution should guarantee the democratic legitimacy of political decisions by establishing essential rules for the political process. It provides that each state should have a republican form of government. And it gives each citizen the political as well as the personal protection of the Bill of Rights and other fundamental constitutional guarantees. The enforcement of these rights would assure Americans that legislative and executive policy would be formed out of free debate, democratic suffrage, untrammeled political effort, and full inquiry.[3]

[3] Eugene V. Rostow, "The Democratic Character of Judicial Review," *Harvard Law Review,* Vol. XLVI, No. 2 (December, 1952), 210.

Anthony Lewis found the constant factor of the activism of the mid-twentieth century in the ethical element—the court has become the guardian of the national conscience in three primary areas: integration, state criminal proceedings, and apportionment.[4] C. Herman Pritchett suggested that one important difference is that for the first time an activist court was pursuing liberal policy goals.[5]

Until 1954 the Supreme Court acted "more like a brake than a motor in the social mechanism,"[6] and the usual effects of judicial review were to retard change and to affirm the social, economic, and political relationships already existing in society. *Marbury* v. *Madison* announced the doctrine upon which all subsequent judicial review has been based, but the immediate practical effect was limited to the litigants of the case.[7]

Political implications of the Dred Scott decision were great, but again the effect was to restore the law that had regulated the ownership and disposition of slaves before the Missouri Compromise. While it disturbed a large part of the population, the decision did not dramatically alter political or social institutions or require changes in the deeply rooted attitudes and practices of the population. Throughout the entire period of judicial activism on behalf of laissez-faire economics, Court action was primarily negative and delayed the social and economic changes the statutes sought to enforce. The Court had so long acted as a brake that this was regarded as its proper function. Pritchett said: "The judicial revolution has changed that. In its dedication to libertarian goals the Court has in several major fields of public policy become the motor, not the brake. It began in 1954 with the Court's epochal decision to rid the nation of the blight of racial segregation and discrimination."[8]

[4] Anthony Lewis, "Historic Change in the Supreme Court," *New York Times Magazine,* June 17, 1962, p. 38.

[5] C. Herman Pritchett, "The Judicial Revolution and American Democracy," paper presented at the University of Kentucky Centennial Conference, April 9, 1965, p. 3.

[6] Felix Cohen, "Transcendental Nonsense and the Functional Approach," *Columbia Law Review,* Vol. XXXVI (1935), 845.

[7] Pritchett made this point when he said: "Not the least of John Marshall's great accomplishments . . . was that he was able to achieve a role of 'active resolution' for the Supreme Court without disturbing the official theory that the justices had 'neither force' nor will.' " Pritchett, "The Judicial Revolution and American Democracy," p. 2.

[8] *Ibid.*, 11.

The segregation cases did not order return to a previous relationship but required legislatures to rewrite statutes dealing with education and create a completely new kind of social relationship contrary to the traditions, mores, and belief systems of many of the communities in which the new order was to prevail. According to Charles Hyneman:

> When to the Segregation decisions are added the later judicial acts extending the new constitutional regime to other places of public assembly, one must acknowledge that. . . . the nonsegregation orders are without precedent for comprehensive and deep-cutting social consequences and for application of judicial method to issues of obligation arising directly out of constitutional language.[9]

Extension of judicial power into the realm of legislative apportionment emphasized the intent of the Warren Court to take an increasingly active role in the affirmative decision-making process of the community. This has consequences for the structure and organization of political institutions which may be largely unknown and unanticipated. Judge Hand did not live to see the Court enter the "political thicket" of legislative reapportionment, but he would have disapproved of this incursion into politics. Justice Frankfurter's last great dissent on behalf of restraint was written in *Baker* v. *Carr*. In this protest he was joined by Justice Harlan, who in subsequent reapportionment cases spoke out in the same tradition. In *Reynolds* v. *Sims*, Harlan challenged the view that

> every major social ill in this country can find its cure in some constitutional "principle," and that this Court should "take the lead" in promoting reform when other branches of the government fail to act. The Constitution is not a panacea for every blot upon the public welfare, nor should this Court, ordained as a judicial body, be thought of as a general haven for reform movements.[10]

The majority opinion written by Chief Justice Warren followed Eugene Rostow's view that it is the responsibility of the Court to protect democratic values as it understands them. The opinion clearly spells out the majoritarian and egalitarian values and the theory of representative government upon which the decision rests:

9 Charles S. Hyneman, *The Supreme Court on Trial*, 199.
10 *Reynolds* v. *Sims*, 377 U.S. 533, 624–25 (1964).

... *Wesberry* [v. *Sanders* 376 U.S. 1 (1964)] clearly established that the fundamental principle of representative government in this country is one of equal representation for equal numbers of people, without regard to race, sex, economic status, or place of residence within a State. ...

Legislators represent people, not trees or acres. Legislators are elected by voters, not farms or cities or economic interests. As long as ours is a representative form of government, and our legislatures are those instruments of government elected directly by and directly representative of the people, the right to elect legislators in a free and unimpaired fashion is the bedrock of our political system.[11]

The very important practical significance of the difference between the views of activism and restraint upon the American democratic system are underscored in this series of cases. The proper definition of judicial review is not merely a theoretical problem. It is a question which has great implications for the lives of millions of Americans, not only in the matter of reapportionment but also in all fundamental issues presented to the Court.

When viewed from the standpoint of the effect upon traditional institutional arrangements and relationships within the system, segregation and apportionment cases may present a new problem. Robert McCloskey believed that the Warren Court made a claim to govern that is different from any such claim made in the past. He regarded the Brown decision not merely as a doctrinal development from holdings such as *Sweatt* v. *Painter* but as a mutational leap which sometimes occurs in the evolution of a species. The old activism of the 1930's was limited to control of the economy. In more recent years the Court voluntarily assumed responsibility for substantive policy in a whole variety of social and political issues which are new to the Court and regarding which there are no fixed public attitudes by which the Court can be guided.[12] Viewed from another standpoint—that of the continually recurring issue of the Court's power to make decisions which have enormous impact upon the social, political, and economic as well as the legal life of the country—the controversy can be regarded as a

---

[11] *Ibid.*, 560–62.

[12] Robert G. McCloskey, "Reflections on the Warren Court," *Virginia Law Review*, Vol. LI (November, 1965), 1240, 1257.

continuation of the older one. This is essentially the perspective from which C. Herman Pritchett viewed the issue in his book *Congress Versus the Supreme Court*. He did not discount the vital importance of the differences between those who support activism and those who urge restraint. He accepted it as a logical controversy which emanates from the constitutional separation of powers and believed that neither extreme position will dominate. The Court always appears to re-establish its empathy with the community as it did when it perceived the threat implicit in President Roosevelt's ill-conceived court-packing plan and withdrew from its negative role. The change in personnel on the present court may be viewed by some as providing an opportunity to bring about some accommodation to public attitudes.

Pritchett pointed out challenges to the Court that reached disturbing proportions. These came in organized form from the Conference of Chief Justices of the States in a resolution approved in 1958, from the resolution adopted by the House of Delegates of the American Bar Association in 1959, and from congressional efforts to curb the Court or to modify its decisions.[13] After 1961, when this book was published, there was a strong but unsuccessful movement in Congress to alter the Court's decision to enforce the one-man, one-vote rule and the school-prayer decision. In spite of the fact that congressional attacks upon the Court have so far been unsuccessful, the petty refusal to raise Supreme Court salaries both in 1964 and in 1965 suggests that there is a residue of animosity that might become threatening under certain conditions. The zeal with which the Senate has investigated the qualifications of nominees suggests a willingness if not an eagerness to attack members of the Court for political as well as judicial reasons. Other less prestigious efforts were made by groups to "impeach Earl Warren" and to agitate for a general reversal of the position of the Court. There can be no doubt that the contemporary concern for "law and order," Nixon's victories in 1968 and 1972, and his opportunity to influence the direction of the Court have been at least partly a reflection of dissatisfaction with Supreme Court rulings.

Whether one regards these issues as unique and somehow decisive (and it is always a temptation to consider contemporary problems as

13 C. Herman Pritchett, *Congress Versus the Supreme Court*, 21 ff.

different from and more critical than previous ones) or as merely another resurgence of an old controversy, it is clear that the different views of the judicial function are significant for the operation of the American democratic system. Hand was always an advocate of restraint. One writer, describing the confrontation of the two views through Justices Black and Frankfurter, noted that "the venerable Judge Learned Hand . . . though not on the Supreme Court, has long been a coach and a comfort to the Frankfurter contingent."[14] In the period during which the dialogue between Justices Black and Frankfurter was carried on, the Court came to serve as the primary forum for debates regarding the proper operating conditions of a free society:

> Disagreements among members of the Court have been caused not so much by differing degrees of belief in civil liberties, as by different concepts of judicial responsibility for the furtherance of these goals. On balance, however, the activist position has been strong enough to project the Court into an unparalleled role of leadership and controversy in the continuing struggle for the achievement of freedom, equality, and justice.[15]

A judicial activist may be distinguished by his concern for the achievement of a specific goal and the right result in a controversy rather than for the judicial process by which the Court achieves that end. For him judicial legislation is not incidental but is the very heart of the judicial process. He is guided by the great ideals and great visions he seeks to impart to the law which he considers instrumental and to be used for the greatest good. His first concern is justice, and he understands it to be his responsibility to impose it if necessary upon other branches of government and the community itself. He feels a personal obligation for arriving at results required by his own sense of justice. This tradition found its expression in Justices Marshall, Stephen Field, Wheeler Peckham, Melville Fuller, George Sutherland, and Black. Many who do not accept this position are aware of the cause it can serve. Wallace Mendelson commented: "Be it, or not, a judge's function, Mr. Justice Black's dissenting struggle in the realm of civil liberty challenges the conscience of the crowd. His restless probing at the frontiers of

[14] Fred Rodell, "Crux of the Court Hullabaloo," *New York Times Magazine*, May 29, 1960, p. 29.
[15] Pritchett, "The Judicial Revolution and American Democracy," p. 10.

freedom may help us to achieve more enlightened notions of public decency."[16] Justice Frankfurter expressed his doubts more tartly when he said, "If judges want to be preachers, they should dedicate themselves to the pulpit, if judges want to be primary shapers of policy, the legislature is their place. Self-willed judges are the least defensible offenders against government under law."[17]

A judge who is dedicated to the exercise of judicial restraint also seeks just results, but he is bound more than the activist by limits on his freedom to judge:

> He is primarily concerned with determining what it is proper for him as a judge to do. To the extent that he submerges himself in a judicial mystique and thinks of himself as dominated by a role with prescribed limitations and expectations, to that degree he loses the freedom to pursue his own goals and feels a lesser personal responsibility for the results achieved. He thinks he has to act as he must, not as he wishes he could.[18]

An activist is more willing to declare acts of the legislature unconstitutional when they do not accord with his own philosophical beliefs or policy preferences than is the advocate of judicial restraint who often searches for some acceptable rationalization for doubtful legislation. The former willingly overrules a precedent, while the latter is inclined to do so only rarely and then reluctantly. The activist considers it necessary and right that legal principles and techniques be used as necessary to achieve justice. For example, he may use the power of certiorari freely to redress a perceived imbalance between the employer and employee in cases arising under the Federal Employer's Liability Act.[19]

Activists are often called upon to create new constitutional doc-

---

[16] Mendelson, *Justices Black and Frankfurter: Conflict in the Court*, 123.

[17] "From the Wisdom of Felix Frankfurter," *Wisdom*, Vol. III, No. 28 (January, 1959), 25.

[18] Pritchett, "The Judicial Revolution and American Democracy," p. 4. Judge Hand said, "For the results he [the judge] may not justly be held accountable; to hold him is to disregard the social will, which has imposed upon him that very quiescence that prevents the effectuation of his personal notions." Hand, "The Speech of Justice," *Harvard Law Review*, Vol. XXIX (April, 1916), as reprinted in *The Spirit of Liberty* (3d ed.), 14.

[19] Mendelson, *Justices Black and Frankfurter: Conflict in the Court*, 41.

trine by which their goals may be achieved. Self-restraint may also require creativity in judging, as was apparent in Judge Hand's career, but because the activists now tend to regard the Court as the motor of the system, their need is more frequent and imperative—and perhaps more dramatic. Finally, activists are much more willing to involve the court in controversial matters and to lead in their resolution:

> An activist judge will take the chance of going beyond the established consensus in pursuit of a policy goal in which he believes. He is not so likely to be deterred from entering "political thickets." He is more likely to have confidence that his judgments, even though controversial, are right and will ultimately be accepted, and so is willing to run the risk of some temporary dangers to the judicial institution on behalf of long-range goals.[20]

The essence of the activist spirit has been vividly caught in the following description:

> Mr. Justice Black understands the power of the elemental. His characteristic tools are the great, unquestioned verities. He draws no subtle distinctions. The niceties of the skilled technician are not for him. His target is the heart, not the mind. His forte is heroic simplicity. His opinions attain great power because they seldom bother with mundane considerations that baffle others—e.g., application of a winged principle in a less than ideal world; or the impingement of one vast Platonic truth upon another. In a word, Mr. Justice Black is an idealist. His wisdom is the wisdom of the great idea. . . . He insists that we live up to our highest aspirations—and when we fail to do so he would save us from ourselves.[21]

Judge Hand's philosophy and career represent the epitome of judicial restraint. It is well to remember, however, that both activism and restraint have deep roots in the American tradition and that neither dominates completely, even in a single judge. Wallace Mendelson has wisely recalled that "eventually, the ardent activist gives way to a rule, just as his counterpart on occasion ignores rules for something deemed transcendental. What is important is the tilt of a judge's mind, his conception of the nature of his function and the depth of his convictions. It is a matter of goal and tendency, not of absolutes."[22]

[20] Pritchett, "The Judicial Revolution and American Democracy," p. 7.

[21] Mendelson, *Justices Black and Frankfurter: Conflict in the Court*, 13.

[22] Wallace Mendelson, "Mr. Justice Frankfurter—Law and Choice," *Vanderbilt Law Review*, Vol. X (1957), 334.

Learned Hand believed that the capacity of the American system to endure as it was created by the Constitution was dependent upon the exercise of judicial restraint and that the power of judicial review was circumscribed by the necessity which justified it. According to this position, judicial restraint serves to maintain the system by preserving the constitutional allocation of powers and by protecting the unique function of the courts. Dispersion of power in the specific manner provided by the Constitution appeared to him to be the essence of the American system.

Hand believed that the Constitution was based on the assumption that ideally decisions should be made rationally and for the common good, but the Founding Fathers also understood that the ideal is rarely if ever achieved and that man needs institutions devised to encourage an approximation of the ideal. The checks and balances and federal system provided by the Constitution and described in *The Federalist Papers* were created specifically with this goal in mind. Hand believed that these limits, if maintained, were sufficient to sustain the system and that those who argue the necessity of additional substantive restraints provided by the courts are in error. He was not unmindful of the advantages that might accrue from some substantive judicial supervision, but, upon reviewing the arguments both pro and con, he concluded, "To me it seems better to take our chances that such constitutional restraints as already exist may not sufficiently arrest the recklessness of popular assemblies."[23]

Hand thought that the men who devised the Constitution had divided the functions of government among the separate departments and intended that the legislatures express the will of the people, who are sovereign. He did not know precisely what the Founding Fathers understood by the "common will," but he did know that the Constitution gave the legislature, not the courts, responsibility for its enunciation. He believed that the great advantages of judicial restraint were that it compels the legislature to assume its proper responsibility for resolving the basic conflicts in society and that the people may have the advantage of the political education which accompanies the resolution of critical issues through the democratic process. Restraint

[23] Hand, *The Bill of Rights,* 74.

helps keep the legislatures responsible and the people alert. If the courts refuse to correct the legislature's errors, they can help force modernization of archaic legislative procedures so that the political branches will be more responsive to the will of the people, and in the world of relative values the legislature should be more representative than the courts. Early in his legal career Hand expressed his position:

> The only way in which the right, or the wrong, of the matter may be shown, is by experiment; and the legislature, with its paraphernalia of committee and commission, is the only public representative really fitted to experiment. . . . the legislature, though less courageous because it is less independent, is more genuinely representative. At present it is prone to evade its responsibility by throwing off all the odium of opposition on the court. If it could not do so, it would be compelled to meet the question more squarely and more fairly; and we should not have the inconsistent spectacle of a government, in theory representative, which distrusted the courage and justice of its representatives, and put its faith in a body which was, and ought to be, the least representative of popular feeling.[24]

There is a contemporary theory that the original separation of powers is no longer functional and that the federal system has outgrown its initial purpose. This position maintains that the evolution of political parties and development of sophisticated interest groups have overcome any separation that may have once existed among the different agencies of government. Some proponents of this view deny that an effective functional separation of governmental power is possible—that policy formulation, execution, and interpretation are so intermingled as to be incapable of meaningful allocation to different departments. This view holds that differences between nation and state are largely obsolete and represent the last stronghold of institutional or vested interests. Old state boundaries are irrelevant. Where geographic problems require regional attention, state lines do not satisfy these needs. Modern means of communication and the nationalization of society have voided the constitutional allocation of power for practical and realistic purposes.

Learned Hand understood this position and the role of parties and interest groups, but he did not believe that they obviated the need for

[24] Hand, "Due Process of Law and the Eight-Hour Day," *Harvard Law Review*, Vol. XXI, No. 7 (May, 1903), 508.

the allocation of powers and functions to separate agencies. The original allocation was made by a constituent act of the people, and if it was to be altered, it should be done forthrightly by amendment and not surreptitiously under the guise of judicial review. He believed that the Constitution did not intend that the courts should serve as a third camera and that judges demean their own role when they attempt to do so. The functions of judge and legislator are quite distinguishable; and although the line which separates them may sometimes appear obscure, there is such a line, and its existence is vital to the American system: ". . . there is a plain distinction in theory between 'interpretation' and 'legislation,' as well as a clear boundary in practice."[25] Both are essential, and the Constitution designed separate branches which are responsible for these functions.

Another widely held contemporary view of American constitutionalism regards the Bill of Rights as higher positive law which it is the responsibility of the courts to use as a substantive standard for judging whether the acts of the other departments and levels of government are within their allocated power. It is often and persuasively argued that Hand's theory of judicial restraint deprives the courts of one of their most important functions in a democratic society: it removes from them power to protect those individual rights and liberties which are essential to democracy and which are guaranteed by the Constitution. Insofar as the Bill of Rights places limits upon the power of the legislatures to infringe upon these freedoms, the courts have a primary responsibility for their protection. This is no doubt the most serious criticism made of his position. John P. Frank, one of many students of constitutional law who has disagreed profoundly and explicitly with Hand's view of the Bill of Rights, wrote:

> My . . . serious difference with the judge is the narrow content which he gives to the Bill of Rights itself. By his definitions . . . in truth it matters very little who is charged with enforcement; there is next to nothing to enforce. . . . The constitutional mandate prescribes that there shall be no laws on a particular subject; Judge Hand equates this with the proposition that any laws on the forbidden subject shall be unbiased.

[25] Hand, "Thomas Walter Swan," *Yale Law Journal*, Vol. LVII (December, 1947), as reprinted in *The Spirit of Liberty* (3d ed.), 216.

HUNT LIBRARY
CARNEGIE-MELLON UNIVERSITY

It is a neat trick. I saw him do it with my own eyes; but I still cannot understand how that metamorphosis was achieved.[26]

Rostow supported the view that the Constitution makes the courts responsible for First Amendment freedoms when he wrote, "In cases dealing with freedom of expression the Court sits as the ultimate guardian of the liberties on which the democratic effectiveness of political action depends."[27]

Learned Hand knew that the liberty embodied in the general principles of the Constitution is essential to the good life as he understood it but believed that it would prevail only as long as it was supported by the community and could not be enforced by the courts. Furthermore, he thought that if the courts accept this responsibility, they encourage a false sense of security, for when a crisis appears the courts are without the capacity to defend these rights. Liberty, he said,

> is the product, not of institutions, but of a temper, of an attitude towards life. . . . It is idle to look to laws, or courts, or principalities, or powers, to secure it. You may write into your constitutions not ten, but fifty, amendments, and it shall not help a farthing. . . . It is secure only in that . . . sense of fair play, of give and take, of the uncertainty of human hypothesis, of how changeable and passing are our surest convictions, which has so hard a chance to survive in any times, perhaps especially in our own.[28]

Further, Hand denied that the Bill of Rights is sufficiently specific when isolated from its original natural-law context to be interpreted by the courts as law. He supported his position by pointing to the wide variations of meaning that these general principles have been given by the courts at different periods and to the heated dissents they frequently call forth from the bench. Nonetheless, his two-level theory of the Constitution, which treats part of it as obligatory and part as hortatory,

[26] John P. Frank, review of *The Bill of Rights*, by Learned Hand, *Tulane Law Review*, Vol. XXXII (June, 1958), 793. Frank also seems to beg the question here, for few if any have interpreted the First Amendment as forbidding all legislation in the areas it seeks to protect.

[27] Rostow, "The Democratic Character of Judicial Review," *Harvard Law Review*, Vol. XLVI, No. 2 (December, 1952), 215.

[28] Hand, "Sources of Tolerance," *Pennsylvania Law Review*, Vol. LXXIX (November, 1930), as reprinted in *The Spirit of Liberty* (3d ed.) 76.

is not entirely satisfactory. Even though the Bill of Rights is too vague to be valid substantive law, as he argues it is, there remains the question of congressional power to legislate in an area which the Constitution sought to make as free from regulation as possible. There seems to be no way, even theoretically, for the courts to avoid all responsibility for enforcement of the Bill of Rights. He was led to this inconsistency— through which he denied that the separation of power should be altered without formal amendment but altered the apparent natural-law implications of the Bill of Rights—by his philosophical denial of higher law and devotion to relative values.

Herbert Wechsler, who delivered the Holmes Lectures in 1959, took advantage of the occasion to disagree specifically with Hand's interpretation of the power of judicial review expressed the year before. Wechsler disagreed especially with Hand's assumption that, because it is not specifically provided for in the Constitution, the power of judicial review must be used sparingly. Yet, interestingly enough, his concern with the necessity for the development of neutral principles is indicative of an uneasiness that seems similar to Hand's. Both men accepted the fact that courts do not act upon neutral principles, and both were concerned. They differed in the solutions they thought possible.

Hand had a profound resignation that man is, for the most part, guided by his passions and his self-interest. He believed that, within the limited scope of judicial decisions permitted by his understanding of judicial review, judges are capable of disinterested and rational judgment but that in larger issues involving choice among incommensurable values judges are as likely as others to be guided by their own predilections. Thus he believed that they should refrain from participating in the resolution of such conflicts.

Wechsler, on the other hand, believed that man can choose on the basis of rational principle even in the most fundamental questions. He said:

> ... whether you are tolerant, perhaps more tolerant than I, of the *ad hoc* in politics, with principle reduced to a manipulative tool, are you not also ready to agree that something else is called for from the courts? I put it to you that the main constituent of the judicial process is precisely that it must be genuinely principled, resting with respect to every step

that is involved in reaching judgment on analysis and reasons quite transcending the immediate result that is achieved. . . . But what is crucial, I submit, is not the nature of the question but the nature of the answer that may validly be given by the courts. No legislature or executive is obligated by the nature of its function to support its choice of values by the type of reasoned explanation that I have suggested is intrinsic to judicial action—however much we may admire such a reasoned exposition when we find it in those other realms.[29]

Wechsler's view of the separation of powers appears to be that the different branches of government are obliged to view the same questions on differing bases. Hand believed that the Constitution allocates different kinds of questions to different departments with fundamental policy issues to be resolved by the legislature within its powers as established by the Constitution. Judicial restraint encourages the system to function according to the original design.

While Judge Hand did not expect complete separation of function among the three branches of government, he believed that each fulfilled a unique purpose which should be its first concern and which should be protected. He would have agreed with Charles Hyneman, who said:

> The main business of the judicial branch of government is to settle disputes between litigants, including the dispute between the governmental official who claims to act under authority of law and one of the governed who contends that law does not authorize what the official proposes to do. We cannot allow our courts to be encumbered with any duties that significantly impair their ability to carry out their adjudicatory function.[30]

Hand sought to define the proper role of the courts by first identifying what he assumed to be their primary function and then enlarging this by the addition of activities which seemed appropriate and necessary to the smooth operation of the system and were compatible with the primary judicial role. The meaning of "compatible" is important. Hyneman has said: ". . . there is incompatibility when there is an unwanted impairment of a valued thing. If the Supreme Court's ventures into policy-making seriously impair the quality of its adjudica-

---

[29] Wechsler, "Toward Neutral Principles of Constitutional Law," *Harvard Law Review*, Vol. LXIII (November, 1959), 15–16.
[30] Hyneman, *The Supreme Court on Trial*, 256.

tory acts, or vice versa, the two activities are incompatible."[31] Hyneman believed that until recently there was general agreement that insofar as an incompatibility was found, the Court should withdraw from policy formation but that there no longer seems to be unanimity on this point. He thought that recent activist literature implies that the adjudicatory function of the Supreme Court should give way if necessary to permit judicial enlargement of constitutional guarantees to individuals.

Judge Hand believed that if the courts attempt too much they dissipate their effectiveness and that if they press their own policy views they invite their own destruction. He assumed that the courts should protect their energy and prestige for the adjudicatory function, which only they can serve in the American system. Justice Harlan Stone expressed this position in a letter he wrote to Justice Frankfurter shortly after Justice Black's appointment to the bench:

> [Black] needs guidance from someone who is more familiar with the workings of the judicial process than he is. . . . I am fearful though that he will not avoid the danger of frittering away his opportunity for judicial effectiveness by lack of good technique, and by the desire to express ideas which, however valuable they may be in themselves, are irrelevant or untimely. There are enough present-day battles of importance to be won without wasting our efforts to remake the Constitution *ab initio*, or using the judicial opinion as a political tract.[32]

Herman Pritchett believes that Hand's assertion that the law "must be content to lag behind the best inspiration of its time until it feels behind it the weight of such general acceptance as will give sanction to its pretension to unquestioned dictation"[33] may describe the relationship that does often exist between law and opinion but that this view "cannot possibly be accepted as stating a guide for a judge to follow. What respect could be accorded a court whose justices felt obliged in deciding cases consciously to lag behind the best thought of the time because that thought had not yet won general acceptance."[34]

31 *Ibid.*, 257.

32 Alpheus T. Mason, *Harlan Fiske Stone: Pillar of the Law*, 469.

33 Hand, "The Speech of Justice," *Harvard Law Review*, Vol. XXIX (April, 1916), as reprinted in *The Spirit of Liberty* (3d ed.), 15–16.

34 Walter F. Murphy and C. Herman Pritchett, *Courts, Judges and Politics: An Introduction to the Judicial Process*, 693.

Similarly, Alexander Meiklejohn believed that the Court should play the part of teacher to the community. Hand thought that this position assumed, incorrectly, that the solutions the courts might find to social conflicts would be better than those which would emerge from the legislature and feared that such a role might interfere with the proper discharge of judicial duties. Wallace Mendelson suggested that the idea that the use of the power of judicial review is a desirable instrument for public education "sounds strange in the mouths of its liberal sponsors. By their standards, most of the Court's teaching in this area has been erroneous. But right or wrong, the fate of the 'nine old men' suggests that judicial precept is somewhat less than effective pedagogy."[35]

Hand had a great affinity for all who sought to defend the institutional integrity of the courts and to preserve them against encroachments. He shared Justice Brandeis' careful adherence to jurisdictional and procedural limits which Paul Freund described:

> [Brandeis] would not be seduced by the quixotic temptation to right every fancied wrong which was paraded before him. . . . He steeled himself . . . against the enervating distraction of countless tragedies he was not meant to relieve. His concern for jurisdictional and procedural limits reflected, on the technical level, an essentially Stoic philosophy. For like Epictetus, he recognized "the impropriety of being emotionally affected by what is not under one's control."[36]

Justice Frankfurter found procedural protections useful in maintaining freedom within the limits of the judicial process and believed that liberty was most often achieved through the observance of these safeguards. In procedural matters neither he nor Hand deferred to the political branches of government, for they seemed clearly within the competence of the courts.

While there is some question regarding Justice Holmes's ultimate intention in First Amendment cases, it is clear that he understood that the protection of any particular liberty cannot properly be allowed to distract from the more comprehensive judicial purpose the courts serve.

---

[35] Mendelson, "Mr. Justice Frankfurter—Law and Choice," *Vanderbilt Law Review*, Vol. X (1957), 341.
[36] *Ibid.*, 336, quoting Freund, *On Understanding the Supreme Court*, 65.

Both Holmes and Justice Brandeis rejected the narrow construction of the First Amendment guarantee of freedom of speech in the majority opinion in *Whitney* v. *People of the State of California* but joined in the decision for procedural reasons. They were accused by some of permitting technicalities to stand in the way of justice and of having no appreciation of the great issues involved. Others supposed that they were well aware of the problem but "deemed themselves not free to do Justice, but bound to do justice under law, i.e., in accordance with that very special allocation of function and authority which is the essence of Federalism and the Separation of Powers."[37]

Because Learned Hand was vitally concerned with preserving the integrity, independence, and authority of the federal judiciary, which he regarded as essential to the well-being of the system, he believed that the courts' hallmark must be judicious and impartial decisions so honest and unbiased that their authority is unquestioned. The authority of law as finally announced by a court comes not from the person of the judge or any faction of society but from the belief that the judge, insofar as he has the capacity, voices the will of the community. Restraint limits the scope of judicial decisions to matters that are amenable to judicial determination.

Hand feared that involvement in "political questions" would deprive the judges of their capacity for impartiality and deprive the courts of the people's confidence in their capacity to decide in accordance with the law. He thought it necessary for the judiciary to remain free from political involvement in terms of both strongly partisan political predispositions and subjection to political pressures and expectations. It is as important that the people regard judges as outside the hierarchy of political power, as that they so regard themselves:

> To interject into the [judicial] process the fear of displeasure or the hope of favor of those who can make their will felt, is inevitably to corrupt the event, and could never be proposed by anyone who really comprehended the issue. This was long held a truism, but it must be owned that the edge of our displeasure at its denial has of late been somewhat turned. In the name of a more loyal fealty to the popular will, we are asked to defeat the only means by which that will can become

articulate and be made effective. To this . . . I submit that there is but one answer: an unflinching resistance.[38]

The implications of increased political involvement which Hand feared were suggested in 1965 in Senate Judiciary subcommittee hearings before the confirmation of James P. Coleman as judge of the Fifth Circuit Court of Appeals. The debate did not concern what his friends and enemies alike termed "a brilliant legal mind and a rare combination of legal and political experience."[39] Instead, he was charged with being a dedicated racist certain to use his judicial position to maintain white supremacy in the South. Attorney General Nicholas Katzenbach was so offended by the violent attacks made on Coleman by integrationists that he made an almost unprecedented appearance on his behalf.

Judge Hand was afraid that it might become the normal and commonly accepted procedure to attack or support nominees on the basis of their views on certain issues and perhaps overlook other qualities which either do or do not commend them as federal judges. When the issue of fitness is debated in this fashion, it is difficult if not impossible to appraise a nominee's capacity in judicial rather than political terms. Hand thought that the public might come to regard judicial appointments as politically inspired regardless of the facts. He knew that there had been political appointments to the federal bench in the past, but it seemed to him that they had been the exception rather than the rule and had almost always been regarded with disfavor. It was the possibility that they might come to be regarded as proper that concerned him. He believed that this trend would lead to the loss of public confidence in judicial lack of bias and might ultimately cause a depreciation of the authority of the courts. He thought that the proper test for a judge was judicial competence rather than political belief and that the independence, integrity, and authority of the courts depend upon this difference. Judges are unsupported by bureaucratic structure, and more than other public officials must draw upon their own resources, moral and intellectual, to sustain them in their search for answers to difficult questions.

[38] Hand, "The Contribution of An Independent Judiciary to Civilization," as reprinted in *The Spirit of Liberty* (3d ed.), 157.
[39] *Wichita Eagle*, July 13, 1965, p. 8a.

Writing shortly after the Fortas affair, Robert H. Bork expressed concern that

> The success of the Senate filibuster that kept Justice Abe Fortas from succeeding Earl Warren as Chief Justice was only the latest, but surely the plainest, signal that the U.S. Supreme Court is in the process of descending in national estimation from a position above the battle to the status of a political institution that may, with complete propriety, be attacked and beaten on political grounds. . . . I am . . . concerned . . . with the fact that political retaliation is increasingly regarded as proper. This raises the question of the degree to which the Warren Court has provoked the attacks.[40]

The move to impeach Justice William O. Douglas seems to have been made at least partly in retaliation for the Senate's treatment of two Nixon nominees. Generalizations regarding the basis of the controversies over the William Haynsworth and G. Harold Carswell nominations are difficult, but it does appear that the vulnerability of the Court which provided the opportunity for the Fortas affair invited attacks upon less well qualified candidates. President Nixon's avowed intention to "balance" the Court and his overriding concern for the political qualifications of his nominees at the expense of their moral and intellectual attributes must cause one at least to pause to reconsider Hand's concern for the Court when it assumes responsibility for resolving major substantive policy matters.

A cogent argument can be made that it is undemocratic for nine men, appointed for life and without direct responsibility to the people, to exercise a veto power over the other branches of government, except in the narrowest, most evident, and most urgent cases.[41] This understanding was expressed by Justice Morrison Waite in *Munn* v. *Illinois* when he said: "We know that this [the political power to regulate] . . . may be abused; but that is no argument against its existence. For protection against abuses by legislatures, the people must resort to the polls, not to the courts."[42]

[40] Bork, "The Supreme Court Needs a New Philosophy," *Fortune*, December, 1968, p. 138.
[41] Anthony Lewis, "Justice Frankfurter, Supreme Scholar of the Supreme Court," *Wisdom*, Vol. III, No. 28 (January, 1959), 5.
[42] *Munn* v. *Illinois*, 94 U.S. 113, 134 (1877).

It appears that Judge Hand was completely in accord with Justice Waite's views, for he too thought it better to let some problems go unsolved than to place the ultimate decision in the hands of a "bevy of Platonic Guardians" who are not responsible to the will of the people and who, perhaps unconsciously, represent the privileged group from which they are largely drawn. He had a profound appreciation of the democratic process and the ability of the people and their representatives to make choices. He could see no justification for upsetting the delicate balance achieved by legislation in the name of greater justice or equality decreed by an institution that is intentionally non-representative.

Judge Hand accepted the judgment of James Bradley Thayer that frequent resort to judicial review is indicative of distrust or lack of confidence in the legislature. Arguments in favor of judicial review appear to be based on the assumption that the popular branches of government cannot be trusted to refrain from abuse of the powers that have been given them. Wallace Mendelson has suggested that commitment to democracy in America is limited by a somewhat inarticulate distrust of it, as is indicated by the

> concentration in a single agency—significantly, that farthest removed from the people—of power to override all other elements of government, whether at the national, state, or local level. Neither Congress nor the President, no administrative agency, no governor, no state court or legislature . . . is immune from the centralized power of judicial review.[43]

It was important to Hand that the courts exercise restraint partly because judges are not directly responsible to the public but more importantly because in the American system they should not be responsive to the immediate will of the people. Representation is the function of the legislature, and the people are free to bring whatever pressure or influence they can in the political resolution of issues. But when these same pressures and influences, no matter how sophisticated and subtle are brought to bear upon the nation's judges, they constitute an attack upon the judges' judicial competence and integrity. It is as much the responsibility of the judges to resist this pressure as it is the obligation of the legislator to take it into account.

[43] Mendelson, *Justices Black and Frankfurter*, 126.

Hand acknowledged that the system did not provide a strict majoritarian democracy when he said that "in a pitilessly consistent democracy judges would not be making law at all."[44] He knew that in the political branches it is often the stronger or "major force" which had the determining voice. He also said that the founders might have left policy choices to the judges "like the Judges of Israel," but the point he emphasized was that it is precisely the division of function between policymaking and judicial interpretation that the Constitution intended to spell out and separate. So, while he would agree that one might have a democratic society in which the judges did exercise a major policy-making function, this explicitly is not the system provided by the American Constitution.

Hand's theory of restraint suggests that the relative finality of judicial decisions in constitutional cases creates an obligation to limit the use of the power of judicial review. While the courts may restrain the powers of others, there is no institution which similarly guards the boundaries of the courts. He regarded judicial restraint as one example of the great self-discipline that a democratic way of life demands of its citizens. Perhaps it is one of the most difficult, for with the power to decide goes the knowledge that a court's judgment is final and beyond correction or reversal except in rare instances. His practice followed his theory, and in constitutional matters he was "unwaveringly faithful to his creed about the limited role of judges in a democracy."[45]

While the relative finality of judicial decisions in constitutional freedoms can be supported in one sense and especially in terms of the short run, it can also be argued that no decision of the Court has long prevailed if it ran against the main stream of public sentiment. It may be that Hand failed to take into account the executive and congressional checks upon the courts that are provided by the Constitution. These may well be adequate to guarantee that courts will be responsible and representative although they are not directly chosen by the people. The restructuring of the Court in the late 1960's and early 1970's has supported this thesis.

[44] Hand, "The Contribution of an Independent Judiciary to Civilization," as reprinted in *The Spirit of Liberty* (3d ed.), 158.
[45] Frank "Some Reflections on Judge Learned Hand," *Chicago Law Review*, Vol. XXIV (1957), 638.

James Bradley Thayer exercised a profound and lasting influence on Learned Hand. Jerome Frank has written that in all Thayer's teachings he stressed the importance of the democratic idea of government by the people believing that the American Constitution anticipated an adult, mature society "in which no one will play father to the citizens, treating them like children."[46]

Frank agreed with this thesis, which he found reflected in Hand's essay "Democracy: Its Presumptions and Realities," and suggested that Herald J. Berman's discussion of Soviet justice provides an indication of where the opposite theory may lead. Berman says that the underlying assumption in Russia is that the

> subject of law, legal man, is not a mature, independent adult . . . but an immature, dependent child or youth, whose law-consciousness must be guided, trained, and disciplined by official legal rules and processes. . . . The Soviet lawmaker or judge is like a parent. . . . [that legal system] may best be characterized as a system of "parental law" in which people are treated . . . as immature, dependent youths . . . for whom rights . . . are . . . gifts. . . . [It is] dangerous not because it is lacking in law and justice, but rather because it is developing a new type of law which, while helping to satisfy men's need for justice in their personal and social relations, is reconcilable with political and ideological tyranny . . . [for it rests on the basis that rights] are conferred by the state as a matter of grace.[47]

Hand followed Thayer in his insistence that the courts cannot be relied upon to save a society or to preserve its freedom, but Hand's interpretation of Thayer is not necessarily the only legitimate one, according to Frank, who prefers the one he believes that Holmes, Brandeis, and Stone followed, which allows the court to deny the presumptive validity of legislation which invades freedom of speech or religious worship.[48] In the Carolene Products case Stone suggested that

[46] *Ibid.*, 686.

[47] Harold J. Berman, *Soviet Justice and Soviet Tyranny*, quoted in Frank, "Some Reflections on Judge Learned Hand," *Chicago Law Review*, Vol. XXIV (1957), 687.

[48] Frank believes that Holmes and Brandeis, who were charged with applying a double standard, were faced with a "dilemma from which, verbally, they never exited." Stone invented a formula for the exit which Frank believes was implicit in Thayer's teachings— that the "vice of judicial demolition of legislation was that it prevented public discussion of policies, thereby keeping the people from attaining that political maturity which democracy required." *Ibid.*, 691.

when a statute impeded the democratic process there should be a presumption of invalidity.[49]

In his tribute to Justice Stone, Hand ignored this explicit acknowledgment of the dichotomy between free speech and property cases and assumed that Holmes, Brandeis, and Stone had each followed his own interpretation of Thayer's teaching.[50] Frank wrote that "Judge Hand, in his account of Stone's constitutional views, disclosed a surprising blind spot—at precisely the point where Stone's views strikingly differed from his own."[51] Hand's position does not appear to be completely without foundation, however, because Stone also wrote:

> My more conservative brethren in the old days [read their preferences into legislation and] into the Constitution as well. What they did placed in jeopardy a great and useful institution of government. The pendulum has now swung to the other extreme, and history is repeating itself. The Court is now in as much danger of becoming a legislative and Constitution-making body, enacting into law its own predilections, as it was then.[52]

Judicial restraint has been objected to on two grounds, which are themselves representative of conflicting views of the role of the courts. It has been argued that undue exercise of restraint fails to take into account the value of slowing down the political process by providing a brake upon the majority until the wisdom of its policies can be further considered or a more comprehensive consensus developed in support of them. A primary consideration in favor of a system of checks and balances provided by the separation of powers was to prevent precipitous action by a majority, and the courts are admirably suited to perform this function. This argument against restraint generally prevailed until the shift in the Court occurred in 1937. Activists are now more inclined to argue that the Court is well suited to move ahead of popular consensus and to serve as the motor of the community, to add impetus if

[49] *United States* v. *Carolene Products Co.*, 304 U.S. 144, 152–53 (1938).

[50] Hand, "Chief Justice Stone's Concept of the Judicial Function," *Columbia Law Review*, Vol. LVII (September, 1946), as reprinted in *The Spirit of Liberty* (1st ed.), 201.

[51] Frank, "Some Reflections on Judge Learned Hand," *Chicago Law Review*, Vol. XXIV (1957), 693.

[52] Mendelson, *Justices Black and Frankfurter*, 118, quoting Alpheus T. Mason, *Security Through Freedom* (Ithaca, N.Y., Cornell University Press, 1955), 145-46.

not to create or originate movement in the direction of certain desirable community goals.

Hand insisted that the very fact that these two opposing arguments can be made against judicial restraint suggests support for his position that to participate in the resolution of basic issues necessarily places the judges in the position of making choices in matters which are incommensurable and which in a democracy should be left to the representative or political departments of government. His position does not offer any solution, however, to a society which needs either a brake or a motor that is not supplied by some other institution.

In an article which defends judicial activism as an affirmatively democratic process, Eugene V. Rostow took issue explicitly with Learned Hand and his "monkish rule of complete abstinence."[53] He believed that the position that judicial review is undemocratic rests upon the erroneous assumption that the Constitution should be permitted to develop without judicial check. This would permit the legislature and the executive to determine the course of its development, a process which would be appropriate in a parliamentary system such as that of Great Britain but is completely inappropriate in the United States. In direct opposition to Hand's position, he reasoned that, since the purpose of the Constitution is to assure a free and democratic society and since the Constitution places certain rights beyond the reach of government, it is within the direct allocation of power to the judiciary to protect the citizens from any encroachments upon these constitutionally guaranteed freedoms. He said:

> It is error to insist that no society is democratic unless it has a government of unlimited powers, and that no government is democratic unless its legislature has unlimited powers. Constitutional review by an independent judiciary is a tool of proven use in the American quest for an open society of widely dispersed powers.[54]

It might appear that Hand's high regard for experience would have led him to accept judicial activism as a useful pragmatic technique. It seems clear, however, that he believed its full impact could not be

---

[53] Rostow, "The Democratic Character of Judicial Review," *Harvard Law Review,* Vol. XLVI, No. 2 (December, 1952), 214.

[54] *Ibid.,* 199.

known until the implications of what he regarded as arbitrary decisions without consistency or justifications were understood by the people and their reactions felt in terms of challenge or support for the Court's authority to pursue an active role in the resolution of basic issues. He believed that the evidence was not all in and that the ultimate danger of judicial activism to the system in terms of loss of confidence and authority was greater than the long-run benefit. He believed that there are several factors which might contribute to the erosion of judicial authority: loss of the judicial mystique of the Court as an unbiased interpreter of the law; politicization of the Court through its participation in major policy questions; an attempt by the Court to become a rule-making body rather than an adjudicatory agency so that many of its rules would go generally unenforced; increasing numbers of dissenting opinions which would tend to destroy the force of its judgments; direct conflicts with other branches of government regarding their constitutional power; and group-by-group alienation as far-reaching decisions sought to resolve or reverse political issues disappointed different segments of the public. These factors do appear to have been present and to account at least in part for a potential reconstitution of the Court. It is too early to tell whether or not changes now in progress will bring renewed confidence in the Court by the American public. Judge Hand understood that the evolution of institutions was a long process but feared that it might not be possible to reverse a trend of critical deterioration in confidence in the courts should it occur.

CHAPTER XII : *Reflections*

That Learned Hand was a great judge is almost universally agreed. He has properly been compared favorably with Justices Holmes, Brandeis, and Benjamin Cardozo,[1] but there remains a question about the residue of greatness that was uniquely his—the contributions he made to American life and thought which distinguish him from other great jurists who were his contemporaries. What was it about Learned Hand the man, the citizen, the judge, and the philosopher that made these contributions possible?

It may have been his profound devotion to his fundamental assumptions and his seemingly relentless effort to live and be guided by them. It may have been his pragmatic philosophy which prepared him magnificently to hold strongly to these beliefs which he thought were justified by experience and yet fortified him with an open mind, a comprehension of the tentativeness of all man's knowledge, tolerance, and humility before contrary beliefs. There can be no doubt about his courage in facing what he understood to be dilemmas of a democratic system or of his attachment to that system as he understood it.

Perhaps more than anything else, Learned Hand posed searching and fundamental questions which irritate the arrogant and trouble the thoughtful. The consistency with which he insisted upon the relativity of man-made values posed in sharp relief the problem of such a philosophy. It is a fundamental question of twentieth-century America. Can

---

[1] "No oracular gifts are required for the prophecy that when the history of American law in the first half of this century comes to be written, four Judges will tower above the rest—Holmes, Brandeis, Cardozo and Learned Hand." Judge Henry F. Friendly, "Learned Hand: An Expression from the Second Circuit," *Brooklyn Law Review*, Vol. XXIX (December, 1962), 6.

a democratic society endure without common acceptance and defense of some ultimate values? Are tolerance and skepticism an adequate foundation? The problem is as relevant and imperative for contemporary man as it is for his society. In his review of *The Spirit of Liberty*, George Wharton Pepper suggested a sense of the inadequacy implicit in a philosophy of relative values when it applies not to a political community but to an individual. It was especially disconcerting to Pepper because he did not think that the skepticism and tolerance expressed by Hand as his personal view about ultimate values was adequate to account for the Learned Hand he knew and admired so warmly. Half in lament and half in consternation he wrote:

> If this were merely a commendation of tolerance of the opinions of others, it might readily be heeded by a convinced believer in (say) the teachings of Nicene Christianity. But if it is intended as a complete statement of a man's whole faith, one is left wondering how in practice it can prove itself to be an effective substitute for convictions and fixed beliefs. As a statement of judicial attitude it is admirable. . . . But the Learned Hand who is beloved and admired by this reviewer and by a great circle of other friends—and who has as many fine qualities as any man I know—must (it seems to me) have within him sources of conviction and wellsprings of feeling far deeper and more soul-satisfying than the faith which he so sincerely proclaims. A man willing "to assure unimpeded utterance to every opinion" might have no beliefs of his own; but unless he had within him things more true and deep than he himself is aware of, he could not be a Learned Hand. Skepticism has had a large part to play, but I feel sure it is only a part of the drama of his life.[2]

There may be no satisfying answer to this profound insight, which questions the pragmatic philosophy to which Hand adhered. There can be no doubt that Hand did have beliefs of his own—beliefs held strongly enough to provide the basis of action in his personal and professional life. His high intelligence and his capacity for tolerance, self-discipline, and self-restraint may have been the qualities which permitted him as an individual to be stout in his defense of his own position and yet understand that it was a matter of personal choice and not necessarily

[2] George Wharton Pepper, review of *The Spirit of Liberty: Papers and Addresses of Learned Hand*, *Yale Law Journal*, Vol. LXII (December, 1962), 135–36.

of universal validity. The strength of character that Pepper knew to be a part of Learned Hand came from his own personally chosen values which were deeply held. Some men who are willing "to assume unimpeded utterance to every opinion" may not have beliefs of their own.

Learned Hand had a rare capacity to distinguish between his personal philosophy and his duties and responsibilities as a judge in the American democratic system—even when that personal philosophy involved his understanding of the role of the judge in society. He knew that his concept of the judicial function had not prevailed; and though he believed that he was right, he understood that, as a judge acting within the framework of the judicial hierarchy, he was bound by the higher court, precedent, and tradition. His opinions are sprinkled with personal protests which gave way to the wisdom of others whom he regarded as properly able to direct and confine the limits of his choice. On the other hand, whenever his specific duty as a judge did not constitute an overriding obligation, he expressed with conviction and enthusiasm his philosophy and his personal conception of the role of the judge in American society. Even in his opinions he was guided by them as consistently as was human insofar as higher authority did not dictate otherwise.

This distinction between personal belief and duty is apparent in Learned Hand's comments about the principles embodied in the First Amendment when those found in his cases are compared with those drawn from his essays and speeches. They appear to represent not so much an inconsistency in his thought as a reflection of his understanding of the function as a judge and the hierarchy of values by which he arrived at decisions in cases at bar.

The essays and speeches reflect his most profound thoughts about the nature of the Constitution and its place in the American system unencrusted by the gloss of decades of court decisions and historical development. It was his appraisal of what "might" or "should" have been, presented in unequivocal terms. In these writings he was free of the stringent obligations of the judge to hierarchy and precedent. In his opinions he felt bound to render decisions in as close congruity to the views of the Supreme Court as he was capable of. Compare, for example, his assertions that the general principles of the Bill of Rights consist of "cautionary warnings against the intemperance of faction and the first approaches of despotism" or "stately admonitions [which] refuse to subject themselves to analysis"; or that they are to be read as "admonitory or hortatory, not definite enough to be guides on concrete occasions"; with his statement in *Dennis*:

> If the defendants had in fact so confined their teaching and advocacy [so that it did not include violent overthrow of government], the First Amendment would indubitably protect them, for its [sic] protects all utterances, individual or concerted, seeking constitutional changes, however revolutionary, by the processes which the Constitution provides.[3]

A corresponding distinction appears in Hand's personal reflections upon the proper role of a judge in the American system and that role in the system as it actually operates. When called upon to make a judgment in a case involving the First Amendment he said:

> In application of such a standard courts may strike a wrong balance; they may tolerate "incitements" which they should forbid; they may repress utterances they should allow; but that is a responsibility that they cannot avoid. Abdication is as much a failure of duty, as indifference is a failure to protect primal rights.[4]

McGeorge Bundy recognized Hand's "devotion to the sternest standards of his trade" and his capacity to divorce his personal views regarding the role of the courts from his obligations as a judge in the federal system when he wrote, "Who else . . . could have reset the language of clear-and-present-danger to make it effective in the world as it is, while at the same time looking skeptically at the whole line of law from which he worked?"[5] Karl Llewellyn emphasized that the fine temper of Hand's mind was a product of his necessity to deal with the tension between his personal philosophy and his strong sense of obligation to his duty as a judge as he understood it:

> His . . . philosophy must, of course, be read against his judicial decisions . . . . he had to wrestle, as for example Mill did not, with the problems of weighing the costs of freedom against its gains, and with the labor of modifying even his own precious single ideal value to take

[3] *United States* v. *Dennis*, 183 F. (2d) 201, 206 (1950).

[4] *Ibid.*, 212.

[5] McGeorge Bundy, review of *The Bill of Rights*, by Learned Hand, *Yale Law Journal*, Vol. LXVII (April, 1958), 949.

account of other values. In these papers—cumulating into "The Spirit of Liberty"—the forces which might limit freedom of expression might seem to be only forces of sect or faction or bigotry; but in the whole range of the man's work, especially in his last years on the bench, one would have to recognize his clean tackling (in the teeth of his own articulate philosophy) of the deeper question of when and how far the values of freedom must yield to the needs of the society on which, and for which, the recent and delicate plant of freedom grows.[6]

Without forgetting the consummate skill Learned Hand brought to the art of judging and his devotion to the highest standards of his trade—achievements which may well have been the source of his greatest personal satisfaction[7]—or ignoring his literary genius, which, though controlled and constrained by the judicial need for simplicity and clarity, "lend to the final saying overtones, sparkle, fragrance,"[8] or the other attributes, both personal and professional for which he is called great, it must be noted that he will also be remembered and honored for restructuring the dialogue about restraint and activism in judicial review so that both must be defended on the basis of the fundamental assumptions about the American democratic system. He sought to

> distill from the decisions [of the Court] . . . conclusions of the widest sort about the nature of justice in our society. . . . [he suggested] that those who would study the relationship between justice and liberty in

[6] K. N. Llewellyn, review of *The Spirit of Liberty: Papers and Addresses of Learned Hand*, *University of Chicago Law Review*, Vol. XX (Spring, 1953), 611.

[7] "His stature as a judge stemmed not so much from the few great cases that inevitably came to him over the years, even on what he delighted to call an 'inferior' court, as from the great way in which he dealt with a multitude of little cases, covering almost every subject in the legal lexicon. Repeatedly he would make the tiniest glow-worm illumine a whole field. I can give testimony how often, having found myself mired in some morass of admiralty, or of copyright or patent law, an opinion, or perhaps only a paragraph or even a sentence, of Judge Hand's, has guided me to firm ground. He did not invent issues that were not there, but his microscope was so powerful and his focus so accurate, that he could see in the slide before him shadings that had altogether escaped the attention of lesser men. Once he had identified the true issue, he would wrestle with it, and worry over the way to decide it, and then would forge his thought into steel sharper and more resilient than Damascus ever made." Friendly, "Learned Hand: An Expression from the Second Circuit," *Brooklyn Law Review*, Vol. XXIX (December, 1962), 13.

[8] Llewellyn, review of "The Spirit of Liberty," *University of Chicago Law Review*, Vol. XX (Spring, 1963), 612.

America must lift their eyes from the cases and consider the whole process of society. . . . [he remembered] that those decisions are not all of society.[9]

It was primarily in his essays and speeches that Hand most dramatically challenged judicial activism and demanded that it be defended upon some neutral basis. Most debates about the scope of judicial review have been guided by personal commitments to the legislation in question or by

> whose ox is being gored at the moment [but] . . . Judge Learned Hand falls outside these traditional patterns. His discussion is lucid and temperate. His attack upon much of what has become traditional judicial review appears to stem not from his personal reaction to the pattern of decisions or the statutes which have been reviewed but from two separate factors. In the first place, long experience as a judge has given him a genuine sense of modesty about the role of judges in society. . . . In the second place, he believes that judicial review is inconsistent with the essentials of a democratic society.[10]

One critic has suggested that Hand therewith disclosed that "his is an aseptic mind, surgically clean and morally sterile. As a lawyer and judge, his concern is only with the skillful use of his professional tools. His mind and interests, insofar as he is a judge, are amoral and non-political."[11] Another believed that

> Judge Hand has contributed to clarity of analysis by reminding us that the relevant comparison is not between the enduring values of free inquiry and expression on the one hand, and transitory measures for the control of property on the other; the problem is harder than that. We are obliged to compare the ultimate values of property with those of free inquiry and expression, or to compare the legislative compromises in the two realms; for laws dealing with libel or sedition or sound trucks or a non-political civil service are as truly adjustments and accommodations as are laws fixing prices or making grants of monopolies.

9 Bundy, review of *The Bill of Rights*, *Yale Law Journal*, Vol. LXVII (April, 1958), 944, 949.
10 Edward L. Barrett, Jr., review of *The Bill of Rights*, by Learned Hand, *California Law Review*, Vol. XLVI (1958), 859–60.
11 Milton R. Konvitz, review of *The Bill of Rights*, by Learned Hand, *Cornell Law Quarterly*, Vol. XLIV (1959), 291.

Judge Hand's insistence on equality of values in constitutional decisions can be matched by a persistent current of political thought.[12]

Hand was criticized, if gently so, by some who chided him for devoting so much thought and energy to defending a position of judicial abnegation, "which has been irrevocably decided [against] by a century and a half of practice,"[13] so that his arguments seemed somehow to be wrong or out of joint. This view failed to take into account Hand's purpose in reviewing the historical conditions surrounding the evolution of judicial review—a purpose which Wechsler seemed to understand fully. Hand was examining the justification for judicial review as a basis for reasoning about just those things that Barrett charged him with ignoring:

> . . . what should be its scope and intensity of its application. How far should the courts go in reexamining legislative choices? Should they apply different standards in testing legislative interferences with economic liberties than they do personal liberties? How fast should the courts go in making their influence felt? What techniques should they use? Is there value in using traditional judicial techniques and keeping reasonably within bounds of precedent or should the primary interest be in achieving a "just" result?[14]

Wechsler, understanding this, attacked Hand's more fundamental position regarding judicial review.[15] Bundy, aware of the elemental nature of the issue as drawn by Hand, wrote: "Yet, even if Judge Hand is wrong in the end, he puts many things sharply right along the way. First, he is right in his appeal to history—the Constitution as it was is parent, at least, to what it is; without a past it has no serious present. Second, he is right in his persistent concern for craftsmanship."[16]

It may be Learned Hand's challenge to comfortable conformity, to unearned belief, to the smug satisfaction that the American democratic

---

[12] Paul A. Freund, *The Supreme Court of the United States*, 34–35.

[13] Barrett, review of *The Bill of Rights*, by Learned Hand, *California Law Review*, Vol. XLVI (1958), 861.

[14] *Ibid.*, 861–62.

[15] Wechsler, "Toward Neutral Principles of Constitutional Law," *Harvard Law Review*, Vol. LXXIII (November, 1959), 2–5.

[16] Bundy, review of *The Bill of Rights*, by Learned Hand, *Yale Law Journal*, Vol. LXVII (April, 1958), 949.

system is preordained to succeed even without discipline and self-restraint, to the easy acceptance of those dogmas that seem to support personal prejudices that is his most distinguishing characteristic.[17] Yet it was achieved without harshness or vindictiveness but in the spirit of one deeply involved and concerned with the success of the common enterprise. After much thoughtful reflection about him, Jerome Frank, a close colleague and friend, wrote:

> Being human, he has his faults. . . . But no other judge has contributed so much of enduring value to his civilization. To borrow the words of Anatole France, "We owe him the gratitude due to minds that have fought against prejudices. . . . Men are rare who are free from the prejudices of their period, and look squarely at what the crowd dares not face." Judge Hand has a kind of courage seldom described and too seldom manifested—the courage to accept the fact that, as man is but a finite creature, there are some incurable defects in the solution of most human problems, and that life presents to us challenging uncertainties. This fact does not daunt him, soften him into a flabby defeatist, or harden him into a crusty cynic. A true liberal, he is no dogmatist.[18]

Bundy surely captured much of the portent and essence of Judge Learned Hand's contribution to American democracy when he mused, ". . . if Judge Hand be wrong, what is right?"[19]

[17] On Hand's seventy-fifth birthday the editors of the *Federal Bar Journal* dedicated an issue to him, saying, ". . . we acknowledge a long standing indebtedness to you for bringing to the law and there maintaining an abhorrence of dogma, a constant challenging of first principles, an instinct, intellect, and wisdom not heretofore known, and most important, a knowledge of, an application of the knowledge of the proper function of a judge in a democratic society." Editors, "To Judge Learned Hand," *Federal Bar Journal*, Vol. VIII, No. 2 (January, 1947), 189.

[18] Frank, "Some Reflections on Judge Learned Hand," *Chicago Law Review*, Vol. XXIV (1957), 703.

[19] Bundy, review of *The Bill of Rights*, by Learned Hand, *Yale Law Journal*, Vol. LXVII (April, 1958), 949.

Bibliography

Public Documents

Fair Labor Standards Act, 52 Stat. 1067 (1938) 29, U.S.C. (1940).
I U.S. *Statutes at Large*.

Books

Aristotle. "Nicomachean Ethics," *The Basic Works of Aristotle*. Ed. by Richard McKeon. New York, Random House, 1941.

Barker, Ernest, trans. *The Politics of Aristotle*. Oxford, Clarendon Press, 1946.

———. *Traditions of Civility*. Cambridge, Cambridge University Press, 1948.

Barrett, William, and Henry D. Aiken. *Philosophy in the Twentieth Century*, Vol. III. New York, Random House, 1962.

Bickel, Alexander M. *The Least Dangerous Branch*. New York, Bobbs-Merrill Company, Inc., 1962.

Boorstin, Daniel J. *The Genius of American Politics*. Chicago, University of Chicago Press, 1953.

Brecht, Arnold. *Political Theory: The Foundations of Twentieth Century Political Thought*. Princeton, New Jersey, Princeton University Press, 1959.

Cahn, Edmond. *The Moral Decision: Right and Wrong in the Light of American Law*. Bloomington, Indiana, Indiana University Press, 1956.

Chafee, Zechariah, Jr. *Free Speech in the United States*. Cambridge, Massachusetts, Harvard University Press, 1948.

Corwin, Edward S. *The "Higher Law" Background of American Constitutional Law*. Ithaca, New York, Cornell University Press, Great Seal Books, 1955.

Danielski, David J. *A Supreme Court Justice is Appointed*. New York, Random House, Inc., 1964.

Frank, Jerome. *Courts on Trial: Myths and Reality in American Justice*. New York, Atheneum, 1963.

236

Freund, Paul A. *On Understanding the Supreme Court*. Boston, Little Brown & Company, 1949.

———. *The Supreme Court of the United States*. New York, World Publishing Company, 1965.

Gray, John Chipman. *The Nature and Sources of the Law*. Boston, Beacon Press, 1909.

Haines, Charles Grove. *The Revival of Natural Law Concepts*. Cambridge, Harvard University Press, 1930.

Hamilton, Alexander, John Jay, and James Madison. *The Federalist: A Commentary on the Constitution of the United States*. New York, Modern Library Edition.

Hand, Learned. *The Bill of Rights*. Intro. by Charles E. Wyzanski, Jr. New York, Atheneum, 1964.

———. *The Spirit of Liberty: Papers and Addresses of Learned Hand*. Coll. and ed. by Irving Dilliard, New York, Alfred A. Knopf, 1st ed., 1952; 2d ed., 1963.

Jaffa, Harry V. "The Nature and Origin of the American Party System," *Political Parties, U.S.A.* Chicago, Rand McNally & Company, 1961.

James, William. "Pragmatism's Conception of Truth," *Pragmatism*. Cleveland, World Publishing Co., 1955.

Kalven, Harry, Jr. "The Metaphysics of the Law of Obscenity," *The Supreme Court Review*, 1960. Ed. by Philip B. Kurland. Chicago, University of Chicago Press, 1960.

Lippmann, Walter. *The Public Philosophy*. New York, New American Library of World Literature, Inc., 1955.

McCloskey, Robert G. "Economic Due Process and The Supreme Court: An Exhumation and Reburial," *The Supreme Court Review*, 1962. Ed. by Philip B. Kurland. Chicago, University of Chicago Press, 1962.

MacIver, R. M. *The Web of Government*. New York, Macmillan Company, 1947.

Mason, Alpheus T. *Harlan Fiske Stone: Pillar of the Law*. New York, Viking Press, 1956.

Mendelson, Wallace. *Justices Black and Frankfurter: Conflict in the Court*. Chicago, University of Chicago Press, 1961.

Murphy, Walter F., and C. Herman Pritchett. *Courts, Judges and Politics: An Introduction to the Judicial Process*. New York, Random House, 1961.

Pritchett, C. Herman. *The American Constitution*. New York, McGraw-Hill Book Company, Inc., 1959.

———. *Congress Versus the Supreme Court*. Minneapolis, University of Minnesota Press, 1961.

Smith, John E. *The Spirit of American Philosophy*. New York, Oxford
  University Press, 1963.
Swisher, Carl Brent. *The Supreme Court in Modern Role*. New York, New
  York University Press, 1958.

Articles and Periodicals

"The Antitrust Campaign," *Fortune*, Vol. XXXVIII (July, 1948), 6367.
Barrett, Edward L., Jr. Review of *The Bill of Rights*, by Learned Hand, *California Law Review*, Vol. XLVI (1958), 859–62.
Berle, A. A., Jr. Review of *The Spirit of Liberty: Papers and Addresses of
  Learned Hand*, *Columbia Law Review*, Vol. LII, No. 6 (June, 1952),
  811–15.
Bork, Robert H. "The Supreme Court Needs a New Philosophy," *Fortune*,
  December, 1968, pp. 138–78.
Bundy, McGeorge. Review of *The Bill of Rights*, by Learned Hand, *Yale
  Law Journal*, Vol. LXVII (April, 1958), 944–49.
Burger, Warren E. "Judicial Restraint, Criminal Justice," *New York Times
  Magazine*, October 5, 1969.
Chirelstein, Marvin A. "Learned Hand's Contribution to the Law of Tax
  Avoidance," *Yale Law Journal*, Vol. LXXVII (1968), 440–74.
Cohen, Felix. "Transcendental Nonsense and the Functional Approach,"
  Columbia Law Review, Vol. XXXVI (1935), 809–49.
Cox, Archibald. "Judge Learned Hand and the Interpretation of Statutes,"
  Harvard Law Review, Vol. LX (February, 1947), 370–93.
Davidson, Bill. "Judge Learned Hand: Titan of the Law," *Coronet*, Vol.
  XXVI (September, 1949), 108–14.
Editors. "To Judge Learned Hand," *Federal Bar Journal*, Vol. VIII, No. 2
  (January, 1947), 189.
Frank, Jerome. "Some Reflections on Judge Learned Hand," *Chicago Law
  Review*, Vol. XXIV (1957), 666–705.
Frank, John P. Review of *The Bill of Rights*, by Learned Hand, *Tulane Law
  Review*, Vol. XXXII (June, 1958), 790–94.
———. "The Top U.S. Commercial Court," *Fortune*, Vol. XLIII (January,
  1951), 92–96ff.
Frankfurter, Felix. "Judge Learned Hand," *Harvard Law Review*, Vol. LX
  (February, 1947), 325–29.
———. "Learned Hand," *Harvard Law Review*, Vol. LXXV, No. 1 (November, 1961), 1–4.
Friendly, Henry F. "Learned Hand: An Expression from the Second Circuit," *Brooklyn Law Review*, Vol. XXIX (December, 1962), 6–15.

"From the Wisdom of Felix Frankfurter," *Wisdom*, Vol. III, No. 28 (January, 1959), 24–30.

Gressman, Eugene. "With Vision and Grace," *New Republic*, Vol. CXXVI (June 2, 1952), 19.

Hamburger, Philip. "The Great Judge," *Life*, Vol. XXI (November 4, 1946), 116–25.

Hand, Learned. "The Commodities Clause and the Fifth Amendment," *Harvard Law Review*, Vol. XXII, No. 4 (February, 1909), 250–65.

———. "Due Process of Law and the Eight-Hour Day," *Harvard Law Review*, XXI, No. 7 (May, 1908), 495–509.

———. Review of *Collected Legal Papers*, by Oliver Wendell Holmes, *Political Science Quarterly*, Vol. XXXVI, No. 3 (September, 1921), 528–30.

Jaffe, Louis L. Review of *The Spirit of Liberty: Papers and Addresses of Learned Hand*, *Harvard Law Review*, Vol. LXVI, No. 5 (March, 1953), 939–43.

Judd, Orrin G. "Judge Learned Hand and the Criminal Law," *Harvard Law Review*, Vol. LX (February, 1947), 405–22.

Konvitz, Milton R. Review of *The Bill of Rights*, by Learned Hand, *Cornell Law Quarterly*, Vol. XLIV (1959), 291–93.

Kurland, Philip B. "Earl Warren, The 'Warren Court,' and the Warren Myths," *Michigan Law Review*, Vol. LXVII, No. 2 (December, 1968), 353–57.

———. Review of *The Bill of Rights*, by Learned Hand, *Yale Review*, Vol. XLVII (June, 1958), 596–99.

———. "U.S. Supreme Court Forges Justice with Links of Past," *Wichita Eagle and Beacon*, September 21, 1969, p. 1b.

"The Law," *Time*, Vol. LXV (May 30, 1955), 13.

Lewis, Anthony. "Justice Frankfurter, Supreme Scholar of the Supreme Court," *Wisdom*, Vol. III, No. 28 (January, 1959).

Llewellyn, K. N. Review of *The Spirit of Liberty: Papers and Addresses of Learned Hand*, *University of Chicago Law Review*, Vol. XX (Spring, 1953), 611–12.

McCloskey, Robert G. "Reflections on the Warren Court," *Virginia Law Review*, Vol. LI (November, 1965), 1229–70.

Mendelson, Wallace. "Mr. Justice Frankfurter—Law and Choice," *Vanderbilt Law Review*, Vol. X (1957), 333–50.

Pepper, George Wharton. Review of *The Spirit of Liberty: Papers and Addresses of Learned Hand*, *Yale Law Journal*, Vol. LXII (December, 1952), 35–36.

Philbin, Stephen H. "Judge Learned Hand and the Law of Patents and Copyrights," *Harvard Law Review*, Vol. LX (February, 1947), 394–404.

Rodell, Fred. "Crux of the Court Hullabaloo," *New York Times Magazine*, May 29, 1960, 13ff.

Rostow, Eugene V. "The Democratic Character of Judicial Review," *Harvard Law Review*, Vol. XLVI, No. 2 (December, 1952), 193–224.

Schmidhauser, John R. "The Justices of the Supreme Court: A Collective Portrait," *Midwest Journal of Political Science*, Vol. III (February, 1959), 1–49.

Strout, Richard L. "Warren Court Philosophy Under Assault: Chief Justice Burger Shapes a Record Living Up to Nixon's Expectations," *Christian Science Monitor*, April 3, 1970, p. 1.

Wechsler, Herbert. "Toward Neutral Principles of Constitutional Law," *Harvard Law Review*, Vol. LXXIII (November, 1959), 1–35.

Wyzanski, Charles E., Jr. "Judge Learned Hand's Contribution to Public Law," *Harvard Law Review*, Vol. LX (February, 1947), 348–69.

———. "Learned Hand," *Atlantic Monthly*, Vol. CCVIII, No. 6 (December, 1961), 54–58.

Unpublished Material

Pritchett, C. Herman. "The Judicial Revolution and American Democracy." Paper presented at the University of Kentucky Centennial Conference, April 9, 1965.

Table of Cases

241

Helvering, Commissioner of Internal Revenue v. *Gregory*, 69 F. (2d) 809 (1934).

Herndon v. *State of Georgia*, 295 U.S. 441 (1935).

Higgins v. *Smith*, 308 U.S. 473 (1940).

Jacobellis v. *Ohio*, 378 U.S. 184 (1964).

Kittle, 180 Fed. 946 (1910).

Knetsch v. *United States*, 364 U.S. 361 (1960).

Lawton v. *Steele*, 152 U.S. 133 (1894).

Lehigh Valley Coal Co. v. *Yensavage*, 218 Fed. 547 (1914).

Lenroot v. *Western Union Telegraph Co.*, 141 F. (2d) 400 (1944).

Loewi v. *Ryan*, 229 F. (2d) 627 (1956).

Loubriel v. *United States*, 9 F. (2d) 807 (1926).

Marbury v. *Madison*, 1 Cranch 137 (1803).

Masses Publishing Co. v. *Patten*, 244 Fed. 535 (1917).

Minersville School District v. *Gobitis*, 310 U.S. 586 (1940).

Munn v. *Illinois*, 94 U.S. 113 (1877).

Murray's Lessee v. *Hoboken Land and Improvement Co.*, 18 Howard 272 (1856).

National Labor Relations Board v. *American Tube Bending Co.*, 134 F. (2d) 993 (1943).

National Labor Relations Board v. *Federbush Co.*, 121 F. (2d) 954 (1941).

Nichols v. *Universal Pictures Corporation, et al.*, 45 F. (2d) 119 (1930).

Phelps Dodge Corp. v. *National Labor Relations Board*, 113 F. (2d) 202 (1940).

Prudential Insurance Co. v. *Benjamin*, 328 U.S. 418 (1946).

R. C. A. Manufacturing Co. v. *Whiteman*, 114 F. (2d) 86 (1940).

Regina v. *Hicklin*, L.R. 3 Q.B. 360 (1868).

Republic Aviation Corporation v. *National Labor Relations Board*, 142 F. (2d) 196 (1944).

Reynolds v. *Sims*, 377 U.S. 533 (1964).

Roth v. *United States*, 354 U.S. 476 (1957).

Schenck v. *United States*, 249 U.S. 47 (1919).

Seelig v. *Baldwin*, 7 F. Supp. 776 (1934).

Spector Motor Service, Inc. v. *Walsh*, 139 F. (2d) 809 (1944).

Stromberg v. *People of the State of California*, 283 U.S. 359 (1931).

Sweatt v. *Painter*, 339 U.S. 629 (1950).

United States v. *A. L. A. Schechter*, 76 F. (2d) 617 (1935).

United States v. *Aluminum Co. of America*, 148 F. (2d) 416 (1945).

United States v. *Andolschek*, 142 F. (2d) 503 (1944).

United States v. *Associated Press*, 52 F. Supp. 362 (1943).

Index

RCA *Manufacturing Co.* v. *Whiteman*: 173

Reapportionment: *see* legislative apportionment

Reason: in Hand's philosophy, 51–53; role of, in judgments, 73; in democratic systems, 196–97

Reasonable man test: 136–37, 146, 148

Reed, Stanley Forman: 28

Regina v. *Hicklin*: 154

Regulatory commissions, judicial role of: 114–16

Republican Party: 203

Republic Aviation Corp. v. *National Labor Relations Board*: 114

Restatement of Conflicts of Law: 43

Restatement of Torts: 43

Revival of Natural Law Concepts, The (Haines): 186

Reynolds v. *Sims*: 205

Rights: property, 136; personal, 136; *see also* man, rights of

Roosevelt, Franklin Delano: 9–10, 203, 207

Roosevelt, Theodore: 5, 9, 17, 203; and Sherman Act, 31–32

Rostow, Eugene V.: on apportionment, 205–206; on First Amendment, 214; on judicial review, 226

Roth v. *United States*: 156–57

Royce, Josiah: 4

Rutledge, Wiley B.: 9–10, 120

Sanford, Edward T.: 145–46

Santayana, George: 4, 15

Schenck v. *United States*: 142, 145

Schmidhauser, John R., on background of judges: 91–92

School-prayer decision: 207

Scientific analysis of political thought: 187–88, 196

Search and seizure: 137n., 161

Search warrants: 38–39

Second Treatise on Civil Government (Locke): 186

Sedition: 144–45

Seelig v. *Baldwin*: 96, 121

Segregation cases: 138, 155, 205–206; *see also* equal-protection clauses

Separation of powers: 111–12; related to presumed-validity doctrine, 18–19; to prevent abuse, 89–90; and judicial review, 106ff.; in Tax Court decisions, 115;

function of, 116–17; in commerce, 117–22; concurrent-powers doctrine of, 120; in due process, 122–29; contemporary theory of, 212–13; Hand on, 216, 222–23

Sherman Act: 6, 31

Skepticism: 53; danger of, 62; Hand's, 229

Slaughterhouse cases: 123

Smith Act: 134–35, 141–42, 147

Soviet law: 224

Speciale, M.: 12

Spector Motor Service, Inc. v. *Walsh*: 93, 121–22

Speech, freedom of: 95, 133; limits of, 142–43, 224–25; *see also* First Amendment

"Spirit of Liberty, The" (Hand's address): 11–12,231

Spirit of Liberty, The (Hand's collected essays and speeches): 13, 229

States: allocation of power to, 117–22; police power of, 123–25

Stoic philosophy: 218

Stone, Harlan: 224–25; on role of judiciary, 217

Stromberg v. *People of the State of California*: 147

Supremacy Clause: 20, 117; directed to states, 104–105

Supreme Court: appellate jurisdiction of, 22–23; original jurisdiction of, 23; authority of, over lower courts, 23–24; role of, 83, 203–207, 217–18, 221–22; background of justices on, 91–92; precedent of, in Hand's decisions, 92–96; and political questions, 107, 206–207, 210; on economic due process, 126–27; on segregation decisions, 138; congressional challenges to, 207; *see also* judicial review

Sutherland, George: 208

Swan, Thomas Walter: 6

Sweatt v. *Painter*: 206

Swindler, William: 16

Taft, William Howard: 5; on Hand, 9

Taney, Roger B., on due process, 123

Tax commissioner, discretionary power of: 27, 29–30

Tax Court: 115–16

Tax law: interpretations of, 26–29; Hand's contribution to, 30; on income, 203

Thayer, James Bradley: 4, 224–25; on judicial review, 222

Thucydides: 15

Index

Tobacco company cases: 34

Tolerance: and freedom, 53; importance of, 53, 55, 67, 75, 198–99

"Top U.S. Commercial Court": see Circuit Court of Appeals, Second Circuit

Totalitarianism: and regimes, 72–73; doctrines of, 188

Truth: as pragmatic concept, 55–56; and advocacy, 57; for community, 74

United States Criminal Code: 35

United States v. A.L.A. Schechter Poultry Corporation: 95, 112, 119, 122

United States v. Aluminum Co. of America: 32–34, 93

United States v. Andolschek: 37

United States v. Associated Press: 32, 93, 167

United States v. Carolene Products Co.: 128, 224–25

United States v. Casino: 38

United States v. Coplon: 38

United States v. Corn Products Refining Co.: 6

United States v. Cotter: 36–37

United States v. Crimmins: 40

United States v. Delaware and Hudson Company: 113–14

United States v. Dennis: 41, 87, 94, 96, 134–35, 141–43, 145–48, 152, 156, 166, 231

United States v. Kennerley: 154, 158

United States v. Kirschenblatt: 38

United States v. Krulewitch: 37

United States v. Levine: 155, 157

United States v. One Book Entitled Ulysses: 155

United States v. Rebhuhn: 159

Valéry, Paul: 8

Values: relative, 48, 54, 58–62, 75–76, 197–98; conflicts in, 54; necessity of, 55, 59–60; and advocacy, 59; ultimate, 61; see also natural law

Vinson, Fred H.: 148n., 152–53

Violent overthrow of government: 134, 147, 151, 152–53

Virginia Electric and Power Company: 94

Wages: 176–77

Waite, Morrison: 221

Ward, Artemus: 69

Warren, Earl: 13, 205, 207, 221; see also Warren Court

Warren Court: 35, 205, 206, 221; see also Earl Warren

Wechsler, Herbert: on interpretation of the Constitution, 163; on neutral principles, 215; on judicial review, 215, 234; on separation of powers, 216

Wesberry v. Sanders: 206

Whitehead, Alfred North: 15, 69

Whiteman, Paul: 173

Whitney v. People of the State of California: 146, 148n., 152, 219

Wickersham, George W.: 9

Williston, Samuel: 56

Winters v. New York: 157

Worship, freedom of: 224–25

Wyzanski, Charles E., Jr.: 138, 148n., 202; on Hand in lower court, 6; on Hand's contribution to antitrust law, 34; on role of judges, 86; on Hand's adherence to precedent, 93; on judicial review, 113

251

The paper on which this book is printed bears the watermark of the University of Oklahoma Press and has an effective life of at least three hundred years.

Date Due